THE SOUL OF ANIME

EXPERIMENTAL FUTURES
Technological Lives, Scientific Arts, Anthropological Voices
A series edited by Michael M. J. Fischer and Joseph Dumit

THE SOUL
OF ANIME

Collaborative Creativity and

Japan's Media Success Story

IAN CONDRY

Duke University Press
Durham and London   2013

© 2013 Duke University Press

All rights reserved

Printed in the United States of America

on acid-free paper ∞

Designed by Jennifer Hill

Typeset in Garamond Premier Pro

by Keystone Typesetting, Inc.

Library of Congress Cataloging-in-

Publication Data appear on the last

printed page of this book.

For Nick, Jackson, and Alec

CONTENTS

ix   *Note on Translations and Names*

1   INTRODUCTION * Who Makes Anime?

35   ONE * Collaborative Networks, Personal Futures

54   TWO * Characters and Worlds as Creative Platforms

85   THREE * Early Directions in Postwar Anime

112   FOUR * When Anime Robots Became Real

135   FIVE * Making a Cutting-Edge Anime Studio:
The Value of the Gutter

161   SIX * Dark Energy: What Overseas Fans Reveal
about the Copyright Wars

185   SEVEN * Love Revolution: Otaku Fans in Japan

204   CONCLUSION * Future Anime: Collaborative
Creativity and Cultural Action

218   *Acknowledgments*
221   *Notes*
227   *References*
237   *Index*

✱ All interviews and sources in Japanese were translated by the author. Japanese names are given in Western order, with given name followed by family name (e.g., Hayao Miyazaki, Mamoru Oshii, Shinichiro Watanabe, Mamoru Hosoda).

A note on name order: The tradition for English-language scholars is to use Japanese order (i.e., Miyazaki Hayao). In contrast, English-language newspapers, magazines, and trade publications tend to use Western order. In my first book, *Hip-Hop Japan* (2006), I went with scholarly tradition. I may have been influenced by my years of Japanese-language study; Japanese order sounds more authentic to me, like reading manga pages "unflipped" (the original Japanese orientation, reading right to left). Scholars tend to make an exception, however, for Japanese authors who have published in English. I suspect this is mainly due to citation practices in academia. If we want to cite the 2009 translated book *Otaku: Japan's Database Animals* and we write the author's name in the Japanese order, Azuma Hiroki (2009), there is a danger that people less familiar with Japanese will look for the reference under "Hiroki 2009," his given name. It is possible that some scholars want to avoid a kind of linguistic imperialism as well. In any case, current scholarly practice creates a confusing system: Western order for Japanese scholars with English-language publications, and Japanese order for everyone else. Given that Japanese scholars are increasingly publishing in English, and moreover they introduce themselves and present name cards (*meishi*) in English using Western order, I have decided to write Japanese names with given name followed by family name. To be honest, it sounds a little strange to me, but if it leads to less confusion, the change will be worth it.

Who Makes Anime?

* *The Soul of Anime* examines the worlds of Japanese animation to explore the ways cultural movements succeed—that is, gain value and go global through forces of collective action. By some estimates, a staggering 60 percent of the world's TV broadcasts of cartoons are Japanese in origin (JETRO 2005).[1] Anime feature films encompass a range of works from mass entertainment, like *Pokémon* and *Spirited Away*, to art-house favorites including *Ghost in the Shell* and *Summer Wars*. Anime ("AH-nee-may") refers to Japanese animated film and television, but the worlds of anime extend well beyond what appears on the screen. Anime is characteristic of contemporary media in its interconnected webs of commercial and cultural activities that reach across industries and national boundaries. In the United States and elsewhere, anime fan conventions draw tens of thousands of participants, many dressed as their favorite characters. Anime clubs on college and high school campuses are becoming as common as sushi in American supermarkets. A vast array of licensed merchandise depends on anime characters as well, characters often born in manga (comic books), but also in videogames, light novels, and even TV commercials. Scholars, fans, and media observers are producing a growing body of literature aimed at extending and deepening our understandings of the diverse field of Japanese animation. What distinguishes this book is my effort to use fieldwork in animation studios and other sites of anime-related production to explore ethno-graphically the social side of media. I start with the logic and practices of making animation and use this perspective as a way to think about cultural production more broadly. I argue that collaborative creativity, which oper-ates across media industries and connects official producers to unofficial fan production, is what led to anime's global success. Put simply, success arises from social dynamics that lead people to put their energy into today's media worlds. This collective social energy is what I mean by the "soul" of anime.

Anime is a success in the sense that it became a sustainable form of creative expression and a style recognized as "Japanese" that went global without the push of major corporations (at least at first) and thus repre-sents a kind of globalization from below. In other words, anime demon-strates the diversity of actors involved in the transformation of a small-scale, niche cultural form into something that reaches wider audiences and influences people around the world. Why did Japan, of all places, become a global leader in animation? How did the cultural universe of anime ex-pand from being a (mostly) children's genre to something of value for teenagers and adults as well, and why did this not happen in the United States until much later? What can anime tell us about the emergence of media forms that depend not only on corporate backing but also on grassroots and independent efforts to extend audiences and impact? These questions give us the opportunity to rethink how we understand the emergence and spread of distinctive cultural forms as something other than a game of "follow the money." Instead, we need to follow the activity, the energy, the commitment of those who care, starting with what is most meaningful to them. Anime is instructive because it reveals the centrality of a kind of social energy that emerges in the space between people and media. For me, the soul of anime does not point to some ultimate, internal essence of the media as an object. Rather, the soul of anime points to this social energy that arises from our collective engagements through media, and as such, it gives us an alternative way to think about what is of value in media. This, in turn, suggests dynamics for producing creative platforms on which to shape new futures.

The book's central thematic is the interplay between an internal logic of anime as a kind of portable creative platform (glossed as "characters and worlds" but somewhat more complex) and the social contexts in which anime gains its meaning and value—what I'm calling the "social side of media," which includes both paid labor and fan activities. By looking at cultural production across categories of producers, we can gain insight into the workings of contemporary media and culture by reflecting on pre-Internet examples of user-generated content, viral media, and the complexities of transmedia synergies. Overall, this is a story of the emergence of a media form that, as it matured and spread, gained both wider mass audiences and deeper, more niche-oriented fans in Japan and overseas. The example of anime is all the more striking, and more provocative in terms of thinking about how cultural movements go global, once we recognize that anime studios succeeded despite relatively modest economic returns. The idea of collaborative creativity enables us to map the broader connections of anime beyond the media forms themselves.

Many studies of animation begin with a question about the object—what is anime?—but I suggest a different entry point: Who makes anime? The chapters of this book can be read as an attempt to understand anime's value in terms of a circle of interaction across categories of producers. Rather than beginning with the contrasts between production and consumption, answering the question "Who makes anime?" starts from a different place, making central not only the roles of anime creators but also the roles of manga artists, sponsors, merchandisers, and fans as part of wider processes of production.[2] In the chapters that follow, I examine, in turn, the making of anime by looking at how professional animators design new anime around characters and worlds (chapters 1–2); the emergence of different approaches to anime, such as feature films versus TV, as a way to think about the transmedia connections that are necessary to make anime successful, notably the key role of manga (chapter 3); how synergies between anime creators and toy companies pushed the development of robot anime that emphasized "real" (i.e., grownup) themes and helped to expand audiences for anime from children to adults (chapter 4); how "cutting-edge" studios design their own workplaces as (more or less) open spaces for creativity (chapter 5); how online file sharing and the practices of "fansubbing" expand the cultural universe of anime amid fierce debates over the legitimacy of copyright (chapter 6); and how Japanese *otaku* (obsessive fans) channel their desire for anime characters, even to the point of wanting to marry them, and whether this should be viewed as a deeper descent into a closed-off niche world or, instead, as an unusual gesture toward mass appeal (chapter 7). In the conclusion, I return to some of the larger questions about how cultural forms travel from niche to

Ethnography and Fieldwork in Anime Studios

As a cultural anthropologist, I approach these issues by attending to some of the nuances of social life and then use those details to develop larger theories about the workings of media and culture. My research centers on ethnographic fieldwork, primarily in several anime studios in Tokyo, between 2004 and 2010. I spent three and a half months in the summer of 2006 attending script meetings, voice recordings, and editing sessions, and I conducted interviews with dozens of creators. In the years before and after, I made one or two brief trips to Japan annually to continue my research. My main field sites were Gonzo, Aniplex, and Madhouse, but I also visited Studio Ghibli, Production I.G., Toei Animation, Sunrise, and several other smaller operations where I observed creators at work. During one voice-recording session, I was even recruited to be a voice actor for a couple of lines (in Japanese) when an extra was needed (see chapter 5). For comparison with practices within the United States, I spent a day at the Cartoon Network studios in Burbank, California, and I interviewed a Korean American anime director who works in the United States, Japan, and South Korea (chapter 3). In Japan, I observed labor at a high-end toy factory (the Bandai Hobby Center in Shizuoka), and I met with Japanese anime magazine writers, publishers, scholars, and fans. My research also extended beyond today's workplaces, both in thinking historically and in other realms of fandom. I attended anime conventions in Boston (2006–2009) and Los Angeles (2011) and the enormous "fanzine" convention Comic Market in Tokyo (August 2006), and I follow many aspects of online anime fandom in both Japan and the United States. I also watched a lot of anime, and I read what other academics, fans, and commentators have to say. I benefited from many discussions with students, at the Massachusetts Institute of Technology (MIT) and elsewhere, regarding anime and other forms of Japanese popular culture.

Fieldwork can be a somewhat haphazard, unpredictable process. As a result, it is often difficult to achieve a perfectly balanced mix of examples and insights. Although I observed a lot, I might mention that in my efforts to visit anime studios, whether through cold calls (via email and phone) or personal connections, I failed to get access or interviews far more often than I succeeded. The collection of examples I report on here arose because of the goodwill of people who often didn't know me well, and for that I am grateful. I hope I'm not *too* grateful. The anthropologist Brian

Moeran (1996) notes an interesting by-product of fieldwork in his ethnography of a Japanese advertising agency—that is, his fierce loyalty to the firm he studied. While he analyzed the meanings of meetings, something I also do, he grew attached to his informants, a finding that I'm sure many fieldworkers can appreciate. Does this distort the findings of a researcher? Perhaps. But the flip side is that if you don't spend time at an anime studio or at an advertising agency, you're more likely to see only the content of an anime or an ad, and there is a risk of ignoring (or underplaying) the people and the labor behind the effort. Is this not a bias as well?

At the same time, I acknowledge that the examples I use lean toward the male end of the anime spectrum. Gender in anime is a topic that deserves more attention than my limited access could achieve. All of the studios I visited had female employees, but except for Studio 4°C, with its female chief executive (see chapter 5), few were in the top positions. Female animators were clearly on staff, but in the meetings between those with more power—such as producers, scriptwriters, directors, and key frame artists—I estimate that about one in five or six (at most, one in three) were women. For anime genres, as well, I note that my discussion of mecha (giant robot) anime and the links with merchandising could apply equally well to magical schoolgirl anime (chapter 4). Whereas giant robot anime excelled as a marketing tool for robot toys, magical schoolgirl anime played a similar role in promoting magic wands and other "transformation" devices as toys (Allison 2006). Of course, gender dynamics mean more than that some anime is for boys and some is for girls. For example, the anthropologist Laura Miller (2011) persuasively argues that the promotion of so-called Cool Japan by the Japanese government is also skewed toward "male geek culture" and thereby ends up erasing the creativity of young women. Gender issues are an extremely important aspect of anime studies. Although the limitations of fieldwork may be a poor excuse for some of the absences here, I had to work with the cards I was dealt. Rather than asserting a questionable objectivity, anthropologists tend to write from a perspective that is necessarily "partial" in both senses of the word: committed to certain ends and incomplete (Clifford and Marcus 1986). I might add that this ethnography of anime creativity at times gives less emphasis to narrative and representation not because I think this is unimportant, but because my aim is to move us toward questions of production, participation, and engagement in particular social contexts.

A Parlor Bet and Other
Social Contexts of Anime Production

Given the substantial international influence of anime, readers might be surprised by the crowded, often disheveled look of the places where animators work. I was surprised by the piles and piles of paper, the intensity of hand-drawn work, and the sheer amount of labor required. I was also impressed by the workers' focus, energy, and commitment to working together on enormous projects. Collaborative creativity is more than jargon for animators.

Most of Tokyo's anime studios are scattered in the suburbs west and north of the city, generally in the pie slice formed by the Chuo train line (heading west from Shinjuku) and the Seibu Ikebukuro line (heading northwest from Ikebukuro). The buildings tend to be nondescript, concrete slabs that could be mistaken for the countless condos and small office buildings extending in all directions from Tokyo's center. For all of its international impact, Japan's anime production remains in many ways a cottage industry. A report by the Japanese advertising firm Dentsu estimates that roughly seven hundred small companies are working in "anime-related production," and of those, four hundred firms are working on "anime production" itself. Some of the larger studios include Toei Animation, Studio Ghibli, Nihon Animation, Shin-Ei Dōga, Studio Pierrot, GDH (Gonzo), Production I.G., Sunrise, and Madhouse, but there are hundreds of others. A studio can employ anywhere from fifteen to a few hundred people, and the studios rely on local freelance animators as well as large offshore animation production houses primarily in South Korea, the Philippines, and China. By some estimates, 90 percent of the frames used in Japanese animation are drawn overseas, although the work of design and storytelling is more often done in Japan. Many anime firms cooperate in production, especially when crunch time comes, and individual animators' career paths can lead through several studios. The studios operate as a fragmented but complexly networked epicenter of what has become an increasingly global business.

Inside the workspaces, the commonalities among the studios I visited—the lived-in atmosphere, the backlit desks for the animators (some of whom, inevitably, were face-down asleep), the rows of computers for others—were reminders of how anime production in Japan has, and has not, evolved since the industry began in the late 1950s. Most of the dozen

1. Friends react with ridicule to the proposition of Winsor McCay (far right) that in one month's time he will create drawings that move, as dramatized in *Little Nemo* (1911).

anime studios I visited were work-worn and bare bones. Although anime studios also had a playful side, with musical instruments and other pastimes lying about, they are places of strict deadlines, where the work literally piles up.

To spend time in an anime studio is to be struck by the labor of making media. My working definition of "animation" is a media form that is created one frame at a time. A tremendous amount of work is required, with painstaking attention to detail, to create *each frame* of film (or, at least, multiple frames per second). It's a crazy idea. In fact, in the film *Little Nemo*, a short from 1911 that mixes animation and live action, the American cartoonist Winsor McCay portrayed his start at "drawing pictures that will move" as a parlor bet against his cigar-smoking friends. In the film, he draws several sample characters on a sheet of white paper and explains that by using film, the cartoons will move. His friends guffaw, rubbing his head to see if perhaps his skull is cracked (see figure 1). The film then cuts to McCay's stylized workplace, and we see the thousands of pages of paper, barrels of ink, and a playful reference to the inevitable missteps of creating animated work. In the end, however, McCay succeeds, wowing his friends with the magic of animation. One wonders, would he have had the energy to do all that work if it weren't for his friends waiting in anticipation?

Let's jump ahead almost a century and take a closer look at work in an anime studio by visiting a morning meeting with an anime director in the early stages of creating a film that went on to win the Best Animated Feature award from the Japan Academy Prize Association in 2010.

Summer Wars Storyboards and the Energy in the Room

In the summer of 2008, the director Mamoru Hosoda was deep into creating the storyboards for his feature film *Summer Wars*. It was a year before the film's scheduled release, and the work was heating up. Hosoda and his co-writer Satoko Okudera had already composed the original story and completed the script; Hosoda was in the process of turning the script into storyboards. He says he works on storyboards in family restaurants (*fami resu*), such as Denny's, where he draws for stretches of six to twelve hours—at least, during the several months it takes to complete them. Hosoda's storyboards are highly regarded among anime professionals, and some are published as books (Anime Style Editors 2006; Hosoda and Summer Wars Film Partners 2009).

Generally, anime directors in Japan are responsible for the storyboards, which are drawn on roughly letter-size pages. Each page is composed of five frames stacked vertically, with space alongside each frame for noting the action, dialogue, effects, and timing of the scenes and cuts. For the hour-and-a-half film, Hosoda would eventually produce a little over five hundred pages of finalized storyboards, with countless drafts discarded along the way. In July 2008, the producer of *Summer Wars* invited me to observe a meeting between the director and his computer graphics team. I was struck by how storyboards help guide the collaborative creativity of anime production in distinctive ways.

On the day of the meeting, Hosoda met me at the entrance to the main offices of Madhouse, then near Ogikubo Station in western Tokyo. A light rain fell as Hosoda led me to a small office building nearby. The producer met us on the sidewalk and led us up three flights of stairs, laughing and apologizing that the elevator was out. Madhouse had rented a floor of the building to be the primary workspace for Hosoda's film. It was not a fancy location. There were shelves with stacks of paper and small desks with a lightboard for drawing on the thin pages used for character movements. Each person's carrel was decorated haphazardly with unique collections of figurines, magazines, and manga.

Feeble air conditioners hummed in the small, muggy room, which was barely large enough for the ten of us around a table. An array of snacks and canned coffee, apparently bought at a nearby convenience store, was spread out in the middle of the table. Work in an anime studio is not glamorous, and a lot of it is solitary. The film's young producer, Yūichirō Saitō, introduced everyone in the room, including me as an observer and a couple of other Madhouse staff members. Except for an assistant producer for Madhouse, the rest of the group were men. Most of the people were from Digital Frontier, a leading computer graphics production company that works in film, videogames, and more. Hosoda began the meeting with comments about the earthquake that had rocked northern Japan the night before, with shocks reaching hundreds of miles away in Tokyo, where my hotel had swayed unnervingly for a long minute shortly before midnight. But this was still three years before the Tōhoku (northeastern Japan) earthquake of March 2011 and the devastating tsunami and nuclear crisis that followed. The quake we experienced in 2008 caused little damage. At the meeting, Hosoda asked whether anyone had injured friends or family, and no one did. "Well, it was just an earthquake," he concluded. Then he lit a cigarette and got down to business.

We each had a stack of paper in front of us: the current draft of the storyboards for the first half of the film. Over the next three hours, Hosoda led us through the roughly three hundred pages, sometimes skimming quickly and sometimes stopping to discuss certain issues in more detail. He discussed "camera angles" (as they would be drawn), the possible effects that could be used, and above all the look and feel that he was aiming for. He noted that some of the scenes should look "cartoony" (*kaatūni*), in contrast to the more photorealistic 3D computer graphics animation (full 3D CG) used, for example, in the film *Appleseed: Ex Machina*, on which several of the CG team members in the room had worked. For Hosoda's film, most of the character movements would be hand-drawn. Many of the backgrounds were hand painted, as well—notably, those featuring the luxurious rural home where much of the action takes place. Even this hand-drawn work, however, would be scanned into computers to be assembled and edited. The computer graphics would be used especially for certain scenes that were best done with computer modeling, such as the virtual world setting (although this was not 3D in the sense of requiring glasses to give the illusion of depth). At one point, Hosoda noted a scene that required a boy to look out the back of a car as it moved down the street. "This scene we're going to need your help on," he said, explaining that it was very difficult to portray a receding landscape without using computers.

As the meeting went on, many drawings were pulled from other stacks of paper on the shelves around us, depicting the designs of characters in various poses, the settings in the vast virtual world (another main location of the film), and other rough sketches of diverse visual elements (a flowchart, a card-labyrinth game) that would appear. The papers were passed around, examined, and commented on, sometimes marked up with red pencil and photocopied. There was discussion of different decisions that would have to be made as the production progressed, especially about how to get the different visual elements to work together. Hosoda listened carefully to people's questions and suggestions, but he also decided things firmly after opinions had been aired. This was Hosoda's third full-length feature film, and he looked comfortable in his role as the director.

Hosoda trained as an oil painter in art college, and his visual sensibility shows through in the nuances of his storyboards. He is adept at shaping the contours and tempo of his films. Consider, for example, two pages of storyboards for *Summer Wars* that depict one of the early battles for the online avatar King Kazuma, a virtual martial arts champion bunny rabbit (Hosoda and Summer Wars Film Partners 2009: 26–27). The scene appears as part of the opening credits sequence. The storyboards convey the layout and the staging of a virtual battle (see figure 2). At the bottom of each page, the director writes the number of seconds of the movie depicted in the five drawn frames. In this example, the left-hand page (scene 5, cuts 11–12) reads "4 + 0," which means four seconds plus zero frames (at twenty-four frames per second). The right-hand page (cuts 13–14) accounts for "2 + 0," only two seconds of film. Note the hand-drawn touches. The picture sometimes spills out of the frame as a camera is directed to pan across a larger background, a process now done by scanning images and manipulating them on a computer. We can see the dialogue (*serifu*) drifting out of its prescribed box. We can sense a little of Hosoda's voice in the multiple exclamation points, the sound effects drawn large, and the drama of the drawings.

Hosoda's storyboards were filled with this kind of kinetic energy. Even in the morning in a sweaty room with canned coffee, we found ourselves

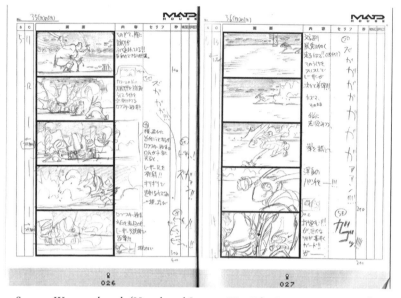

2. *Summer Wars* storyboards (Hosoda and Summer Wars Film Partners 2009: 26–27).

being pulled into the world of the film. We sensed the tension between the characters as they faced their respective challenges. We flipped through the storyboards, page by page, scene after scene, and the visual storytelling was clearly taking shape in the minds of the CG team. But to be honest, the film did not really take shape for me. I found it very difficult to imagine, based on the sketches and scribbled directions, what the final product would actually become (see figure 3). Here, too, a personal history of certain experiences was required to make sense of the drawings, and I lacked that experience.

Even so, there was something about being in a meeting like that, with others in the room intensely focused on the project at hand, that has a galvanizing effect. The collective attention helped build connections, bring focus, and clarify the roles of the many people needed to complete such a large project. Such meetings did more than convey abstract information about a mechanical process of production; they helped reinforce a sense of engaged commitment. The energy in the room was contagious, and this energy begins to give a sense of something larger than the media object itself, something emerging from a collective commitment among those who care. Storyboards helped achieve that focus of attention, and that focus began to take on a life of its own.[3]

3. King Kazuma (crouching) battles a lobster tank in *Summer Wars*.

By the end of the three-hour meeting, the members of the computer graphics team had an understanding of the scenes they would have to design, at least for the first half of the film that was discussed. Hosoda and his producer had a clearer sense of things that still needed to be worked out. Meetings like this regarding background paintings, characters' movements, special effects, voice acting, music, and so on, would continue in the months that followed. After the meetings, the more solitary work of drawing and constructing the scenes would continue. Much of the practice of animation is focused downward, toward a page of paper or a computer screen. As an ethnographer, however, I found the meetings indispensable because they clarified some of the underlying logic of making animation and allowed me to experience the energy of working closely with others—sharing information, working out goals, dividing up the labor.

Storyboards are intriguing because they are integral to the process of production, but in the end they are regarded as waste, a useless by-product, and in most cases are thrown away. This highlights something we intuitively know: What we see on-screen represents a small slice of the labor involved in the overall projects. Hosoda's job is to guide much of that work, but it was readily apparent that problem solving, creativity, and innovation would be required, to a greater or lesser extent, at many stages in the process. Moreover, success itself depends not only on production inside studios, but also on many factors the creators cannot control. This fundamental unpredictability requires creators to take a leap of faith into projects when they are uncertain of the outcome. Both history and futurism play a role in guiding the creative action that flows through anime projects, revealing how our cultural assumptions go into creating the worlds we inhabit. Writers about anime get the luxury of knowing how things turned out, but this can give a false impression of the perspective of working in media worlds. In this regard, anime gives us a concrete example to think through the social dynamics of purposeful creativity in a global context. Anime exists not only as media but as labor and energy that connects creators, businesses, and fans. Collaborative creativity can offer a way to rethink the value of contemporary media, not only as content, but also as connection. In turn, it allows us to extend analyses across locales, platforms, and kinds of producers.

This doesn't mean that anime creators are getting rich. The value of the cultural success of anime as a global phenomenon and the energy of the participants are not easily translated into monetary rewards for the studios. This means low salaries for animators; it also has broader significance. Japan, like other advanced industrial nations, is facing the challenge of developing new industries, especially now that manufacturing increasingly is moving overseas to low-wage nations. When I began this project in the early 2000s, I imagined that the "content industries" (the Japanese term for media, publishing, and entertainment) might be a powerful engine of economic growth; the reality is more complicated. Although the work of creating scripts and storyboards, designing characters and background artwork, and drawing key frames is generally done in Japan, much of the drawing of "in-between" frames by lower-wage animators is done overseas in South Korea, the Philippines, and China. Depending on how you measure it, "Japanese" animation is made mostly outside Japan. For the Madhouse producer Yūichirō Saitō, however, that really isn't an issue as long as the quality of work is solid. "We just want to make good animation; we are not so concerned about national origins," he said.[4] Still, given the budget constraints of making animation and the tremendous amount of work required, we find that cultural success and economic success mean different things. Some people are quick to blame unauthorized online access to anime as the culprit, but other factors are important, too, including how low budgets are related to the history of Japanese animation and the terms set by early TV series like *Astro Boy* (see chapter 3).

For workers, the pressure of working quickly and cheaply, combined with the uncertainty of the success, adds to the precarious nature of the business. When I spent time at Gonzo and Madhouse in 2006, they both occupied entire floors of flashy corporate buildings, but they have since moved, and Gonzo was forced to downsize. When I visited Production I.G. in the summer of 2010, it had just relocated a few months before. The new digs took up five floors of a small building and included a large metal model of a plane that had been made for a promotional event and had appeared in Mamoru Oshii's film *The Sky Crawlers*. The CEO of Production I.G., Mitsuhisa Ishikawa, said that some people complained that the space was too clean to be an animation studio, but he implied that it wouldn't take long for the place to get that cluttered and messy, even a little grimy. Of course, all studios have some kind of newfangled face for meetings with media, potential sponsors, and others. The waiting areas are replete with posters, pamphlets, and merchandise pushing their current projects. But backstage, as it were, animators work among piles of paper. Stacks upon stacks of drawings are organized in large manila envelopes. At Toei Animation, a powerhouse in children's programming, a longtime key-frame animator took time out from his work to show me his drawings and said he was happy that he had remained in anime work (see figure 4). He acknowledged that after almost eight years working on the same series, he was a little tired of drawing digital monsters who do battle, but he wasn't complaining. Such is the reward of certain kinds of success.

For many, a career in anime can be short-lived. According to an article in the *Wall Street Journal*, nine out of ten animators leave the industry within three years to move to other areas of work. The average salary for animators in their twenties was estimated at $11,000 per year and only twice that for animators in their thirties (Hayashi 2009).[5] Long hours are the norm, and many animators work freelance, moving from project to project, often without benefits. Most animators burn out or simply can't make a living on the pay they receive for their drawings. Those who remain tend to be the ones who work quickly and who can handle the grueling pace.

In terms of economic success, anime seems more of a cautionary tale than a model of entrepreneurial innovation. The same *Wall Street Journal* article noted that some animators leave the business for more lucrative work in videogames. In fact, when several representatives from the Japanese videogame company Square Enix visited MIT in March 2009 to give a seminar on the making of the *Final Fantasy XII* game, I was excited to

4. Key-frame animator, Toei Animation, August 2006.

share my insights about the workings of characters and the intriguing parallels between anime and videogame production. But the director, Hiroshi Minagawa, also had something to ask me about my study of anime: "Why are you studying such an old-fashioned and unprofitable industry?" Good question.

Why Study Anime?

For me, the answer to the question "Why study anime?" lies in an interest in uncovering the dynamics of cultural movements that don't rely on the promise of exorbitant wealth as the measure of success. Anime has become a globally recognized style—or, more accurately, a generative platform for creativity—despite relatively modest economic returns. Some researchers describe animation as a business, with a kind of "follow-the-money" approach (Raugust 2004; Tada 2002). But in an era of user-generated media, when amateur productions can rival those of professional studios, we need a wider perspective to map how emergent cultural forms develop and take hold. Japan, as the world's third largest economy and a robust epicenter in the import and export of popular culture, provides a useful location for unraveling the dynamic political struggles over the meanings of popular culture, both as cultural resource and as commercial product.

But what leads to success? Malcolm Gladwell argues that we have a strong tendency to misconstrue stories of success because we place too much explanatory weight on the individual abilities of remarkably successful people. These successful people, Gladwell (2008: 19) says, "may look like they did it all by themselves. But in fact, they are invariably the beneficiaries of hidden advantages and extraordinary opportunities and cultural legacies that allow them to learn and work hard and make sense of the world in ways that others cannot." Both the Beatles and Bill Gates had "extraordinary opportunities" in the sense that they were able to practice their skills for many, many more hours than their peers and competitors. Hard work, yes, but Gladwell brings attention to the serendipity of being in the right place at the right time (something that can be said for global media). So far so good. But his notion of "cultural legacies" gives too much credence to essentialist stereotypes, and in making the case that social context is integral to any success, he doesn't take his argument far enough. He describes remarkably successful programmers, lawyers, and musicians and how they benefited from their surroundings, but in the end we see primarily successful *individuals*. If the trick to understanding success is grasping the crucibles in which people ended up being successful, then shouldn't those crucibles be our scale of analysis? And, if so, what scale is that? In the case of anime, there are good reasons to argue for focusing on any of a number of levels: the auteur animator, the innovative studio, the larger pop culture scene, the national characteristics of Japan, or a transnational realm of animation art and entertainment. In this book, my aim is to give a sense of the interaction of these different levels. Let's start with Japan as a nation.

What Is the Relationship between "Japan" and Anime's Success?

It is easy to understand why the nation itself seems to define the key crucible of creativity, in part because many people, Japanese and foreigners, make the case that anime represents Japan. In English, "anime" means "Japanese animation," although in Japan, it more commonly means all animation worldwide, with "Japanimation" used to specify national origin.

The Japanese government occasionally uses anime and manga characters in public diplomacy efforts. In 2004, the Japanese government sent water-tank trucks to Iraq as a form of overseas development assistance and placed the flags of Japan and Iraq on the side. The Iraqis noted, however, that the Japanese flag might not be recognized by local citizens. In response, the Japanese government decided that it would also include on each of the donated trucks a large sticker of Captain Tsubasa, the title character of a soccer manga and anime, who is well known to Iraqis and others in the Middle East as "Captain Majid."[6] Compared with Japan's flag, the anime character was a more readily recognizable image of Japan (Asō 2007).

Some government officials hope that the overseas success of anime will constitute a kind of "soft power," which is, as the political scientist Joseph Nye (2004) describes it, the ability to influence other nations through the attractiveness of a nation's culture and ideals. In March 2008, Japan's minister of foreign affairs named the Doraemon character (a futuristic blue robot cat featured in manga and anime) a "cultural ambassador." Since the character is very popular in China but largely unknown in the United States, the choice clearly reflects an orientation toward Asia rather than America. At the ceremonial event, a person dressed in a Doraemon costume declared, "I hope through my cartoons I will be able to convey to people overseas what ordinary Japanese people are thinking, what sort of life we are leading and what sort of future we are trying to create!"[7] I find this rather silly, of course, but given my own country's efforts to gain international influence through Predator drone strikes, I have to admit that these examples of Japan's attempts at cultural diplomacy, even if they are a bit dubious, have the advantage of doing less harm than air-to-surface missiles. Even so, what, exactly, anime might mean for the future of Japan's foreign policy is unclear. The cultural studies scholar Koichi Iwabuchi (2002b) sees a worrisome new "soft nationalism" that aims not only to spread Japanese culture abroad but to define the boundaries of authentic culture at home.

Japanese popular culture certainly is a driving force in youthful interest in Japan overseas (a boon to Japan studies programs everywhere), but I am skeptical that it can have a deep influence on support for Japanese government policies. Or, rather, when foreigners feel a connection, it is to the Japanese people or Japanese "culture" rather than to the national government. The earthquake and tsunami of March 11, 2011, and the nuclear crisis that followed clearly brought an emotional outpouring from people around the world, but whether this brings support or outrage toward the Japanese government will depend on how that government's response is ultimately viewed. For this and other reasons, the transnational intimacy toward Japan is more about the people (or an image of the people) than the government (Condry 2007). Besides, there are other things anime promotes, such as an understanding of how transmedia franchises can work, that are likely to be more influential than a vague connection to the national interest. In other words, when people assert a connection between Japan and anime, we might bear in mind the question of what ideological commitments are served. The questions we ask can shape how we view the objects we study. So if a simple link to Japan is not enough, then what explains the popularity of anime overseas? Some locate success in the internal characteristics of media, but I would argue that can be only a partial explanation.

"What's so special about Japanese popular culture? Why is it gaining such popularity outside Japan?"[8] Questions posed this way encourage us to think that there are some general, overall characteristics of Japanese popular culture that explain its success, regardless of whether success is defined in terms of aesthetic excellence, market achievements, or impact with an audience. Lasting success is often theorized in terms of a kind of resonance with audiences or eras. There are many examples of this, but let's consider one by the Asian studies scholar Timothy Craig (2000). He makes good points about the processes by which Japanese popular culture drew inspiration from overseas to speak to everyday concerns of Japanese people, but I worry about overarching national or ethnic assertions of cultural resonance as a way to explain popularity. For example, Craig proposes the following: "Japan pop speaks in special ways to Asia and the West. For other Asians, Japan's pop culture has a resonance that is derived from ethnic similarity and from shared values, tastes, and traditions. . . . For Western pop culture consumers, much of Japan's pop appeal comes not from its familiarity but from its *difference* from what we are accustomed to in our home cultures" (2000: 15–16).

Although the idea of resonance can hinge on either similarity or difference, it tends to reinforce what the cultural studies scholar John Whittier Treat calls the "stalled historicity" of Japan studies by Westerners, whereby European and American scholars are "motivated to produce Japan as the cultural counterpart or rival (and thus both similar and different)" (1996:

1). We can also see this in *A Reader in Animation Studies*, which includes an essay pointing to "constants in Japanese television serials" such as the presence of a heroine who is an orphan or of other characters without family (Raffaelli 1997: 124). Notions of resonance need not always distort history by reinforcing ideological assertions of national uniqueness, but resonance does tend to imply a static relationship between individuals and media or performance. This is not a problem when the resonance is small-scale (again, how far to extend this scale is an interesting question). The social energy in Hosoda's storyboard meeting can be viewed as a kind of "resonance," and I am very interested in the meanings that can arise from that kind of intersubjective vibe. But when "resonance" is used to explain much larger formations—that is, when the success of a certain pop culture franchise is explained by its resonance with a kind of cultural background —I become skeptical. Yet this style of cultural analysis is widely used, and it relies on a particular assumption that culture should be viewed as widely shared patterns characteristic of a whole society.

This theory of cultural resonance is not unique to the United States or "the West," either. In an issue of the Japanese magazine *Nikkei Entertainment*, the editors propose that it is the power of a certain style of popular culture—namely, a "circle of friends" mode—that explains what they identify as a recent trend in Japanese pop culture hits. They contrast this with an earlier era's *Zeitgeist* centered on "charisma" (*karisuma*), which in Japan emphasized having a standout personality as a path to success:

> There was an era [the late 1990s] in which charisma was the word getting all the attention. . . . The TV drama *Beautiful Life*, featuring [the pop idol] Takuya Kimura as a charismatic beautician, was a remarkable hit (recording a 41.3% rating in the Tokyo area). At the time, it was the middle of the "lost decade" after the economic bubble burst. People wanted to see their dreams realized again, and they were drawn towards a desire for "charisma." But in the 2000s, the recession further deepened. Charisma could no longer be depended upon. It may be that what began to pull at our hearts was the idea of a "circle of friends" (*nakama*) that drew together its strength for a common purpose. (Kanai and Hirashima 2010: 21)

This reproduces the idea of cultural resonance as an explanation for media success, though here it is not a resonance with "Japan" or "Asian tastes and values" but, rather, a resonance with a particular era within Japan. Same logic, different scale. The editors of *Nikkei Entertainment* offer several examples to prove their point, including the manga and anime *One Piece*, a pirate adventure where the characters work together to solve problems, and K-Pop (Korean pop music) singing groups with many members. The problem is that there are many other examples of circle-of-friends-type works (*nakama mono*) that do not become hits. In that case, the important "resonance" was not only the characteristics of things that succeeded or only in the overall spirit of the times. The question of what differentiates hits from also-rans requires a more dynamic model of success. Cultural analysis itself can and should be more subtle than overarching claims of resonance suggest (Yoda and Harootunian 2006). The context of Japan is different from that of other countries in crucial ways, but that doesn't mean that all pop culture forms from Japan are successful overseas. So taking "national culture" as an explanation for success doesn't make sense; it would be better to try to understand Japan as a context in which certain media forms could develop in distinctive ways, energized in part through fan relationships (Kelly 2004). A contrast between manga in Japan and comic books in the United States is a case in point.

How is it that Japanese manga is so diverse, speaking to wider audiences, and constituting so much more publishing volume than comics in the United States? History provides clues. In the 1940s, American comic books dealt with extreme themes, including gruesome violence and salacious romance. But an uproar surrounding the presumed negative impact on children led a consortium of magazine publishers to establish a Comics Code in 1954 that regulated the content of comic books so they would be appropriate for children (Hajdu 2008). In Japan, manga was a cheap and accessible form of entertainment that took off in the postwar period. Manga dealt in a variety of extreme content, and there were occasional uproars among parent–teacher organizations in Japan, but no similar authority was established (Schodt 1983, 1996). Manga artists were freer to develop works that spoke to teens and adults than were their counterparts in the United States, although, as Sharon Kinsella (2000) points out, commercialism in the manga industry in the 1980s put something of a damper on counterculture themes that thrived in earlier decades. Roughly 60 percent of anime productions are based on popular manga. The deep catalogue and the wide range of characters with a devoted fan base create an important comparative advantage for Japan vis-à-vis the United States. In this way, we can see how the emergence of anime is related to the context of Japan but relates to a finer level of detail than the overall "culture" of Japan. Clearly, popular culture with adult themes has a "reso-nance" in both Japan and the United States, but institutional and com-mercial forces guided the development of the world of comics in distinc-tive ways (see chapter 3).

In contrast to assertions of cultural resonance, I propose exploring in more detail the feedback loops that enable new styles to emerge and be sustained. The idea of emergence can help elucidate the connections be-tween creators, businesses, technologies, and fans and the ways in which energy flows between them to sustain a variety of projects and activities. I borrow the term from the work of the anthropologist Michael M. J. Fischer, though many others are experimenting with similar ideas (see, e.g., Clarke and Hansen 2009; Johnson 2001). Fischer reminds us that culture is not a "thing" or an unchanging pattern of norms and values, as por-trayed in, say, Gladwell's "legacies" or the *Nikkei Entertainment* editors' characterization of eras. Rather, culture is better viewed as "a methodolog-ical concept or tool of inquiry" that has been refined over the years to "allow new realities to be seen and engaged as its own parameters are changed" (Fischer 2007: 3). In this regard, ethnography provides the tools to look for cultural dynamics in local settings in terms of their practical impact in guiding behavior and beliefs.

Fischer finds inspiration in analogies drawn from new techno-sciences, especially life and information sciences, which can help us think of cultural and social patterns as "emergent out of mutations, assemblages, viral tran-sivity, rhizomic growth, wetwares and softwares." New information tech-nology and media environments can be viewed as "culturing new connec-tivities" (Fischer 2007: 31–32). Animation offers its own sets of metaphors of creativity, from storyboards to key frames and voices (at the level of studio production) and then extending across vehicles of conveyance for the characters and the worlds they inhabit, whether as videogames, toys, or cosplayers (short for "costume players"). In other words, rather than start-ing with "Japanese culture" as the explanation for creativity, and in con-trast to using resonance with a cultural backdrop as the explanation for media success, I want to draw attention to how cultural forms emerge from social practices and how value depends on multifaceted uses. From this perspective, the crucibles of creativity have to be understood at a finer level of detail than simply "Japan" and particular studios; we need more broadly to understand anime as a "field," in Pierre Bourdieu's (1998) sense, of communication and competition. This idea of emergence works in tandem with a notion of social energy, a kind of unseen force, or dark energy, that best explains the expansion of the anime universe. An ethnographic lens zeroes in on the ways people organize their activities around media. The social in media is connected to cultural action. A brief visit to an anime convention in Boston can show what this means.

Anime Music Videos

At the Hynes Convention Center in Boston, an enormous room with about six hundred people was filled to capacity, including many of us standing around the back and sides. It was May 2006 at the Anime Boston convention, and we were watching the Friday night session for anime music videos (AMVs). The energy in the room bubbled as we watched parodies, action sequences, and dramatic videos with complex love triangles. Participation was integral, too, since we were each given a sheet of paper to mark our votes for the best in a range of categories.

Anime music videos use clips from anime edited together with the music of a popular (or obscure) song. At anime conventions in the United States, the AMV events are usually packed with people and excitement. That Friday night, we had gathered to watch the twenty-six finalists in the AMV contest. The crowd was quiet and watched politely, though occasionally exploding with laughs and cheers when particularly clever connections were made. The video that drew the most laughs of those I saw was a spoof on the opening credits to the American TV show *Friends*, which combined the theme song and actors' credits (Jennifer Aniston, Matthew Perry, etc.) with images from anime. Another AMV re-edited the opening to *Batman Begins* with *Naruto* (action ninja anime) clips. The level of proficiency in the video editing was spectacular. The AMV that won the "Best in Show" award was made by a female video editor living in Italy, who had combined clips from the series *Princess Tutu* (2002) with the Swedish pop song "Håll om mig" (Hold me now) by Nanne Grönvall. The video displayed great ingenuity in portraying the tension between characters in the anime, and the images flowed with the emotional rise and fall of the song. Even people worried about copyright infringement can recognize the creativity of such an AMV, but does our appreciation of such creative works erode the foundation of intellectual property?

Where should the line be drawn in terms of the circulation and control of AMVs? Here the world of anime does not provide a single answer.

Manga publishers and anime studios tend to reject the idea that the "free publicity" generated by unauthorized distribution of AMVs outweighs the losses they attribute to unlicensed downloading and streaming. When forced to choose, they care more about control than publicity. Nevertheless, participatory communities of fans of all kinds appear to feel increasingly empowered to make things and put them online. There is simply too much out there to police fully, and since much of the sharing is noncommercial, there is not much benefit to the industry to pursue lawsuits, especially given the experience of the Recording Industry Association of America in the United States. The RIAA sued some and threatened to sue tens of thousands more consumers accused of downloading music illegally. This effort is widely regarded as a public relations disaster, and it failed to curtail downloading. With AMVs, some bands and record labels have asked that their work not be used (a request that is largely granted by AMV creators). At AnimeMusicVideo.org, a website that helps support AMV creators by making videos available for downloading, sponsoring contests, and providing a forum space for discussions, each time you download an AMV a disclaimer appears that reads, "This video is purely fan-made and is in no way associated with the musical artist or anime company in any way."[9] The phrase "in no way associated" might be better read as "unauthorized, but please don't sue us." The description of each AMV generally lists the artist and title of the song (and, often, the lyrics), as well the anime productions that were sampled for it. Many AMVs lovingly portray scenes from a single series, but some sample dozens, even more than a hundred different shows (e.g., "Jihaku" by Fantasy Studios or the "AMV Hell" series). Disclaimers aside, AMVs gain some of their value from an association with the songs and anime that they feature. Familiarity with a song or anime does something in terms of drawing us in.

At the same time, this world of AMVs is an intriguingly hybrid space, ignoring copyright in some regards but asserting the importance of authorship. The cultural space of AMVs is neither a free-for-all defined by disrespect for copyright nor a postmodern utopia of share-and-share-alike pastiche. The participants still hold strong opinions about originality, authorship, and fairness, even if those principles contradict copyright law. When you sign up to become a member of AnimeMusicVideo.org, which is free, you are greeted with a range of stipulations about the types of works that will be accepted. A submitted AMV must be created by the author or group that is submitting it (i.e., it has to have been edited by that person or group). The clips must come directly from a file of the anime, not from other people's AMVs. The rules also stipulate that you should not use pirated software, or "warez." (Although this rule is unenforceable, I imagine it could discourage discussion on the AnimeMusicVideo.org site of where to get free copies of expensive video-editing software.) On one hand, one could argue that these gestures at ethical behavior are too limited compared with the damage done by further encouraging copyright infringement through sampling and remixing. On the other hand, as many people point out, good AMVs can introduce both anime and songs to new audiences and amplify the affection fans have for long-running anime. I and at least a few others were introduced to *Princess Tutu* and the Swedish pop singer through the AMV, which gained attention because of its fine workmanship. Shouldn't some credit go to the AMV artist? More broadly, if we are to grasp the value of anime, shouldn't we acknowledge the hard work of organizing conventions, as well as the openness of fans in attending AMV screenings and voting on the winners? To grasp the complexity of production and value, I explore a range of perspectives and ultimately draw the conclusion that the greater the circulation is, the more value is created (see chapter 6).

If we also consider the thousands of fans who dress as their favorite characters, where should we locate the force of desire for this kind of participation in anime? Cosplay, a Japanese contraction of "costume" and "play," illustrates the centrality of "characters" as a kind of platform on which others can build, yet that process of building itself becomes a personal expression (Allison 2006; McVeigh 2000; Steinberg 2008). Dressing as a character, sometimes performing *in* character, is rewarded by the attention one receives. Fan conventions are a space where dressing up is *appreciated*—note the language of value—in terms of an ethic that accords status to do-it-yourself costumes above store-bought wear. We shouldn't underestimate the value of cosplay as a social lubricant, as well. Fan conventions are certainly about a love for anime, but that frisson of excitement around flirting with others often seems to be an important part of the scene. Costumes facilitate conversation, acting as a visual celebration of alliance with specific worlds of anime fandom but also working as an ice breaker for people who haven't met. Even for people unaccustomed to the thrill of cosplay as practitioners, it is easy to observe and feel the energy at an anime convention. Collaborative creativity raises the question not only of who makes anime but also of what anime does. The answer depends on what we think of media and culture.

Media and Cultural Studies: Contexts, Not Borders

Anime can provide insight into recent shifts in media and cultural studies. In some ways, media studies is morphing from a focus on individual technologies (radio, film, television, the Internet) to the study of what moves across media—characters, celebrities, brands, stories, worlds, civic action, for example. Those of us who work in "area studies" such as Japan studies face an analogous shift as we adapt cultural studies to an age of globalization. Just as media can no longer be defined by what happens within a particular technological platform, so, too, can culture no longer be defined solely by national or ethnic boundaries (Gupta and Ferguson 1997b). Some of the most interesting theorizing of media and culture over the past two decades wrestles with these issues in some way.

At the same time, anime studies has been developing as an intellectual field, in part because anime provides such fertile ground for a variety of disciplinary angles. Many scholars offer nuanced readings of anime texts, taking varied approaches to questions of identity, technology, sexuality, and power and often wrestling with our unease regarding the future. The number of studies of anime has grown exponentially in recent years, reaching across genres and forms, including claymation, computer graphics, and hand-drawn "cel-type" animation. "Cel" is a reference to transparent celluloid sheets that were used for animation in the past. Characters would be drawn on these sheets, laid across background images, and filmed using a multiplane camera (see LaMarre 2009). By contrast, Winsor McCay drew movements and backgrounds for every frame in *The Sinking of the Lusitania* (1918). The literature and film scholar Susan Napier is among the pioneers in arguing for scholarly recognition of the art of anime, of the deep philosophical themes that much Japanese animation explores. Her work also traces the continuities in the desire for Japan by Westerners, from Impressionist artists in the 1800s to anime fans more recently (Napier 2005, 2007). Many scholars offer nuanced readings of anime, often relying on a mix of interpretation of the narrative content of certain works along with consideration of the technology of making animation (one frame at a time, the illusion of movement based on a series of still drawings, and so on), and this takes many forms (Brown 2010; Looser 2006; Lunning 2006, 2007, 2008, 2009, 2010; Macwilliams 2008). Although much scholarly research on anime emphasizes the interpretation of narratives within films or series, a wider variety of work is appearing to deal with varieties of fandom and cross-media synergy with things like science fiction writing and the character merchandise business (Bolton et al. 2007; Poitras 1999; Ruh 2004; Steinberg 2008). Into this mix, my aim is to add insights to be gained from ethnographic fieldwork. Just as we can learn from considering anime in relation to audiences, so, too, can we see scholarly studies of animation as efforts to build a certain kind of field of debate, another gambit in the process of determining what makes anime important. Textual interpretation and ethnographic fieldwork are clearly complementary approaches.

Anthropology's commitment to participant-observation fieldwork shines a light on the active relationships and dynamics of production, and this can bring a new perspective to anime studies and to media studies more generally. The media scholars W. J. T. Mitchell and Mark B. N. Hansen (2010: viii) identify two broad methodological approaches to media studies: the empirical and the interpretive. For them, empirical studies, especially from sociology, economics, and communication, tend to focus on mass media and their political, social, economic, and cultural impact, particularly by attending to what gets distributed to audiences. The interpretive approach, associated with the humanities, including literary theory, film studies, and cultural studies, tends to focus on "the constitution of media" and how this shapes "what is regarded as knowledge and what is communicable" (viii). Mitchell and Hansen, however, hope to go beyond these binaries of empirical and interpretive and "to exploit the ambiguity of the concept of media—the slippage from plural to singular, from differentiated forms to overarching technical platforms and theoretical vantage points" by using media as "a third term, capable of bridging, or 'mediating' the binaries." Even with this definition, however, we can see that both the empirical and the interpretive approaches primarily analyze media as particular kinds of objects with the capacity to convey cultural understandings. Media is seen as a collection of "affordances," that is, the capabilities of technologies to relate information or enable interaction in particular ways, for example, in the differences between Twitter and a massively multiplayer online videogame. To take seriously this notion of media as a "third term" that mediates binaries, we need to view media in its multiplicity of roles: as a conveyer of meanings, as a platform for others to build on, as a tool of connection, and as a process that can activate collectivities. In this respect, anthropologists tend to spend less time with the interpretation of media content than with the practices around media and how these interactions, modes of communication, and day-to-day lived experience generate meaning in terms of behavior and beliefs.

Raymond Williams (2006 [1980]: 141) has commented that what is striking to him is that "nearly all forms of critical theory are theories of consumption. That is to say, they are concerned with understanding an object in such a way that it can profitably or correctly be consumed." Although he wrote this in 1980, noting that questions of "taste" and "sensibility" dominated discussions of texts, the criticism remains apt, particularly in the many studies of Japanese popular culture that start with the story from a particular media text and then discuss its significance. This approach can play a useful, critical role, but it also portrays only part of the workings of media. Williams implies a different question: What would it mean to develop a critical theory of production?

Media anthropologists have attempted to redress the overemphasis on consumption by looking in more detail at how institutions, transnational pressures, and a diverse range of actors negotiate the complex challenges of making their productions, whether it is Bollywood films (Ganti 2002), Kazakh soap operas (Mandel 2002), or amateur videos by Miao ethnic minorities in China (Schein 2002), to name a few important studies. Faye Ginsburg, for example, traces the complex tradeoffs that occur when aboriginal groups in Australia attempt to use television to recuperate their collective stories and histories. While access to media outlets for the aboriginal community does provide some measure of redress for the erasure of many of these stories from national Australian narratives, she finds that "retelling stories for the media of film, video, and television often requires reshaping them, not only within new aesthetic structures but also in negotiation with the political economy of state-controlled as well as commercial media" (2002: 40–41). From these perspectives, media production is a site where agency, structure, and power intersect in contested negotiations over meaning and representation.

My own sense is that something may be gained if we shift from a concern with the "cultural power" of media toward a critical theory of production that explores how "value" is produced. The anthropologist David Graeber proposes moving beyond the definition of value in terms of the economistic individual evaluating objects' exchange value or use value, and beyond the overly holistic and static structure of a society's "values," because neither is much help in developing social theory that can accommodate people's efforts to change society purposefully. Instead, he encourages us "to look at social systems as structures of creative action, and value, as how people measure the importance of their own actions within such structures" (2001: 230). This approach is useful for thinking about anime because as we map the "structures of creative action" as social systems, we can observe some of the ways value materializes through collaborative creativity. "Soul" as a collective energy gestures toward ethnographic insights that begin with *that which is most meaningful*, in the hope that if we start from there, we can begin to see how people value media and use it as a means to help organize their social worlds. Indeed, the transformation of social media may be not the online networks themselves but, rather, the paradigm shift in consciousness that accompanies a sense of media as something we participate in through our activities in particular social networks. As Einstein wedded the Newtonian duality of space and time, so, too, we might see the interconnection of media and culture not in terms of vehicle and representation (technology and message) but, rather, as an integrated actualization of the social.

This brings into focus the *social in media*. In what ways is media part and parcel of our social world? Beginning a look at anime in terms of labor and production is more apt for our social media moment, because it reminds us that conveying "messages" and "images" is only part of the work that media does. Yet the easy response that social media is all about "connection" tends to be too general and too limited to act as a convincing theoretical advance. Although "social media" is often taken to refer to a certain kind of online platform, it makes more sense to me to think of the social as an analytical perspective on what media is and does. Anime's dependence on a *collaborative creativity* makes it a useful test case of the dynamics that lead to what some are calling "spreadable media"—that is, media that moves across particular channels of communication (Jenkins 2009a). But what happens if we turn that concept of spreadable media on its head? Rather than emphasizing the media object that is spreadable, might we gain a different perspective by thinking in terms of the people who do the spreading, the economic and social motivations that drive those actions, which ultimately lead to a nuanced co-creation of value? Value can mean very different things, depending on whether the context is a storyboard meeting or an AMV contest. This multiplicity complicates analysis and begins to give a sense of the distributed innovation that provides force to anime as a cultural movement.

An ethnographic perspective on anime offers tools for media research in terms of socially committed actors, looking at how media provides a center of gravity for certain kinds of interests and activities. These themes are explored by others, as well. Following Jonathan Zittrain (2008) and his interest in the potential of an open, participatory, customizable Internet, I view anime characters as a generative platform of creativity. The anthropologist Brian Larkin (2008) works in similar directions in his concept of "infrastructure." Thomas LaMarre (2009) argues that the "anime machine" can point the way to rethink our relationship with technology. Henry Jenkins (2006) theorizes in terms of the design of transmedia storytelling. Anne Allison (2006) gauges the interaction between play and consumerism in Japanese toys. What these approaches share is a sense of media technology less as a guiding structure than as something to build on and push in innovative directions. Our understandings of value are what guide these energized efforts.

Collaborative creativity, social energy, generative platforms, and value in specific contexts—these are the tools of cultural analysis that I use to explore anime in terms of the emergence of a cultural movement. I use the term "soul" to reflect on ethnographic insights that begin with the energy and intentions of those most deeply involved in this cultural world, to focus on *that which is most meaningful*—or, less holistically, *what matters to people*, a kind of shorthand for deep meaning. If ethnography aims to understand the perspectives of the participants in a cultural community, this seems a good place to begin. I would underscore that this "soul" is not some kind of internal essence, like the problematic notions of the "soul of Japan" or the "soul of the samurai," as if there is some unchanging central, generative core that explains everything about anime. Quite the contrary: The soul I refer to here is best envisioned as a kind of energy that arises from the ways anime connects people; a connection that operates as a conduit of interest and activity; a soul, in other words, that arises out of collective action. I hope this can illuminate the power of ideas manifested in material production but that gain life across media platforms and across categories of producers. The value of media emerges in places that can be far removed from the locales of production and beyond the specific content of the media forms themselves.

Put another way, rather than looking primarily *into* anime media to understand the resonance of the content, I explore anime by looking outward at the social relations, emergent business networks, and day-to-day activities that expand the cultural universe of anime. I see the driving force as a kind of "social energy" that pushes outward while being guided in patterned ways. Such a perspective suggests that the energy works locally in terms of being activated through relatively intimate social networks rather than across national settings or wide categories of people as a whole. It may be that our places in our smaller social worlds and networks provide the key to the emergence of new systems of value.

Outline of the Book

To get a sense of what collaborative creativity means for anime, we need to look at diverse spaces of production and various understandings of success. Professional animators, toy companies, manga artists, transnational youth, and specialized otaku all contribute in their own ways to the making of anime, and they bring distinctive perspectives on understanding anime's value and meaning.

Chapter 1 expands on the theoretical underpinnings of this ethnographic approach to anime. I go more deeply into the work of Mamoru Hosoda to observe practical steps in creating animation and to see how he explains the bigger picture. There are technologies of direction and control (the storyboards, checklists, deadlines), as well as complexly distributed labor and expertise. This extends the discussion of a critical theory of production that centers on value within structures of creative action. Hosoda's recent work converges on a seemingly paradoxical trend in society, especially in his films *The Girl Who Leapt through Time* (2006) and *Summer Wars* (2009). New communication technologies enable wider collaborative networks to form around solving complex tasks, but at the same time, we find ourselves facing increasingly personalized, individual futures. This further sets up the theme of thinking about relationships between niche and mass.

In chapter 2, I discuss how new anime projects are built up around characters and worlds and propose that we think of this combination as a kind of creative platform. Indeed, what anime studios make is not only audiovisual narratives but, more fundamentally, long-lasting characters (and their worlds), which ideally can be spun off across media forms for years to come. We visit script meetings for a children's anime called *Zenmai Zamurai*, and I discuss the logic of two other samurai anime aimed at teens and adults: *Samurai Champloo* (2004) and *Afro Samurai* (2007).

In chapter 3, I explore the development of early postwar anime (late

1950s and 1960s) and the contrasts between the production of feature films and that of television. While some creators, such as Yasuo Ōtsuka at Toei Animation, focused on the joy of animated movement in feature films and pioneered styles of full animation, others, such as Osamu Tezuka and Mushi Productions, worked on radically limiting the number of frames needed in order to deal with the budgets and schedules of television animation. Both approaches speak to the artistry of animation but communicate differently and tend to rely on different connections across media. This divide deepened as sponsors and merchandisers recognized the marketing potential of cartoon entertainment. Outside influence was integral, as well, and we consider the influence of Disney and the central role of manga. Some argue that the media world of manga is an ideal of democratic capitalism in that the most successful comics are also the best comics. Why? With low costs to produce and consume and tight feedback loops between publishers and readers, manga developed in an intense field of competition generated by a combination of skilled creators, a deep catalogue, and a ready-made fan base. I would argue that the emotional attachments people build with characters over the years is part and parcel of the platform of characters and worlds. The platform that anime builds on, therefore, is not only characters and worlds but also the social energy that attaches to them.

In chapter 4, I discuss mecha (giant robot) anime and the transition from children's series to those aimed at teens and adults (1970s–90s). Although anime is sometimes regarded as significant because it provides particular kinds of fantasyscapes—virtual worlds of possibility, realms of unbridled imaginative leaps—I would argue that anime is equally important for the connections it makes to the "real." In fact, the term "real anime" increasingly became a means to talk about grownup themes. As creators and audiences matured, new styles of anime emerged, a process we can see in the shifts over time among *Astro Boy, Mazinger Z, Gundam,* and the works of Gainax, such as *Neon Genesis Evangelion.* Fieldwork at a Bandai brainstorming session rounds out the discussion of anime and toys in terms of both nostalgia and futurism. Given the example of *Gundam,* which initially failed on TV but then succeeded through outside activities of fans and merchandisers, we are faced with the fact that sources of success clearly don't lie solely within the media form. This adds another dimension to thinking about platforms and contexts.

In chapter 5, I discuss fieldwork at the Gonzo studios, where I observed the making of *Red Garden* (2006), a late-night TV series aimed at teens and young adults. As in chapter 1, I describe some of the day-to-day labor and what I heard about the bigger picture from the director Kou Matsuo and from Shin Ishikawa, chief executive of Gonzo. Along with making comparisons with Studio Ghibli and Studio 4°C, I explore the question of what makes a studio cutting edge. How does a studio make something new but that also has a foundation on which others can build, a kind of "avantcore"? I focus on the idea of openness, of creating a space for others to fill, as an important element in collaborative creativity, not unlike the space between frames of a comic strip ("the gutter").

Where do overseas audiences fit into the picture? In chapter 6, I examine how transnational anime fans provide a fascinating perspective on digital technology and the copyright wars. The phenomenon of fansubbing, whereby fan groups translate the most recent broadcasts of Japanese anime and make them available online for free, constitutes a kind of civil disobedience aimed at improving the anime industry. There are heated debates about whether this is a legitimate practice and if it is, under what circumstances. Fansubbing extends our understanding of the social energy around anime fandom and is emblematic of a wider range of fan activities. But is this aspect of collaborative creativity better seen as debilitating destruction? Although the copyright wars tend to be judged on the basis of "the effect on the market," the history of media illustrates that "the market" is such a hodgepodge of legal and ethical systems that one person's "piracy" can be seen as another's legitimate activity. In the early twentieth century, Hollywood (an antipiracy torchbearer today) was established as a renegade industry, avoiding Thomas Edison's patents. Today, the fierce debates about fansubbing among anime fans point to the possibility of a social resolution to online sharing (i.e., the emergence of a largely agreed-on set of values guiding sharing, use, and commodification). I'm not alone in seeing this as a better fix than the variety of technological or legal solutions proposed otherwise.

In chapter 7, I consider some niche Japanese fans, stereotyped as the notorious otaku, some of whom argue for the benefits of an awkward revolution: falling in love with anime characters. I begin with a discussion of an online petition asking for legal recognition of marriage with a 2D character, one offshoot of a larger world of "*moe*" (pronounced "moh-ay") attractions. How are we to interpret the deep-felt emotion people have toward virtual characters? Might this niche attitude gain mainstream respectability? Some theorists see in *moe* a radical break with other forms of media consumption, but I see this as a further extension of collaborative creativity. The *moe* phenomenon seems to imply an intensely personal subjectivity, a cul-de-sac where emotional attachments flow only inward, without reciprocity. A closer look, however, reveals the enduring connection to broader social collectives—for example, in the desire to have emotional attachments publicly validated and thereby to rethink ideas of manhood, consumption, and love.

In the conclusion, I discuss some of the insights of collaborative creativity. I return to the themes of collaborative networks versus personalized media, the value of anime from a laborer's perspective, and the possibilities for overseas expansion of audiences for anime and Japanese film. In the end, I consider what this ethnographic approach to anime production can tell us about globalization from below and about wider possibilities for emergent cultural action in the future.

For me, anime offers a solution to some of the analytical puzzles that arise from media's fluid mobility today. Instead of looking for some core or essence within media, I would encourage instead a look at how logics of production build a kind of generative platform and how this collaborative creativity operates across categories of producers. Anime provides a distinctive, though not unique, approach to the question of *what moves across media forms*—namely, characters and worlds (and the emotional attachments that build energy around them). Anime also offers a perspective on the *movement of culture* across borders, specifically by showing how boundaries are less important than questions about how people use media in specific social settings. There are multiple, networked crucibles of creativity, and we can learn about their dynamics through participant-observation fieldwork.

In sum, collaborative creativity aims to bring into focus the multiplicity of modes of production and what, exactly, collaboration means.[10] Who is collaborating with whom? Who "owns" the results of collaboration? Whose creativity is valued and whose is recognized and within which spheres? How is collaboration something more than mere circulation, and in what ways does it overflow the categories of production and consumption? Collaboration tries to hold in dynamic tension the objects, the related people, and the contexts. As we will see, this reshapes the ways to think about the "Japaneseness" in the globalization of anime by showing that origins are less important than the contexts. Let's return to the work of Mamoru Hosoda to see where these ideas lead.

ONE

Collaborative Networks, Personal Futures

In March 2010, the anime director Mamoru Hosoda visited MIT to screen his feature film *Summer Wars*. When the credits rolled and Hosoda skipped down the steps of the enormous classroom, physics equations still scribbled on the blackboard, the audience of 450 people broke into thunderous applause. Hosoda and his extended production staff had clearly created a film with a global and contemporary appeal. They had done something more, as well. In both *Summer Wars* (2009) and in his previous feature, *The Girl Who Leapt through Time* (2006), Hosoda and his team developed characters and worlds that dramatized broader developments in media and culture. The two films highlight seemingly paradoxical trends: today's increased potential for collaboration and networking in contrast with an increasing personalization and individualization of our media worlds. New kinds of mass culture are emerging, sometimes made by amateur producers, at the same time that niche obsessions are becoming more specific and widespread. These developments suggest shifts in the workings of economic and political systems as well. We get pulled in two directions at once, encouraged to individualize our media experiences, whether by choice or through automated filtering systems (Pariser 2011), and at the same time motivated to reach out to others through networked interactions across platforms (Benkler 2006; Jenkins 2006). How is the future trending in terms of the individual and the collective? A look at Hosoda's work in animation—and specifically at how he envisioned his films—provides ethnographic context for the films and introduces perspectives on the work that characters and worlds can do.

Summer Wars opens with a seventeen-year-old boy from the city who is asked by a female upperclassman to accompany her to her family's home in rural Japan for a part-time job. It turns out that the "job" requires him to pretend to be her fiancé. As a math geek who has never had a girlfriend, he is hardly the type. Moreover, he has to play the role in front of her entire extended family, who have gathered in the family's main house in the Nagano countryside to celebrate the matriarch's eightieth birthday. Birthday plans are thrown into disarray, however, when trouble comes to Oz, a vast online realm that facilitates communication, entertainment, and a wide variety of official transactions. A rogue online artificial intelligence (AI) bot known as "Love Machine" starts causing havoc in the online metaverse of Oz. The repercussions extend throughout society—not only in Japan, but around the world—as traffic and commuter systems, water and power supplies, emergency notification systems, and so on all go haywire as a result of the malevolent program. The boy and girl and her extended family find themselves embroiled in a potentially life-threatening battle with the AI. They each draw on their own social networks and their own resources, bringing together computer equipment, power from a fishing boat, and ice from a shop (among other things) to wage war with the evil troublemaker. The film draws on metaphors from various games, from online fighting games to *hanafuda*, an old-fashioned but still popular card game. The world is interactive and networked in a digital sense, but in the end, it is a matter of engineering the social world that makes the difference.

An anime fan and MIT graduate student at the time described her appreciation of Hosoda's film this way: "I really liked the ways the whole family worked together to hack their surroundings and solve problems." She noted that many hacker movies follow a formula of a good-looking teen boy solving most of the problems while helped by a few "sidekicks." But in *Summer Wars*, she noted, "There were teenagers and older folks working together. Even the eighty-year-old grandmother did some good old-fashioned social engineering using a rotary telephone." For the student, the film portrayed something new: an extended-family approach to hacking the world.

After the screening, Hosoda spoke to the audience about his goal to create a film with a different kind of hero. Heroism is often portrayed in terms of the courage and talents of an individual, he explained. In *Summer Wars*, heroism arises from the collective efforts of a range of characters, each with specialized capabilities, whose connections and collaborative work generate solutions to seemingly intractable problems. In this, the premise of the film offers a metaphor for the collective labor that goes into making animation. It also suggests an effort to redesign the ways heroes, and problem solving, are imagined. One of the film's posters emphasized this idea in the catch phrase "Connection itself is our weapon" (*Tsunagari koso ga bokura no buki*) (see figure 5).

It's interesting that Hosoda presents the potential of connection as both frightening, as when the rogue AI runs amok, and empowering, as when the family pulls together. The language of "virtual worlds" and "cyberspace" as places apart from our living social worlds is gradually disappearing as a way to think about our connections online. *Summer Wars* dramatizes that process of shifting. As Hosoda explained to the MIT audience, "We tend to see the virtual world as 'fake (*feeku*)' and our family relationships as 'real,'" but we are coming to the realization that virtual worlds are spaces with real relationships with real consequences. There are often real people behind those avatars.

The Making of the *Summer Wars* Characters

In making animation, part of the challenge of creating characters is giving the sense of a real person when none in fact exists. How did Hosoda create the characters that appeared in *Summer Wars*? In a published interview, he laughed at the intensity of the process. Hosoda worked with Yoshiyuki Sadamoto, who also designed the characters for Gainax's *Neon Genesis Evangelion* and other projects. The process was grueling and involved holing up in a hotel room away from all distractions. "Yes, we were living together, twenty-four hours a day. . . . We did that four times, usually four days at a time," Hosoda said. The goal was to work out the characters for all of the relatives who would appear in the film, and he and Sadamoto did that by talking about their own families. This in itself introduced some tension, Hosoda says, because "Sadamoto was from a main family house (*honke*), and I was from a branch house (*bekke*), and generally the branch house doesn't get along with the main house." But Sadamoto introduced Hosoda to the challenges of residing at an extended family's main house, where the bulk of the action in *Summer Wars* takes place. Sadamoto had a

5. *Summer Wars* poster that reads "connection is our weapon."

keen sense of the weight of the responsibilities that fall on the main house: "We were drawing as we were talking, on and on, and we realized we were making a family story (*kazoku mono*). Up to now, I really hadn't thought much about families for my animation. Even though there were families [in *The Girl Who Leapt through Time*], the protagonists were a high school girl and two boys. But for this film, the hero was going to be a family. . . . We realized that would make this a very different kind of work" (quoted in Hobby Shosekibu 2009: 125).

In thinking about how characters operate as a platform of creativity in anime, what can we learn from *Summer Wars*? As Hosoda and Sadamoto struggled to draw the characters, they realized that working together successfully meant connecting their drawings to a wide range of experiences. For example, Hosoda described the challenge of making Kenji, the eleventh-grade boy: "Despite being a genius at math, [Kenji] is the kind of kid who doesn't recognize his own abilities. How do you draw that?" The problem was even more complex because Natsuki, the twelfth-grade heroine, had to like Kenji. "Since he's an underclassman boy (*kōhai*), he had to seem somehow cute to her, and we had to think about what that might mean," Hosoda said. With Natsuki's character, he and Sadamoto went against the grain of anime generally: "In normal anime, the hero is the most flashy and conspicuous character, the person who has to display the most amazing skills." Even though Sadamoto tends to draw gorgeous-type characters, Hosoda pressed for a different direction:

> Sadamoto and I had worked together on *The Girl Who Leapt through Time*, so he knows I tend not to like decorative styles. I think the protagonist should be as simple as possible. After all, the camera is going to follow her through the whole movie, so there's no need to create a drawing where everything gets explained in one glance. Besides, a variety of audience members have to get close to her (*yorisotte miru*), so it should be someone who people feel they can contribute their own feelings to. That's why we made the characters simple. (quoted in Hobby Shosekibu 2009: 126–27)

This logic of character design emphasizes an idea of openness so audience members can add something of their own to the characters.

The characters were central to how Hosoda and Sadamoto conceived of making the film, but the challenge was to really understand those characters as people. "We didn't just draw pictures, and we didn't just think up personality types (*kyara*)," Hosoda said. "Instead, we thought, 'If this person was actually around, what kind of person would she be?' That's what we thought about while drawing" (quoted in Hobby Shosekibu 2009: 129). They also watched a lot of Jūzō Itami movies, partly because, as Itami does in his films, Hosoda and Sadamoto wanted to include many characters without relying on the star power of celebrities to define them. Hosoda notes that his approach to creating feature films contrasts in some ways with TV series work: "For TV series, you have to think in terms of the character goods business," especially when it comes to design. "You might even think of the character business as driving what happens in TV anime." For standalone, original films, the character businesses aren't well established, he said, "because films are only in theaters for one or two months. In that period of time, you can't say, 'Let's make a lot of money on character merchandise!' Obviously, in the case of features, the films themselves are the merchandise" (128–29).

Hosoda's dramatization of heroism partly reminds us of how collaboration in anime extends production from the studios through thinking about audiences. Hosoda said he did not want to make a film that focused on a hero saving the world while everyone else said, "Thank you!" He wanted to make "a movie where normal people put their strength together" (130–31). Early in the design, he realized the film was going to contain "family action," Hosoda said, "even though I had no idea what that would mean." A benefit of this approach was to allow people in their twenties, thirties, and forties—"not just teenage girls"—to see characters their age in anime. In this, Hosoda hoped to push anime in new directions, especially by thinking in terms of filmmaking rather than just in terms of anime. "That's how I want to expand the possibilities for animation," he said. "Especially with anime, it has to be made by everyone, so we all have to get on board. With many different kinds of people watching animation, we want everyone to feel a kind of joint ownership (*kyōyū*). When I say everyone, I don't mean just the anime world, but for everyone in Japan, and around the world too, I want to spread the message of the wealth of potential in animation" (131–33).

Revisiting Intellectual Contexts for Cultural Analysis

Hosoda's comments about *Summer Wars* reflect a common mode of discussion about directors and films. As he looks back over the process of production, he explains, in retrospect, how it unfolded and to which larger ideas, even philosophical realms, the film speaks. As a tool of cultural analysis, however, we can use these musings to explore the making of cultural worlds: not only within the film but also in everyday life. "Cultural analysis has become increasingly relational, plural, and aware of its own historicity," says Michael Fischer (2007: 40) in his overview of a century of anthropological theory and practice. This openness makes it capable, "like experimental systems, of creating new epistemic things." The "jeweler's eye" for ethnographic nuance and conceptual experimentation, he adds, often provides insight into both "local crucibles of cultural conflict" and "multisited detailing of networks and transduction from localities to transnational players" (2007: 40). In other words, a goal of ethnographic methods today is to portray these crucibles, along with their broader networks, to see in the making of cultural worlds the possibilities for innovation.

The cultural anthropologist Anne Allison brings a particular perspective to questions of world-making through her study of Japanese toys, such as Power Rangers, Sailor Moon, Pokémon, and Tamagotchi (virtual pets), and the ways they promote a certain kind of global imagination. She finds that children use these play worlds as kinds of platforms for socializing, but children are also taught to view certain logics of consumerism as natural. Ultimately, Allison sees something hopeful but also "chilling" in "this capitalist dreamworld." In particular, "The drive to press forward is ever-present," she says, but "one can never definitively reach the goal, given that it is a frontier stretching out endlessly" into ever more consumption of toys, games, and merchandise. But she sees a glimmer of hope, too, "something more promising and possibly new" in the imaginative strategies provoked by Japanese toys. Pokémon centers on "morphing and disassembling (and reassembling) ... [and thus] offers kids a way of dealing with a world and identity premised on flux" (2006: 278–79). Thus, the cultural workings of capitalism are reproduced and naturalized through children's play, but they also can give children tools to subvert dominant logics through a sense of multiplicity and self-fashioning. This provides a nice contrast to—or, perhaps, extension in a new direction of—Fischer's inspiration from biologists' making of new organisms to "write with biology," whereby Allison shows how both corporations and children might be said to *write with play*.

In *The Anime Machine*, Thomas LaMarre (2009: 15) takes a somewhat different tack toward questions of world-making when he explores the "material essence or specificity of animation." He is careful to note that his point of reference is "the moving image not the apparatus." Still, he draws inspiration from the apparatus of animation, namely the animation stand, which allowed a movie camera to film multiple still images stacked in adjustable layers. The animation stand, says LaMarre (2009: 302), "channeled the force implicit in the succession of moving images into the gap between planes of the image—through the animetic interval." Through this focus, he aims to create a "media theory of animation" that understands anime in terms different from that of live action cinema, for example, in the latter's focus on a ballistic, monocular camera rushing through space. LaMarre emphasizes a different perspective that arises from the multiplane camera that looks down through layers of drawn cels so that the movement of the cels in relation to the other layers is what gives the sense of motion and life. Thus, animation offers a different perspective on worldmaking by emphasizing the relationships between layers of drawn material, for example, characters and background. This, too, we should note, is quite a different theory of animation from one that focuses on the movements or actions of the characters (e.g., in the contrasts between full and limited animation). In this respect, LaMarre also concerns himself with the disciplined structuring of creativity. "By allowing animators to work with the relation between layers, the animation stand at once highlighted the animetic interval and promised to control, contain, or harness it" (2009: 303). Because different studios made different uses of this potential, for example, LaMarre uses the contrasts between the work of Studio Ghibli (especially Hayao Miyazaki), Gainax, and CLAMP (an all-women group) to portray alternative ways anime can help us think through our "relationship to technology"—or, as he puts it, "how anime thinks technology." It's a provocative approach, and he includes a challenge to those of us who think more ethnographically: "If we do not consider the material essence of animation (the animetic interval) in its divergent series, we have no way to think about the relation between animation and communication networks; we risk doing no more than endlessly amassing anecdotes about studios and commodities, producers and fans" (2009: 312). What is at stake is a question of what counts as theory and, in turn, what constitutes evidence and findings. One might counter, however, that the material essence of anime could also be viewed in terms of labor and collective action so that fieldwork "anecdotes" are precisely what are required to help us think about the relations between animation and communication networks.

At the same time, LaMarre does not quibble: His book is about "how to read anime" (2009: ix), and in this he offers what Raymond Williams has referred to as a critical theory of consumption. But if we look for a critical theory of production, the materiality of anime (though not its "essence") would better be seen through the social in media, whether commercial or noncommercial activities. In this case, theory could not proceed primarily from a machinic constraint on production, but rather, a multiplicity of entry points, so that "endlessly amassing anecdotes" is not a pitfall but a necessity in trying to portray the multidimensionality of creativity in today's media worlds. At the risk of underplaying the centrality of this animetic interval, I opt to extend the platforms of creativity in other directions. That said, LaMarre makes a strong case, especially in driving at the heart of what distinguishes animation from other media forms, and in doing so, he offers a constructive model of how to conceive of anime as a particular kind of crucible of creativity.

Henry Jenkins (2006) works in a different direction, looking at how new and old media converge in the minds of fans, who through their participation extend and reformulate the works of media industries. Fans are no longer simply "consumers." Rather, participation is understood "as part of the normal ways that media operate"; the current debates center on "the terms of our participation." Jenkins argues for examining our trans-media future by considering fan reworkings, reminding us that studying fan culture has helped us to understand the "innovations that occur on the fringes of the media industry" and that fan communities may show us "new ways of thinking about citizenship and collaboration." The "political effects of these fan communities come not simply through the production and circulation of new ideas (the critical reading of favorite texts) but also through access to new social structures (collective intelligence) and new models of cultural production (participatory culture)" (Jenkins 2006: 246). With this, Jenkins brings us full circle, locating the crucibles of creativity in smaller networks, even the fringe groups of fandom, to grasp what innovation with media can mean. Having observed a range of work in anime studios, I am struck by how anime making depends on divergent "models of cultural production," so that the social side of animation can be mapped in terms of a networked, collaborative productivity.

What these intellectual approaches to contemporary media studies share is a desire to grasp both the structuring aspects of media and the creative potentials that can emerge sometimes unpredictably and sometimes in unlikely (or unrecognized) places. They also resist the urge to link a form of popular culture with a simple resonance with a broader community. By trying to map the spaces and styles of production, the cultural analysis used by these scholars often assumes that change can happen by identifying a kind of untapped resource—an energy, perhaps, that if guided in new directions can reshape, even animate, dormant potential. This does not do away with the insights to be gained from thinking in terms of resonance, but it points us toward exploring how this vibration can lead to action, that is, how a look at making media can transform our understanding of how media works.

"I Thought My Career in Animation Was Over"

Mamoru Hosoda grew up with a love of anime, but he gained a new perspective when he caught a glimpse of the process of producing films. Hosoda was born in 1967 in Toyama Prefecture and says that his view of anime changed when he was twelve. After watching the theatrical release of the feature film of *Ginga Tetsudō 999* (Galaxy Express 999, dir. Rin Tarō, 1979), Hosoda purchased a picture album (*roman arubamu*) of the film. He said it was a revelation: "Up until then, I had only thought things like 'anime is amazing' or 'I really enjoy this.' But once I had that picture album in hand and I saw the director Rin's storyboards, my thinking about anime changed. Actually, I started to think that it wasn't so much the films themselves, but rather it was the creators who were cool. It was the storyboards that symbolically conveyed that to me. Rin's storyboards made a huge impact on me" (Hosoda and Summer Wars Film Partners 2009: 504). This is an epiphany that comes from a conceptual shift from anime as something to be enjoyed (read, interpreted, consumed) to anime as a cool process of production.

Hosoda's career has meant extending his youthful interests in art and drawing. He pursued the formal study of oil painting as a student at Kanazawa Art College. His appreciation of modern art shows through in one of the visual themes that appears repeatedly in his films—namely, the image of a jet trail streaking through the sky, as in *Digimon Adventure*, or of a boat trail through the water as seen from high above, as in the title sequence of *One Piece: Omatsuri danshaku* (see figure 6). He relates this image to his interest in the painter Lucio Fontana, whose solid color canvas paintings have distinctive stripes across them. From a distance,

6. Title sequence of Hosoda's *One Piece*, with boat slicing through water.

Fontana's paintings look as though the stripes are painted on, but as you approach, you can see that they are in fact razor slices in the canvas. This break in the two-dimensional space of the painting implies a world beyond what we can see and beyond our expectations.

I first met Hosoda in the summer of 2005. This was not long after the release of the pirate adventure feature film *One Piece: Omatsuri danshaku to himitsu no shima* (Baron Omatsuri and the secret island, dir. Hosoda, 2005) based on the long-running *One Piece* manga series by Eiichirō Oda. I vividly recall our first meeting when he discussed the film's dark second half. "I imagined it something like *Westworld* [dir. Michael Crichton, 1973], which begins happily then turns dark" when an amusement park staffed by robots turns life-threatening. Similarly, Hosoda's *One Piece* film begins with playful competitions but turns dangerous for the pirate crew. Eventually, the pirate captain, Luffy, is separated from his friends, and in his isolation he questions his ability to go forward. In a violent scene, Luffy's magical limbs are restrained, impaled by arrows in a rock, and we witness a dark scene of helplessness and despair. This had special meaning for Hosoda at the time: the scene grew in part out of his experience of trying to work on *Howl's Moving Castle* at Studio Ghibli. He had spent six months on the project and had assembled a staff who were expecting to take it to completion, but he was removed from the project (for reasons left unspoken, but I assume "creative differences," an inadequate term for the heated conflicts I suspect were the cause). The staff he had assembled were dispersed, and Hosoda saw his credibility at grave risk: "I felt my career in animation was over." But, somehow, like Luffy, Hosoda found a way to keep moving ahead, returning to Toei Animation to create the sixth in the series of feature films in the *One Piece* series.

Thanks to a mutual friend, I met with Hosoda at least once a year after that. Gradually, I was able to observe more of the work of designing his films. For example, I sat in on a meeting to discuss the art direction (painted backgrounds) for Hosoda's *The Girl Who Leapt through Time*, which won Best Animated Feature Film from the Japan Academy. The five-hour meeting centered on how to design the leading heroine's room. The art director, Nizō Yamamoto, who helped design the lush forest backgrounds for the film *Princess Mononoke* (dir. Hayao Miyazaki, 1997), discussed the pros and cons of different design choices. How would the room be shared with her younger sister? What objects should be on the shelves? What kinds of desk lamps should appear? Should there be musical instruments, and, if so, which ones? Yamamoto, Hosoda, and the producer Saitō looked at magazines showing what girls could buy to furnish their rooms, and they even watched a documentary about a high school girls' volleyball team in rural Japan in the hope that a scene would show a "real girl's" room, which in the end appeared for about thirty seconds. Meetings like this were a combination of thinking from a blank page and also working from examples from elsewhere, including magazines, TV shows, and personal experience.

Hosoda's *The Girl Who Leapt through Time* gives another example of the circular movement of collaborative creativity and the idea that characters work as a kind of generative platform. In an interview in March 2006 at the Madhouse anime studios, Hosoda discussed with me the then forthcoming *Toki o kakeru shōjo* (the original Japanese title of *The Girl Who Leapt through Time*). He noted the challenges of reinterpreting a story that had already been remade seven times since the 1960s. Originally a novella by Yasutaka Tsutsui (2003 [1967]), a writer revered as one of the "three greats" of Japanese science fiction, the story revolves around a high school girl and two male classmates. After a regular school day, the girl suddenly finds she has a remarkable ability: she leaps backward in time, reliving the previous day. With the help of the two boys, she gradually unravels the mystery, discovering that one of her male friends is in fact a time traveler from the future who has mistakenly given her the power to travel through time. The short story published in 1967, the well-known live-action film version of 1983, and Hosoda's anime version in 2006 all share the emphasis on the anxieties associated with high school crushes, the love triangle between the girl and the two boys, and the sadness surrounding one boy's inevitable return to the future.

When Hosoda faced the challenge of remaking the film, he was surprised by something he found while rereading the original science fiction story and watching the live-action film: The future isn't what it used to be. In creating the anime, Hosoda transformed the character premise (*kyara settei*) in a way that he felt spoke to the sensibilities of today's generation of young people.

How did Hosoda change the characters? In Tsutsui's original story, the boy from the future comes to the present to retrieve plants that no longer exist in his time. His aim is to help society as a whole. We learn that although the boy is young, he is also a scientist with a doctoral degree who needs the plants to make medicine. Thus, the original premise that defines his character can be related to early postwar Japan's anxieties concerning environmental degradation. By the late 1960s, the awareness of mercury poisoning in Minamata had become just one example of how economic growth seemed to be producing a variety of ecological and health threats (George 2001). Tsutsui's story portrays youth as instrumental in tackling societal problems in the form of creating medicines.

Hosoda's time-traveling male character is different. He has come from the future not because he is on a quest to help society but to see something in the flesh. Hosoda constructs an alternative vision of the future that hinges on a different understanding of the sources of social change. Thinking partly in terms of people like Osamu Tezuka, who imagined the future with cars flying through the air, Hosoda explained: "My idea was this. For people like us, born in the 1960s and 1970s, the future was going to go on and improve, if not by us, then by people around us, like the Apollo mission group. The idea of the tube going through the air is about infrastructure, and the way an organized society is needed to accomplish that. It is a picture of a big society working together, and how that will happen. But today, it's more like young people have individual pictures of the future, not collective visions overall."[1] But Hosoda reasoned that if today's young people have more individual visions of the future (*kojinteki na miraizō*), then he would have to think of a different reason for the boy of the future to come to our present. "He won't come back for plants. I imagine that he will come back for a more individual reason, something to do with his inner self (*kokoro*). So in this version of *The Girl Who Leapt through Time*, why did the boy from the future come to our era? To see a painting."[2] Hosoda imagined the painting as a Buddhist picture (*butsuga*) painted "perhaps four hundred or five hundred years ago, say in the Muromachi period, though it really isn't specified in the film" (see figure 7). The word for "inner self" (*kokoro*) refers to a kind of "heart and soul" idea, and this ability of a picture to help a tormented self can be viewed as a kind of productive power of art.

Such Buddhist paintings are not meant to be shown in public. Instead, their purpose is to be an object of meditative reflection, to soothe the heart during troubled times. Hosoda explained, "The boy comes back to see a painting as a way to overcome (*norikoeru*) the horror of his times." The boy in Hosoda's film is important not because he produces something but because he consumes something in a way that will make him a better person, more at ease in his heart, even though he faces a world filled with trouble.

Hosoda also changed the heroine of the film. In the original short story and in the live-action film, she could not control her power to leap through time. In Hosoda's version, she learns that she can control her leaps. In the interview, Hosoda explained that young women in Japan today have more sense of their ability to control their own destinies, and he wanted to portray that change. Figure 8 shows the storyboards depicting the scene in which Makoto makes her first willed leap through time. This segment of the storyboards depicts about twelve and a half seconds of the one-and-a-half-hour film. Hosoda moves from the image of a rock skipping across a river to a closeup of Makoto and to her view as she takes a run toward her first leap. Hosoda leads us through shifts in perspective and imagery, moving back to the rock skipping, then to sound effects and an image of a digital clock, and finally to a splash moving backward in time.

I can explain those steps in words, but if you faced the task of drawing it yourself, you can imagine the many questions that would have to be answered: How close are we to the rock we are looking at? What does Makoto see when she looks out at the river? What kind of clock is it? How should the reverse-time splash be drawn? How do the scenes relate to the dialogue? The storyboards aim to clarify some of the uncertainties in reating such a group project as an anime film, but they also offer a reminder

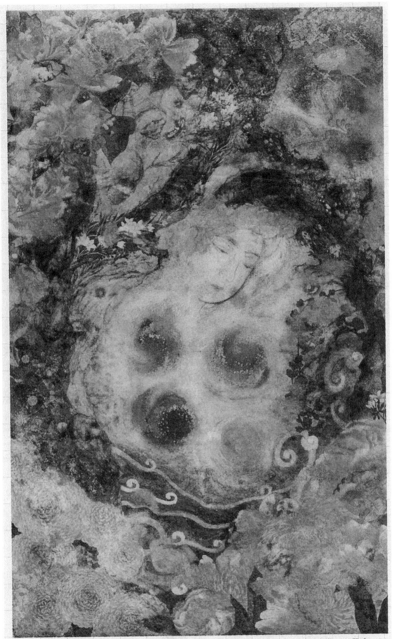

▲原画は極彩色も使われたビビッドな色使い。劇中ではデジタル加工であえて劣化した風合いに

7. Fictional painting made for Hosoda's film (Furukawa and Editors New Type 2006: 34).

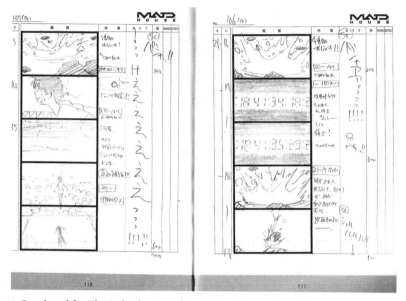

8. Storyboard for *The Girl Who Leapt through Time* (Anime Style Editors 2006).

that anime is a layered multiplicity. Some argue that media forms are always built up from other media so that media production is always a case of "remediation" (Bolter and Grusin 1999), and anime is no exception.

From this perspective, Hosoda's version of *The Girl Who Leapt through Time* conveys some of the multiplicity of media analysis, as well. The movie emphasizes finding one's own path and Makoto's control over her own destiny, as well as the independent-minded boy from the future's desire for the personal, internal solace in a painting. But in the end, both find that the friendship of peers is what gives their lives the most meaning. In Hosoda's film, the boy from the future finds solace not in the painting but in the friendships he develops with the girl and the other boy. The independent and empowered Makoto discovers in the end that she wants the boy's love, even though she initially rejected it. The enduring commitment to a community of peers soothes the pain in their hearts and makes our present worthwhile.

Fieldwork as Collaborative Research
Both Onstage and Backstage

Hosoda's efforts to explain how his films relate to a view of changing audiences, and to the relationships among media, technology, and the future, are analogous in interesting ways to much of interpretive media studies. Like others who look on a completed work and explain it, Hosoda uses the benefit of hindsight to package and contextualize what was eventually produced. I don't doubt his sincerity in describing the logics of production, but having witnessed some of the complexities of what unfolds in script meetings and other moments of dialogic interaction, I recognize that such explanations can capture only some of what goes on in a collaborative process of production. As we saw in Hosoda's meeting with the computer graphics team, there are other aspects to a vibrant work environment that are shaped less by a logic, structure, or method than by a process of interaction that is inclusive in the sense of being an open space for participation. At its best, this is one of the things that ethnographic fieldwork can provide.

Fieldwork forces researchers into a collaborative mode, developing research questions and pursuing leads amid an ongoing and dynamic world. I find that a different perspective arises from looking at media in the process of being made, compared with analyzing the finished product. For example, in my research at anime studios, I was always struck by the air of uncertainty that hangs over projects as creators make their best guesses about how to solve various challenges, from designing characters and stories to thinking about pop music tie-ups and other transmedia marketing strategies. There are few "sure hits" in the entertainment business, and in most cases, people are gambling that their predictions will pan out. Yet scholars of media tend to work from already completed works, whose success or failure is already known, and from which they draw conclusions, all along making assumptions about what matters and what doesn't. Fieldwork is a valuable tool for testing those assumptions.

Here's a concrete example: "What do Japanese anime creators think about overseas audiences when they are creating their works, and how does that affect the anime that gets produced?" When I was designing this research project and writing grant proposals, I included a version of this question. Given that anime has become a global phenomenon, I expected creators to have an increasingly transnational image of their audiences. I also expected that this would be observable in their work meetings. Having sat in on script meetings and interviewed writers, directors, and producers about their projects, however, I can say that in my experience, anime creators talk little, if at all, about overseas audiences. They rarely talk about Japanese audiences, either. In general, I found that the professionals in the room viewed *themselves* as the audience that mattered. This makes sense, having seen it firsthand, but I have to admit that as a fan I was disappointed. I liked the idea of media creators thinking about *me* (or people like me) when they make their works. Plus, it was supposed to be one of my research questions.

I later discussed my reaction with Hosoda. He laughed gently and said that I was looking at things the wrong way. "It's not that I don't care about what the audience thinks," he said. "It's that I respect audiences and expect them to have all kinds of reactions that I can't predict and that I don't want to control. When I say, 'I don't think about the audience,' I simply mean that I trust the audience to see things and understand things that even I don't understand about the work."[3] I sense that this kind of openness to diverse interpretations is common among artists, many of whom bristle at the idea of defining and explaining the *meaning* of one's work. But when anime directors are in the position of having to explain their films to magazine writers, journalists, and even the occasional ethnographer, a different mode of reflection seems to take over, and the effort to appeal to an audience is more readily apparent. Fieldwork can help us understand some of the dynamics of the before, during, and after aspects of imaginative production, which is also related to differences between onstage and backstage types of labor.

I was working with an implicit model of how anime was related to audiences, Japaneseness, and globalization drawn in part from what directors say about their work. Seeing the creators in action, however, expands the perspective. Although it may bring us no closer to an "ultimate truth," it does help us see how explanations themselves unfold in specific contexts. After seeing animators at work, I had to recalibrate my understanding of where (and when) audiences fit into the equation. Fieldwork produces this kind of collaborative research process, whereby questions and findings are generated through an ongoing engagement with the dynamic, and sometimes contradictory, views of those we are trying to understand.

Conclusion

This look at how the anime director Mamoru Hosoda created two award-winning feature films—*Summer Wars* and *The Girl Who Leapt through Time*—brings a concrete perspective to the organization of labor through collaborative creativity. Fieldwork can elucidate the social aspects of media production by showing how relationships develop and how energy is channeled through working together. Over time, drawings on the page become entangled with creators' lives, and in the space between the page and the people is where I would locate the vibrancy of meaning and value. These social relationships are guided not only by to-do checklists, but also by conceptual structures that help determine a logic of anime creativity that centers on characters and worlds, which together act as a kind of generative platform that can be shaped by anime creators but also, as we will see, can be extended across other media businesses and fandoms.

Hosoda's work is shaped by a kind of social theory about media and cultural change that we can see in these two films—namely, divergent views of how we view collective action and individuality today. In *Summer Wars*, Hosoda emphasizes the importance of a new idea of the hero not as a spectacular individual but, rather, as emerging from groups of people working together to solve otherwise intractable problems. In *The Girl Who Leapt through Time*, Hosoda portrays what he sees as a different trend—namely, how communication technology is encouraging what might be viewed as a personalization of visions of the future. Taken together they portray a central tension in the cultural dynamics of media today.

TWO

Characters and Worlds
as Creative Platforms

> You get hooked (*hamattyau*). You like the characters. They
> become like friends, and you want to spend time with them.
> —MASUO UEDA, producer of *Zenmai Zamurai*, on the
> attraction of script meetings

✳ In script meetings for the children's TV series *Zenmai
Zamurai* (2006), the five writers would sit somewhat
uncomfortably while awaiting their turns. The director, producers, original character designers, and various others
joined them around a rectangular table to evaluate the new scripts
and plot ideas. The director Tetsuo Yasumi led the meeting,
choosing from the stack of printouts in front of the fifteen or so
people (a third of whom were women). During the summer of
2006, the meetings were usually held on Wednesdays at noon at
Sony's Aniplex offices near Ichigaya Station in central Tokyo.
After the director chose, we all read the script or synopsis, and
Yasumi began the discussion, sometimes with direct questions to
the writer: "Does it have to be oil in the character's hair? Can't it
be honey?" Sometimes he opened a space for more freeform discussion: "Does a soccer game really go with the world we've created?" For the scripts in final drafts, the director would commonly make changes to dialogue or comment on the length of
speeches. Some of the most interesting discussions came during

the brainstorming of new ideas, thinking about the main character's love interest or rival, considering the central gag or conflict, fretting over the resolution, or wondering whether the plot could be easily understood by the young children who were the target audience. After observing about a dozen of the script meetings for *Zenmai Zamurai*, I came to see how a logic revolving around characters and worlds formed the basis on which scripts were constructed and evaluated. Of course, "characters and worlds" can be viewed as a common approach to narrative creativity more generally—certainly, literature, live-action cinema, videogames, and more can be interpreted in these terms—but I would argue that this dynamic is especially important for grasping transmedia potential and for seeing alternatives to "story"-centered analysis, although, of course, this is a matter of degree rather than a completely new foundation. The goal of this chapter is to explore how this logic works in the case of anime production, beginning with fieldwork examples and focusing on the emergent stages of production—that is, when new episodes are created or how new series are designed. To extend the discussion of the idea of a "creative platform," I will look at how characters and worlds provide a way to conceptualize what, exactly, moves across media.

Script meetings are only one part of a multilayered process with diverse participants that extends over many months. In the case of *Zenmai Zamurai*, it would commonly take six months to go through the steps of developing the plot, writing the script, creating the storyboard, drawing the frames, recording the voices, and editing the final video. The first meeting I attended for *Zenmai Zamurai* in June 2006 included initial ideas for the end-of-the-year special to air in December. Unlike the majority of anime, which is built on manga series, *Zenmai Zamurai* was an original anime with the stories of future episodes still being worked out as the initial episodes were airing. What had already been designed, and what formed the basis of the work to follow, was a set of conceptual tools that help define the making of anime, primarily characters and worlds but also a curious middle-term "premises" that can refer to either characters or worlds, or to the links between them. These foundational concepts not only help to organize the collaborative creativity of anime, they also give us a way of thinking about how the cultural worlds around us come into being.

In the course of doing fieldwork, I was struck by certain aspects of production that contradicted my assumptions about what gives anime value. When I began my research, I tended to view the distinctiveness of anime in terms of the complexity of the stories. Fans I spoke with at anime conventions in the United States often explained their appreciation of anime in terms of stories, as well, for example, drawing attention to plot lines that extended over an entire year (or more) and that avoided simplistic renderings of good versus evil. Scholars who write about anime frequently begin by explaining the story of a particular series or film and then analyze how it reveals something about Japan or gives us insight into cultural politics regarding gender, technology, history, youth, and so on (Brown 2006; Lunning 2006; Napier 2005). As I observed anime creators at work, however, I came to see that the story was often a secondary concern; moreover, it was only one element of a broader range of conceptual tools they used in designing new projects. This applies most often to "original anime"—that is, animation projects that are not based on manga —although sometimes anime film and television adaptations of manga take established characters and worlds but imagine new stories to go with them.

More central than the story itself in organizing the collaborative production of anime was a different set of concerns—specifically, the design of characters, the establishment of dramatic premises that link the characters, and the properties that define the world in which the characters interact. This combination of characters (*kyarakutaa*), premises (*settei*), and worlds (*sekaikan*) generally came before the writing of the story per se and thus can be considered a platform of anime creativity.[1] By "anime creativity" I mean that, compared with viewing anime as a collection of texts, the form can be interpreted somewhat differently if we conceive of anime as an approach to creative production—that is, a way to define and put into practice particular processes of world making.

How do our interpretive methods change if we consider not primarily the stories of anime but the combination of characters and worlds? How might this alter our understanding of what anime is about? In this chapter, I focus on several TV series, including three that use samurai as main characters. At one level, a samurai evokes the idea of a character (a warrior with a sword), a premise (samurai are guided by honor and empowered by swordsmanship), and a world (historical Japan, generally 1400s–1800s). As the late Harold Bolitho (1984) eloquently shows, these images have some truth and much myth. Nevertheless, it is often at this level of generality that samurai are seen as representing Japan—or, at least, Japanese manhood, symbols of loyalty, skill, and perseverance. But just as the equating of samurai with Japan is overly simplistic, the idea that a samurai equals a character is too simplistic for understanding what defines a character. To dig deeper, I discuss diverse character formulations mostly around samurai —namely, the *Deko Boko Friends* and *Zenmai Zamurai* anime series for young children and, for adults, *Samurai Champloo* (dir. Shinichirō Watanabe, 2004), which mixes hip-hop and samurai, and *Afro Samurai* (dir. Fuminori Kizaki, 2007), a "fusion anime" designed in Japan but starring American voice actors. Through this comparison, we can observe some of the calculus that goes into designing new shows around characters and worlds.

Henry Jenkins (2006: 2) argues that what connects new and old media is a cultural phenomenon called "convergence," by which he means "the flow of content across multiple media platforms, the cooperation between multiple media industries, and the migratory behavior of media audiences who will go almost anywhere in search of the kinds of entertainment they want." As a successful example of transmedia storytelling, Jenkins points to the *Matrix* franchise, which includes not only the trilogy of films, but also animated shorts, comic books, and videogames, each of which fills in part of the story: "In the ideal form of transmedia storytelling, each medium does what it does best—so that a story might be introduced in a film, expanded through television, novels, and comics; its world might be explored through game play or experienced as an amusement park attraction" (2006: 96). But as I suggested in the introduction, we might benefit by turning this formulation around. To use Jenkins's terms, instead of looking at "what each medium does best," we might focus instead on the social energy that arises through media connections. An aspect of this is Jenkins's "migratory behavior of media audiences," but we can also observe how anime often attempts to create characters and worlds that can migrate and that creators are drawn together—even attracted—by the characters they create. Rather than transmedia storytelling, we witness a kind of transmedia character telling.

This brings us back to the idea of thinking of anime characters as a kind of generative platform of creativity. In media studies, the term "platform" is increasingly used these days to draw attention to the capabilities of different kinds of cultural vehicles. In the book series they edit for MIT Press, the scholar-artists Nick Montfort and Ian Bogost define "platform studies" in computer terms of digging beyond the level of software code "down to the metal" of hardware—that is, "to promote the investigation of underlying computing systems and how they enable, constrain, shape, and support the creative work that is done on them" (Montfort and Bogost 2009: iii). But one can think of platforms not only as mechanical or digital structures of conveyance but also as ways to define and organize our cultural worlds. This perspective shares a concern with the structuring of creativity, but we need not be focused primarily on a particular hardware configuration. In fact, focusing that way may limit our understanding of transmedia dynamics. In other words, we can also draw inspiration from the idea that platforms are more or less "generative," as the Internet scholar Jonathan Zittrain discusses. In his analysis of the creeping forces of discipline online, he worries about proprietary communication gadgets that cannot be customized or built on. He makes a persuasive argument for the importance of designing and protecting the "generative systems" of personal computers (and the Internet more generally), and preventing a future dominated by "sterile appliances tethered to a network of control" (Zittrain 2008: 3). Characters offer a way to think about anime as a "generative platform," especially in the sense that they can exist somewhat independently of the storytelling to follow. This is important because in the case of anime, it is seldom narrative coherence—the story—that provides the link across media. Rather, the characters and the worlds provide that link. But that raises more questions: How "controlled" and how "open" does such a platform need to be to succeed? The anthropologist Brian McVeigh describes this two-sidedness of Hello Kitty, the commercial powerhouse for Sanrio and an "eminently cute icon of popular culture." Hello Kitty attracts and connects. As McVeigh (2000: 240) says, she is "a symbolic lightning rod that collects electrical currents from other territories of social life," including socializing and labor. But this openness comes with a cost, because Hello Kitty can reinforce "a tendency to aesthetically 'soften' controversial, sensitive, or troublesome issues." Platforms are enabling and constraining, but not for everyone in the same ways. I was curious about how anime creators viewed their spaces of creativity, where they needed new ideas, and how they fit new ideas into preexisting structures. We come back to questions of emergent "structures of creative action," which are not just organizational (e.g., anime studios) but also conceptual (e.g., characters and worlds). Anime making is a nice example because it is so structured and deadline-dependent. By mapping the processes through which creators take original ideas and turn them into ongoing projects, we can grapple with the tensions of choosing projects in the midst of great uncertainty about what will succeed. Moreover, by looking at the design of characters and how they are used to create new stories, we can come to a deeper understanding of this kind of platform and the tensions between creativity and control.

Deko Boko Friends: Characters, but No Story

Let's begin with the anime TV series *Deko Boko Friends*, which stands out as an extreme example of how characters themselves, rather than the stories about them, can be the driving force of some shows. In April 2002, *Deko Boko Friends* began airing as interludes in the hugely popular children's show *Okaasan to issho* (Together with Mother), broadcast weekday mornings on the educational channel of Nihon Hōsō Kyōkai (Japan Broadcasting Corporation; NHK), Japan's public broadcasting network. Funded by publicly assessed fees, NHK is somewhat connected to the Japanese government; in this regard, it is different from a commercial broadcasting company and arguably is more focused on serving the public interest (Krauss 2000). Even so, NHK has a commercial side—for example, it takes an aggressive role in developing anime that not only is educational but that can also sell DVDs, such as *Major*, the baseball-themed anime aimed at teens (Kubo 2005). The network works closely with major publishers such as Shogakukan and with major studios such as Sony's Aniplex, an interesting example of the linkages between public broadcasting and commercial production.

In the case of *Deko Boko Friends*, the target audience is preschool and young elementary-school children. Each short is thirty seconds long. They always begin with a red door set against a white background and a musical phrase of the characters singing the words "Deko Boko Friends." Then comes a "knock knock." The door opens, and one of the show's characters comes out to talk to the TV viewers. An unusual feature of the series is that the characters don't interact with each other. Instead, each episode hinges on the relationship between the character and the young viewer. Plus, there's an element of surprise. As one of the creators explained to me, "Children never know what's going to come out of that door, and that's part of the fun of the show."[2] The DVD releases include a function that randomizes the order in which episodes are shown, reproducing the unpredictability of the TV broadcasts.

9. Screen capture of Prince Egg from *Deko Boko Friends*.

In each episode, a character—for example, a cactus-shaped boy who is so shy his needles fall out—introduces himself or herself. Another character throws holes on the ground, dives into and out of them, and then gathers up the holes like dishes. Yet another can blow up his nose like a balloon, and another can play his teeth like a piano. Each character faces a minor crisis or has an adventure that is resolved by the end of the thirty-second episode. For instance, in one episode, a boy in a red shirt whose head is an egg comes out and says, "Hello. I'm Tamago Ōji (Prince Egg)" (see figure 9). When he looks down, he sees that he's wearing one yellow sock and one green sock. "Oh no," he says. "I came out wearing the wrong sock. I'm so embarrassed!" He grits his teeth and seethes. Steam rises from his head, and his egg cooks, suddenly cracking at the very top. Then little eggshell pieces fall on the floor. This surprises the boy, but he's not hurt. Now he is doubly embarrassed because of his display of anger. He bows and says, "I'm sorry," then sweeps up the eggshell, and the episode ends.[3]

Deko Boko Friends is intriguing because it distills the elements of a series into only the characters. A red door and white background are all that make up the world. No dramatic premises link the different characters. This is pure character-based media. The series was the brainchild of a two-person design team that calls itself "m&k." After graduating from art colleges, Momoko Maruyama ("m") and Ryotarō Kuwamoto ("k") began working at Hakuhodo, the second-largest advertising company in Japan, on a variety of campaigns and scored a big success with the character Qoo. Initially designed for Coca-Cola's ad campaigns in Japan, Qoo has since been incorporated into the company's global marketing strategy. If you haven't lived in Japan, it may be hard to appreciate how ubiquitous the images of characters are. They advertise everything. Cutesy characters often adorn the business cards of employees of serious companies and even government agencies. Sometimes they advertise services for which endearing characters might seem inappropriate. Once I received a flyer for a private detective agency that specialized in trailing wayward spouses suspected of having affairs. The flyer showed teddy-bear-like characters, one wearing a trench coat and using binoculars to spy on a teddy bear couple entering a love hotel. (I should clarify that m&k had nothing to do with that particular design.) What can we say, then, about how characters work as media objects?

Characters versus Brands and Celebrities

Some characters are little more than logos that identify corporate brands. Does this mean, though, that characters should be thought of simply as a variation on brands? Although there are parallels, the differences point to the importance of considering characters a separate category. The sociologist Adam Arvidsson (2006: vii) argues that brands are "an institutional embodiment of the logic of a new form of informational capital—much like the factory embodied the logic of industrial capital." Brands put to work the capacity of consumers "to produce a common social world through autonomous processes of communication and interaction" (vii). As with the idea of collaborative creativity, we begin to wonder: How "autonomous" are the processes, and how shared is "the common social world"? The media scholar Celia Lury (2004: 1ff.) argues that brands constitute a "new media object" that organizes and promotes certain types of interactivity between consumers and products. In this sense, characters and brands share some interesting features in highlighting the collaborative relationship between consumers and producers in producing their meanings.

Characters and brands move fluidly across media, and both are recognizable as connected to larger worlds. But while brands speak back to corporate underpinnings, characters tend to emerge from particular worlds. Moreover, brands can be associated with virtually any kind of object or experience but are valued in relation to the objects associated with them (e.g., sneakers, T-shirts, vacations). Characters are more like people in that they have some kind of bounded identity. In this sense, characters operate more like celebrities. Celebrities can come to stand for certain franchises of media—Bruce Willis for *Die Hard*, for example, or Pikachu for *Pokémon*. But there is something about celebrities being real people that introduces a different relationship between media and celebrity. After all, a celebrity goes home, lives a life more or less scandalous, and (often, at least) can move among different generic worlds of fiction. There is always a disjuncture of some sort between the person and the roles he or she plays. Indeed, the anthropologist Gabriella Lukacs (2010) persuasively argues that the success of certain Japanese TV dramas in the 1990s depended on the match between the stars' on-screen roles and off-screen lives. When the match was poor, certain TV series failed. But characters don't have "outside lives" in the same way. They are associated with their own worlds, but they can also move among "realities." They are replicable celebrities without the baggage of a real life. One wonders, how are characters made? What brings a character into existence?

As a manga artist and teacher, Eiji Ōtsuka says he is accustomed to meeting people who want to be manga artists (*mangaka*), but he has recently noticed a marked increase in the number of young people who say their ambition is to become a "character designer" (Ōtsuka 2008: 14). That is a job description today, and such employment opportunities are likely to increase with the projected growth of the content industries of anime, manga, and videogames. Yet he expresses frustration at the limited way in which aspiring artists often imagine their role as designers: "They spend a lot of time on the hair, the clothes, and the outer appearance of characters in an effort to bring out their individual personalities (*kosei*)" (Ōtsuka 2008: 17). What they don't seem to grasp is that the visual "design" of outward appearance is only one part of what is actually required to "make" (*tsukuru*) a character, he says, so he published a book explaining how to make a character.

Characters can never be separated from their story (*monogatari*), according to Ōtsuka (2008: 18–19). There are exceptions, he acknowledges, but he contends that popular characters almost always develop because of their larger stories. In a similar vein, the media studies scholar Yasuki Hamano (2003: 52) draws on a Hollywood adage to propose that there are three requirements for a hit: story, story, story. I sympathize with Ōtsuka's frustration with those who equate character design with visual design. At the same time, however, "story" is not the only way to understand characters as a platform, although I should add that Ōtsuka's notion of a story shades into the idea of an underlying world.

Still, some of the exceptions Ōtsuka refers to are instructive. Consider the virtual idol Miku Hatsune. Released in 2007 by Crypton Future Media, a small company in Sapporo, Miku Hatsune started out as a voice character in the music synthesizer software Vocaloid, which allows users to enter lyrics and melody that the software can "sing." Crypton released an illustration and some body characteristics (height, weight, etc.) to go with the character, but interestingly, the company allowed the image to be used by anyone. Many Vocaloid users created songs and uploaded them to the Internet—for example, to the video-sharing website Nico Nico Douga (literally, "smile video"). Many of the uploaded songs were made into music videos with either moving or still images of the Miku character. This is an excellent example of how a character can be a "platform of creativity." Certainly, if we followed the lead of Montfort and Bogost (2009), we could learn a lot about how the Vocaloid software and hardware interact and the kinds of creativity that are enabled thereby. But the phenomenon around Miku shows that the character, more than the music software, is the platform on which people are building. I was one of seven thousand people who attended the sold-out, one-day "Vocaloid-only" fan convention at the Sunshine City department store complex in the Ikebukuro section of Tokyo in November 2010. Almost five hundred fan groups had gathered to sell their wares—mostly CDs but also DVDs, books of drawings (*irasuto*), posters, videogames, jewelry, costumes, manga, and more. These activities cannot be explained only by the capabilities of the voice synthesizer software, or in academic terms, the affordances of a computational platform. Rather, the creativity grows out of social energy arising from a collective interest in Miku. We should note that this creativity is guided in important ways too—especially visually with the depiction of Miku as a character with long blue hair in two ponytails—even if the content of Miku—her background, her interests—is left open for fans to interpret as they like.

It would be tempting to see this kind of creativity as located primarily in the fan world, where remaking other people's pop culture works is an important aspect of what fans do. But in the professional world of anime studios, a similar kind of dynamic is at work. Anime scriptwriters often have to work from the characters and worlds of others. How do the character designers conceive of their design work, and, if not storytelling and visual design itself, what moves their projects forward?

How Did m&k Create New Characters?

In July 2006, I had a chance to sit down with m&k at a tea shop in Jimbocho, an area of Tokyo notable for having dozens of small bookstores crowded along narrow streets. According to Kuwamoto, they developed the characters by "auditioning" about sixty of them—that is, drawing up a wide range and selecting from them. "We avoided average characters and aimed instead for those who were in some way unbalanced," he explained. Indeed, this is one meaning of the Japanese term *deko boko*: uneven or rough. They also didn't start with the visual image of the character but, instead, thought in terms of a character's distinctive flavor (*mochiaji*) or special skill (*tokugi*). This reflects a distinction made by the manga theorist Gō Itō between *kyarakutaa* (character) and *kyara* (the character's personality). Itō (2005: 94–95) argues that "the personality (*kyara*) precedes the character itself, evoking the feeling of some kind of existence (*sonzaikan*) or life force (*seimeikan*)." When m&k selected characters from among the many they auditioned, they emphasized extremes: one character is extremely shy; another is extremely speedy; another is an exceedingly elegant older woman who sings traditional sounding songs; another is so big he can't fit through the door. The life force of characters is also conveyed through particular drawing practices. When I visited the small studio in Yokohama where the animator Akiho works, she showed me how she animates the characters using a brush pen. "When I copy over the lines to make the in-between frames," she explained, "I can't perfectly match the pressure on the brush, even when I trace directly on top of a frame underneath." She does this on purpose so that the edges of the characters oscillate slightly to give them "a living feel" (*ikite ru*).

Significantly, in *Deko Boko Friends*, the relationships between the characters are never a plot point. In fact, the characters never interact with each other. "We only think about the relationship between the character and the child watching the show," Kuwamoto explained. "Because we use such different characters, we hope to show how there are all kinds of ways to be in the world. There's nothing wrong with being very shy or always in a hurry and so on." In these ways, the show illustrates how characters themselves, without stories around them and without relationships between them, can in themselves generate a dramatic series. *Deko Boko Friends* became so popular that it has aired in the United States on television as part of the NickJr programming slot on Nickelodeon; DVDs are available for purchase from the publisher, Shogakukan, and a wide range of merchandise is available. The success of *Deko Boko Friends* gave m&k the opportunity to design a slightly longer series. When I first met m&k in the summer of 2006, their second animated series, *Zenmai Zamurai*, had been on the air for three months and was doing very well. The series was somewhat more complicated than *Deko Boko Friends* and allows us to factor in the concepts of premises and worlds, in addition to characters, to understand anime creativity.

The Making of *Zenmai Zamurai*

"It's kind of a secret," confided Kuwamoto, "but Zenmai was one of the *Deko Boko* characters that didn't make the cut."[4] Zenmai's second chance came when NHK approached m&k to make a longer-format series (albeit still only five minutes, including the opening and closing credits). *Zenmai Zamurai* (Turnkey Samurai) debuted in April 2006, and NHK and Aniplex were very pleased by the response. It was a hit. The series began as a five-minute-long short aimed at an audience of younger elementary schoolchildren and aired daily without commercials on NHK's educational Channel 3, once at 7:50 AM and repeating at 5:40 PM. It follows the adventures of a samurai boy with a wind-up turnkey on his head (hence, his name and the name of the series). In addition to attending script meetings around *Zenmai Zamurai*, I conducted interviews with the director (Tetsuo Yasumi), the animation director, a writer, and a producer, and I observed the voice recording and the evaluation of licensed merchandise. At each level, different people contributed something to building up the "life force" of the characters, but they also worked within the designers' models.

In explaining the design, Kuwamoto pointed out, obviously enough, that it is the wind-up key on Zenmai's head, in place of a topknot, that makes him special. "What does that topknot symbolize?" he asked rhetorically. "That life is limited (*kagiri no aru jinsei*)." The first episode of the TV series, "The Birth of Zenmai Zamurai (*Zenmai Zamurai no tanjō*),"[5] ex-

10. Zenmai Zamurai with Mamemaru, his ninja sidekick.

11. Character-centric plush dolls and dictionary of 181 *Zenmai* characters.

plains the origin of the odd topknot and establishes the dramatic premise: One day, while walking through town, Zenmai's sidekick, Mamemaru, a child ninja in training, asks the samurai how he ended up with the *zenmai* on his head. Zenmai tells the tale. "Oh, that was over two hundred years ago," he begins. As a boy, "probably junior high school age," according to the creators, Zenmai was caught stealing *dango* (rice dumplings) and during the chase that followed, he fell into a well. Suddenly, an enormous smiling god told him he had died. Zenmai was understandably upset. All was not lost, however. The god, who spoke only in rap, offered Zenmai a second chance—not unlike the second chance m&k gave him—on the condition that Zenmai had to promise to do good. He did, and the god took a wind-up turnkey from his belt and put it on Zenmai's head, explaining, "You can live as long as the turnkey stays wound up. If you do something good, the turnkey winds up. If you do something bad [e.g., get angry or quarrel], the key winds down." If it wound down too much, Zenmai would die. Kuwamoto later explained, "Children may not be overly concerned with the mortality of Zenmai, but it does add a kind of seriousness to the show."[6]

Zenmai, who is already an unusual kind of samurai character, also has an unusual prop: a "must-laugh rice-dumpling sword" (*hisshō dango ken*), or a sword with multicolored rice dumplings on it that are endlessly replenished (see figures 10 and 11). In the first episode, the god explains, "When a person eats one of these dango, he or she will experience a warm feeling of good fortune (*shiawase na kibun*)." The "character premise" (*kyara settei*), therefore, involves the turnkey, the sword, and the agreement with the god, all of which help define the logic of the series. Zenmai's world includes a female love interest, Zukin-chan, who always wears a bandana because she is embarrassed by her Afro hairstyle; a rival, Namezaemon, who is obsessed with his wealth and his extra-long topknot; and others, such as the granny-age proprietor of a rice dumpling shop who specializes in striking "sexy poses." Adventures ensue, each reaching resolution after four and a half minutes.

World Rules: Clockwork Old Tokyo

In addition to the characters and the premises, m&k thought long and hard about the "world" (*sekaikan*) of *Zenmai Zamurai*—that is, the background or context of the series. In general, the world can refer to the technical look and feel of the animation (e.g., hand-drawn or 3D computer graphics), as well as symbolic references to particular eras (e.g., an imagi-

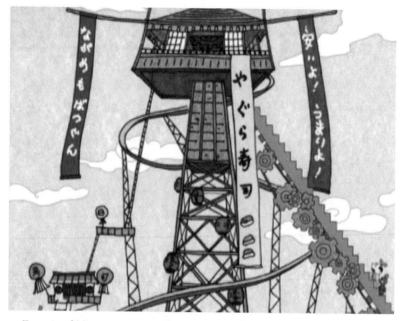

12. Zenmai and Mamemaru visiting the rotating sushi bar.

nary Edo era, 1600–1868, outside of history, in contrast to a futuristic space fantasy). In other words, the *sekaikan* defines the stage on which the dramas of the characters and premises unfold. For *Zenmai Zamurai*, m&k described the world as *karakuri ōedo*, which can be translated as "clockwork Old Tokyo" (see figure 12). Kuwamoto explained, "What makes this world unique is that there is no 'black box.' . . . We live in a world where we've become used to the idea that we don't know how things work. Things like this [pointing to the iPod I was using to record the interview]. We have no idea how the thing works, and we don't find it strange that if it broke, we would have no idea how to fix it." Kuwamoto lamented our accommodation to this unfortunate state of affairs, a kind of willing ignorance.

In the world of *Zenmai Zamurai*, there is no electricity, and one can see how things are connected mechanically. In one episode, Zenmai and his ninja sidekick, Mamemaru, visit a rotating sushi bar at the top of a tower. The escalator on the way up shows the gears driving the steps. Inside, the customers rotate, thanks to a giant windmill at the top of the building. The world helps define the rules in which the drama unfolds. A closer look at script meetings will allow us to explore in more detail how these building blocks—characters, premises, and world—were put into motion to create the stories.

Script Meetings to Create Stories

During the weekly script meetings, the combination of characters (Zenmai and friends), the premise (Zenmai must do something good, and he has a magic sword), and world (clockwork Old Tokyo with no black box) formed both the raw material and the rules within which plots and scripts were evaluated. Spending time in such script meetings was a constant reminder of the collaborative process of media creation: It was there especially that questions of "power" seemed less revealing than analyzing what people valued and why. There were certainly power differences among the participants. Among the fifteen or so people in the meetings, six were women and the rest were men, but the importance of their comments reflected their place in the hierarchy rather than gender. A female executive from NHK often had the final say in terms of what was "appropriate for children," because she was the highest-ranking person from the broadcast network. The flow of the meeting and the final decisions were guided mostly by the director. But a good idea or thoughtful criticism could come from anyone. In this sense, the value of the ideas rather than the power of the participants provides a better guide for ethnographic analysis. A pointed, "Um, I wonder . . ." could move the conversation in an entirely different direction.

The script meetings included the five writers (four men, one woman), who would arrive together, usually bringing their tiny laptops. The writers never commented on each other's work; instead, they waited silently until Yasumi chose their scripts to examine. Once the discussion of a particular writer's work was finished, he or she would leave. Many of the writers were working on several projects, often for several different studios at once. The writer Satoru Nishizono, for example, was working on *Zenmai Zamurai*, a children's show, as well as on the edgy late-night spoof *NHK ni yōkoso* (Welcome to NHK), a send-up of *hikikomori* (youth shut-ins) and their love of erotic videogames, among other themes. In an interview, Nishizono described his efforts to find the emotional core of characters and the ways his thinking about scripts was happening all the time. "Sometimes, I get my best ideas in the bath," he said.[7]

A proposal of Nishizono's that received a lot of attention during the meetings I attended was "Zenmai's Big Slump," which centered on the idea that the "must-laugh sword" was no longer working. As opinions arose around the table, it was clear that people liked the idea. A female producer at Aniplex liked that the story gets serious, even a little upsetting, but then resolves. Others, however, were worried about showing the main character having trouble. "What would be the reason for the slump? How would it resolve?" they asked. "Maybe it's because he has his shoes on the wrong foot?" Or "Perhaps because he's wearing the wrong size underwear (*fundoshi*)?" The debates went on for several weeks as Nishizono developed the plot idea into several versions of scripts.

Although the particular combination of characters, premises, and worlds that defines *Zenmai Zamurai* was a constant theme in the discussions, that does not mean there was a common formula for developing the episodes. Some plot ideas were moved forward simply because they included a clever pun. For example, one proposed plot line involved an extraterrestrial alien whose spaceship resembled a pot (*okama*). What the spaceman would do with Zenmai and his friends was uncertain, but quite a few people enjoyed the idea of the pun that would end the show: As the friends thanked the alien, he would say, as he flew away, "*okamai naku*" ("Don't worry about it"), which has the double meaning of "the pot goes away" (*okama inaku*). Kuwamoto often sketched as discussions were under way; in this instance, he provided a sketch of the pot-shaped UFO that could appear in the episode. At other times, some visual gag seemed to provide the forward momentum for a concept, as long as it fit in the world. For example, one episode revolved around the idea of "butt-sumo," in which massive sumo wrestlers would force each other out of the ring by banging their huge bottoms together. During the summer of 2006, Japan was swept with World Cup fever, and one writer proposed an episode with a soccer match. In the end, however, the idea was rejected because a soccer game was deemed ill-suited to the world of clockwork Old Tokyo. The conclusion was that a different game that related better to the world should be played. In sum, we can see in *Zenmai Zamurai* some of the touchstones for anime creativity. They depend less on well-formed stories than on arrays of characters and premises that give the characters dramatic tension. The world fills out the vision of the artists by providing the frame in which the story unfolds.

Character Goods Businesses

After the script meetings, the companies that were making licensed merchandise for *Zenmai Zamurai* brought in their boxes of goods—board books, dolls of all sizes, little pachinko games, puzzles, lunchboxes, food plates, and on and on. The goods circled the table, with m&k checking the drawing of the characters and, to some extent, the design of the products. The problems that arose mostly concerned the likenesses of the reproduced characters. When I asked m&k how they, as the character designers, felt about the weekly avalanche of licensed goods, Momoko Maruyama remarked on her mixed feelings: She was happy because the interest of so many companies in making merchandise was evidence of widespread appreciation for the characters, but she also worried that not all the goods accurately reflected the world they had created. "The goods that seem to be of clockwork Old Tokyo, that's fine," she said, "but a lot of the things are completely unrelated."[8] Even in the character goods business, the tension remains—at least, to some extent—in reproducing not only the visual design but also the larger worlds in which characters come to life. This collaboration around the characters and worlds of anime, which extends outward through an enormous range of licensed goods, is an important element in transmedia thinking, but it's not necessarily decisive. The designers m&k seemed to have a lot of power in deciding what could be stopped, but they rarely exercised it.

The media scholars Scott Lash and Celia Lury (2007) would describe this merchandise as the "thingification of media." By this they mean the ways brands' logos, such as the Nike swoosh, are increasingly becoming embedded in larger, more encompassing media environments—for example, the spectacular shopping complexes of a Niketown. In this they see a transformation of media from the realm of "representation" to that of the "real," which shares some affinity with my emphasis not on reading the texts of anime but, rather, on examining production through collaborative creativity. But I tend to disagree with the idea that video is "representation" while toys are "real." This distinction between material and digital in terms of physical presence runs counter to my experience. Once while my youngest son was playing Pokémon on a Game Boy in the back of the car, he asked his brothers to read the dialogue on the screen to him (he was too young to read at the time). When his brothers refused (indelicately), he started punching, and pandemonium broke loose as we sped down the Massachusetts Turnpike. If virtual monsters in a videogame can lead to fisticuffs, in what sense are they not "real"? It makes more sense to think of media's reality (or actualization) in terms of an emotional response than in term of a physical object. As one of the *Zenmai* producers says, the characters become like friends, and you want to spend time with them. This emergent social energy can be viewed as a kind of materialization, as well, that connects people across media.

In this respect, characters and worlds provide a way to understand what connects anime to a wider universe of merchandising. The market for licensed merchandise based on fictional characters is ten times that of anime itself (DCAJ and METI 2005). In some ways, producers of licensed merchandise are at a great advantage because they can work from things that have already succeeded in one realm. This is one reason to consider that what the anime industry ultimately produces is not so much TV series and films but, more important, fictional characters and dramatic premises that can be parlayed across diverse media. This worked in unprecedented ways with the explosion of interest worldwide in properties such as Pokémon and Yu-Gi-Oh! But Japanese producers have had trouble repeating those successes in recent years.

Why hasn't Japan been able to produce big hits in the anime character business recently? This is the question posed by Masakazu Kubo, a producer at Shogakukan who heads the publisher's Character Business Center and who helped promote the global Pokémon phenomenon, managing the franchise's transition from videogame to television, film, and more. In a study (Kubo 2005), he addresses a number of the issues facing anime as the flagship content for "Cool Japan." He notes that while there are many new anime being produced, few recent anime series have had much longevity. In April 2005, seventy-two weekly anime TV series were produced, of which sixty were shown on the main TV stations, six were shown on local TV stations, and six were shown on cable or satellite channels. He notes with concern that turnover in series was high, with twenty-seven series (37.5 percent) being new and only three crossing the two-year threshold (Kubo 2005: 13). This tendency toward rapid turnover tends to weaken the companies that help support the anime business, including producers of toys, videogames, clothing, stationery, and other licensed merchandise and DVD and video packagers. Kubo describes the dangerous death spiral that can occur when licensees invest in new productions, see them canceled quickly, and find themselves overstocked with merchandise for largely unknown and uncared-for characters. In contrast, Kubo also points to the positive feedback loop that emerges when anime characters continue for two or three years, because this allows companies to manage the supply of goods, spend time developing high-quality goods, and generally control the market. "To prevent the worst-case scenario, there is no other policy solution than creating long-lasting characters (*iki no nagai kyarakutaa*)," he concludes (Kubo 2005: 22). As examples of Japanese-made anime (*nihonsei anime*) that have achieved this status, he lists *Sailor Moon, Dragon Ball, Doraemon, Pokémon, Yu-Gi-Oh!,* and *Ham Tarō*. How does this kind of thinking about characters alter our understanding of transmedia stories?

Transmedia Anthropology

A productive tension exists in media studies between media as object and media as social practice. By looking at transmedia in terms of the social in media, I believe we can view some of the issues in new ways. Consider the contrast with Henry Jenkins, whose focus has shifted through the years from a concern with *Star Trek* fans as "textual poachers" through an interest in participatory culture and collective intelligence to questions of media convergence and transmedia storytelling. He argues for a shift in the core assumptions of media and cultural studies: "We need to move from a politics based on culture-jamming—that is, disrupting the flow of media from an outside position—towards one based on blogging—that is, actively shaping the flow of media" (Jenkins 2004: 36). So it is appropriate that Jenkins views transmedia as a movement—in his words, as "a driving cause" in the creative and intellectual lives of an increasingly "passionate and motivated community of artists, storytellers, brands, game designers, and critics/scholars." For Jenkins, convergence represents a "significant shift in the underlying logic of commercial entertainment . . . [that] has to do with the interplay between different media systems and delivery platforms (and of course different media audiences and modes of engagement)." According to his definition, "Transmedia storytelling represents a process where integral elements of a fiction get dispersed systematically · across multiple delivery channels for the purpose of creating a unified and coordinated entertainment experience" (Jenkins 2009b). As Jenkins continues this discussion, however, he notes that the question of how to theorize this "unified and coordinated entertainment experience" remains a complicated puzzle. What, if anything, is the unified core? If elements of a fiction are "dispersed systematically," how much and what kind of control is necessary to keep the system working? Does unauthorized sharing and remixing of digital media always add value or not? How can we know?

If we view media in terms of energy and connection, then Jenkins's musings on transmedia point a way toward amplifying that energy and extending those connections. In that sense, Jenkins, like other media scholars, illustrates the productivity of fandom and extends our discussion of the particulars of putting that collaborative creativity into action. He proposes seven principles of transmedia storytelling, mapping a range of dimensions for thinking about how his approach to media making can proceed. The principles highlight characteristics of different media works, thinking both in terms of how they can be designed and how they are used by fans. Sometimes these characteristics are offered in binary pairings; sometimes they are not:

1. *Spreadability* (fans are encouraged to circulate media) versus *drillability* (fans are encouraged to dig more deeply into media worlds).
2. *Continuity* (coherence, systematicity) versus *multiplicity* (openness, contradiction).
3. *Immersion* (fans enter into fictional worlds) versus *extractability* (fans take stories away as resources).
4. *World building* (media forms that exist in a world with its own logic, practices, and institutions).
5. *Seriality* (transmedia as hyperbolic version of the serial, where the chunks of meaningful and engaging story information have been dispersed across media systems).
6. *Subjectivity* (exploring other dimensions of a fictional world by seeing through alternative sets of eyes).
7. *Performance* (fans and producers will actively identify sites of potential performance in and around transmedia narrative where they can make their own contributions). (Jenkins 2009b)

Each of these principles points to things that media creators can consider in designing new works. We can also view transmedia in terms of fans' desires and their uses of media.

Such principles can also be the source of extensive discussion about how they work in the worlds of anime. Consider, for example, the potential for transmedia storytelling to explore multiple subjectivities of a fictional world. The manga *20th Century Boys* by Naoki Urasawa is a masterly example of this possibility, as he explores the faulty memories of a range of childhood friends as a way to unravel a mystery of global consequence. The series, which comprises more than twenty volumes, undermines a common hero-story format by revealing early on that the ragtag group of good guys doing battle with an arch-nemesis will ultimately lose their fight. The suspense thus arises not from finding out "what will happen" but rather from piecing together the details from the perspectives of different characters. The "story," in other words, is less central than the attraction of exploring the diverse subjectivities of different participants.

Jenkins's formulation of the characteristics of transmedia storytelling offers a way to conceptualize media design and fan practices. One can ask questions about the kinds of stories that will work best across media formats and how much the elaborations should be guided from above or below. What is it about Harry Potter that is better for a film or for an amusement park? What kinds of performance spaces can be designed to allow fans their own realms of creative interaction? Given Jenkins's interest in shaping, rather than simply critiquing, the flow of media, it makes sense to theorize around the kinds of questions that producers would ask about designing projects.

As an ethnographer, I want to take these insights in a particular direction—namely, to think more about the points of contact between these media objects and the people who provide the impetus for the flows. The fact that someone would drill into a media form and immerse himself or herself in a particular world, or take away part of a media form as a resource and spread it, certainly says something about how the media was designed. But it also says something about the social worlds in which those activities have meaning for specific people. An ethnographic perspective on media can show us how these networks form and what they do, in David Graeber's words, as "structures of creative action" (2001: 230). From this perspective, we can look outward through transmedia phenomena to see the emergence of social groups that are connected through their appreciation of media. The concept of the soul is meant to hold these collaborative social networks and the media objects themselves in a kind electric tension—close enough, in other words, to charge each other.

The centrality of characters in anime, as in manga, videogames, and more, also provides an alternative perspective to that of transmedia storytelling. Notably, the characters are seen in terms of their tension with others and in the ways they shape the worlds in which they move. From this perspective, the questions of storytelling and unified experience take on a somewhat different cast. If the characters and worlds are the more or less open platform for creativity, then only some of that creativity hinges on storytelling. Fans who make (fake) encyclopedias and timelines related to the giant robot anime franchises are an example. At Comic Market 2006, an enormous, twice-yearly event for selling fan-made works, I purchased a book written in exam form that tested one's knowledge of trivia in the novel and anime series *The Melancholy of Haruhi Suzumiya*. If we think of the soul of anime as a collaborative project, we open up the question of other kinds of coherence beyond the story of the media franchise itself. For me, this is when analysis becomes interesting, because the "coherence" need not reside in the media. It can reside in the collectives that emerge—the structures of creative action—in which both anime studios and fans play important roles.

Media anthropology aims to engage the social processes set in motion through media. The focus on "media" tends to be organized around *what people do in relation to media*, particularly in terms of media production and consumption. There is less concern with the content as text and more to content as it is created or enlivened by producers, policymakers, broadcasters, and fans. This raises the question of how one gains access to this social life of media, especially because we want to understand both that which is most inner (our deepest feelings toward media) and that which is most extensive (the public world of media). Faye Ginsburg and her colleagues propose these kinds of questions for the field of media anthropology: "how media enable or challenge the workings of power and the potential of activism; the enforcement of inequality and the sources of the imagination, and the impact of technologies on the production of individual and collective identities" (2002: 3). From this perspective, the media is about practices and ideas and the intersections with identities of class, race, gender, nation, and more.

Collaborative creativity can offer insights into our understanding of such cultural politics of media, however, by drawing attention to the small-world networks that facilitate (or hinder) the achievement of certain goals. I have often considered these questions in terms of categories of people within larger social groups or institutional settings. It might be said that much work in cultural studies tends to center on an analysis of individuals as part of such larger social groups, especially race, class, and gender. Yet it might be beneficial to reconsider our scales of analysis in the process of doing ethnographic research by thinking in terms of relatively small social networks. Many small social networks map onto larger social categories, but the innovative potential of social networks is heightened when these networks cross traditional categories.

Some new findings in the science of social networks suggest that social influence operates through three degrees of separation. My friend and I constitute one degree of separation, so three degrees of separation is a connection of four people. If each of us is connected to twenty people, that is an eight-thousand-person network. Nicholas Christakis and James Fowler (2009) show how certain kinds of behavior, such as weight loss and gain, quitting smoking, and political views, seem to be contagious through such three-degree networks. This is rather remarkable, because it means that each of us is influenced by the beliefs and actions of a friend's friend's friend (four of us all together with three degrees of separation between us). If these insights were more fully incorporated into fieldwork and ethnography, and if Christakis and Fowler (and the many studies they cite) are correct, then this could have a wide influence on how we envision social action and social change. Because it is often the flows of information across "weak links" rather than "strong links" that can have the most influence—for example, in terms of life-changing opportunities such as finding a career or a spouse—the process of identifying "who matters" should shift in important ways. Cultural anthropologists' dependence on ethnographic fieldwork makes us sensitive to the subtleties of face-to-face interactions. Thus, ethnography tends to emphasize forms of analysis that arise from one-degree-of-separation interactions and then to extend these insights to say something about larger social groups (e.g., "If you are an in-between animator who is an unmarried woman, then . . ."). But the three-degrees-of-influence rule suggests that we need analysis that considers individuals' larger networks (outside meetings, workplaces, etc.) yet are smaller groups than those defined by "identities." This adds another element to thinking about scales of analysis when it comes to crucibles of creativity (Graeber's "structures of creative action"), because we can think about how links between producers and consumers are part of a common, collaborative enterprise.

Collaborative creativity, therefore, can be understood as a way to define these social networks in terms of what they accomplish. In a strange way, this both extends and limits our scale of analysis in trying to theorize transmedia anthropology. This perspective extends in the sense that we look beyond anime studios (or professional creators, however defined), but it also imposes new limits by encouraging us to think in terms of particular networks rather than primarily in terms of broad social categories of people. Given the overlaps between "broad social categories" and "three-degree networks," it would make sense that some research approaches would see little change. However, if we pursue research that takes as its premise a three-degree network of influence as the size of the "social world," then we might find new significance in the places where our social networks cross over into social categories other than our own. This, too, indicates the importance of media and cultural analysis that starts from a different place from "production versus consumption" to explore instead emergent collaborations across categories of producers.

Other research points in similar directions. The media scholar Keith Negus (2006) draws attention to the dangers of assuming that the locus of creativity in media worlds can be reduced to what happens within the confines of the content industries. He urges us to acknowledge that the dynamics of creative production do not take place "simply within an industrial context structured according requirements of capitalist production or organisational formulas, but in relation to broader culture formations, economic practices, and social divisions" (Negus 2006: 202). Negus wants to draw attention to the broader contexts in which creators struggle, not only with the demands of their companies, but also in their desire to shape their own lives and society around them. Two more brief examples of samurai anime provide an opportunity to begin considering some of these connections from the perspective of characters and worlds, particularly to emphasize that premises articulate with broader cultural formations—producing networked connections, we might say—of which some relate to global styles, such as hip-hop, and others arise from cult-level circulation of specialty goods such as figurines.

What Makes a Hip-Hop Samurai World?

Consider the premise of the TV series *Samurai Champloo* (2004), which rethinks samurai by using hip-hop music. Rather than using hip-hop primarily as a background element, the director, Shinichirō Watanabe, chose to use it as a way to think about cultural production. In March 2005, just before a party to celebrate the airing of the final episode of *Samurai Champloo* on Japanese TV, I had a chance to sit down with Watanabe in a coffee shop near the historic, now shuttered, Koma Theater. Asked how hip-hop inspired him, he said:

> First of all, sampling. In pop music these days, there's a lot of sampling of phrases from old jazz and soul records, placing the needle in just the right

spot, using cut and paste, and mixing them with a beat of today. In that way, they create a new kind of music. I wanted to make a period piece using samurai, which is a style that's been around in Japan a long time with a lot of classics. I wanted to use these classics, not to copy them, but to sample them.[9]

The creativity of hip-hop DJs involves using samples, adding a beat, moving the crowd. In a way analogous to thinking about anime creativity in terms of characters and worlds, hip-hop creativity (at least in the DJ/music producer realm) involves sampling and remixing. This cut-and-mix style is used to introduce the characters and the premise of the show in the opening episode of *Samurai Champloo*. To the scritch-scratch sound of the DJ's turntable the series moves back and forth between the three main characters—namely, two masterless samurai and a tea shop girl. Intriguingly, sampling as a creative practice is expanding across other media forms, as well, arguably driven in part by digital technologies but also clearly part of a widening recognition of the creativity of remixing, as we saw with anime music videos (see the introduction).

Watanabe's work reminds us that defining the premise of a series can include connections beyond the Japanese Edo–era world itself. Although the overall story is vaguely defined as a "search for the samurai who smells of sunflowers," and the themes draw from the stock characters of samurai period pieces—evil toll guards, lords with a penchant for guns, molls in the pleasure quarters—the premise is also connected to things outside the world of the series. According to Watanabe, hip-hop provided a key concept beyond sampling that underlies the premise for *Samurai Champloo*:

> There's also the idea of "represent"—you know, writing it in *katakana* [the Japanese syllabary for foreign words]. Many Japanese people nowadays aim to be inconspicuous. By far most people tend to hide themselves in the group, and people say this is the Japanese style. But in the old days, it wasn't like that. In the samurai era, people would use their one sword and represent (*repurizento suru*). It seems to me that was similar to today's hip-hop style.[10]

The "mook," or magazine book, about the series describes the concept of "represent" in terms of characters: "people who have a strong sense of themselves and who can't be confused with anyone else" (Kato and Furukawa 2005: 2). Of the two samurai, Jin is the honorable, straight-ahead swordsman, but he is running from a murky past with his old master and school. Mugen is a wild and rambunctious swordsman from the Ryukyu Islands (present-day Okinawa). Fū is a fifteen-year-old girl with the strength of character to keep the trio on their quest. Each character is meant to stand out as a particular kind of personality.

Premises then can have this characteristic of moving across eras, technologies, and social settings not only to reformulate the worlds of anime, but also to speak back to contemporary concerns. The use of the Edo era in *Zenmai Zamurai* provided a way to think about technology—that is, "no black box." This is a theme we can observe in other reworkings of samurai-related anime, such as *Samurai 7*, which adapts Akira Kurosawa's film *Seven Samurai* by introducing giant fighting robots, and *Oh Edo Rocket*, which imagines an alien who has crash landed and enlists a fireworks maker to build her a rocket (at a time long before space travel). *Samurai Champloo* includes references not only to hip-hop but also to baseball, Impressionist painting, Andy Warhol, and graffiti art. *Samurai Champloo* is remixed samurai and as such opens up possibilities for thinking through complex cultural relationships. There is a home for hip-hop in Japan, just as there is a home for anime around the world. What we can see in Watanabe's work, then, is an emphasis not on "Japanese culture" as something separate from "foreign culture." He remixes not only between East and West but also within Japan—for example, by setting the suave anime-style character Jin against a backdrop of stylized paintings that represents the Edo period more than two centuries ago (see figure 13). *Samurai Champloo* uses hip-hop as a tool to rethink creativity via sampling and "represent" as touchstones through which to imagine characters and worlds.

Afro Samurai as Fusion Anime

The unusual story of the birth of the TV miniseries *Afro Samurai* (2007) illustrates another way in which the idea of a character can launch a project. According to Eric Calderon, vice president of creative affairs at GDH International, the parent company of the Gonzo anime studio, he was hired to develop "fusion Japanese animation, which is Japanese animation that is made in collaboration with Western talent or Western companies in order to make something that is more marketable for the world rather than just the Japanese market" (Epstein 2007a). Calderon says he first became aware of *Afro Samurai* when he saw a figurine on a colleague's desk at Gonzo. He was told that the toy was inspired by the fanzine

13. Edo-style desktop wallpaper of the character Jin from *Samurai Champloo*.

(*dōjinshi*) *Nou Nou Hau*. The original, limited-edition comic was originally only six pages long; after months of negotiations with the manga's creator, Takashi Okazaki, Calderon got the green light to develop an animated short pilot film. Once it was completed, he shopped copies around Hollywood, until, reportedly, the actor Samuel L. Jackson saw it and declared, "You tell them, I'm Afro Samurai" (Epstein 2007a). Spike TV, a U.S. cable channel aimed at men, began airing the show in January 2007. The five episodes were edited together and released as a feature film in theaters in Japan (in English with Japanese subtitles). At least, this was how Calderon, the producer, told the story later.

According to Takashi Okazaki, the creator of the original manga, his inspiration goes back to his longtime love of music. "I've been hooked on African-American music like hip-hop and soul since I was a teenager and that's when I started doodling African-American cartoon characters on things like Kleenex boxes. Then I threw in elements of samurai which had also been my fascination and eventually the character of Afro Samurai was created" (Epstein 2007b). Okazaki especially cites Kurosawa's films, as well as *Zatoichi* and *Lone Wolf and Cub*, as inspirations (Epstein 2007b).

14. *Afro Samurai* character by Takashi Okazaki in DVD, CD, and manga.

What makes the example of *Afro Samurai* interesting is that it shows how the glimmer of a character can be enough to get a project going. Okazaki made a small, cult-level comic that was picked up by a cult-level figurine maker; the figurine wound up on the desk of a worker at an anime studio and caught the eye of a producer looking for new ideas. According to the producer's telling of the process, it was the image of the character Afro Samurai that provided the spark—hence, the power of a transmedia character even without a story (see figure 14).

Conclusion

In this chapter, we saw how characters and worlds can alter what matters in transmedia analysis. If we move away from the "story" as the coherent system and look instead at the emergent creativity, we can see that the work of character designers, scriptwriters, directors, and others who work within studios share a kind of collaborative, working from others' work aspect to production that we commonly associate with fans. By extending our notion of social networks beyond coherent social categories, we also become sensitized to the leaps across "weak," or unexpected, links that can be the impetus for radical rethinking. This raises somewhat different questions for analyzing the dynamics of how a media form goes from niche to mass. The path from niche to mass may first involve jumps from niche to niche. Indeed, this might be the key to a more accurate definition of "mass": to see it as networked niches acting in unison (see also Ito, Okabe, and Tsuji 2012). Just the glimmer of a character in a small-run figurine of Afro Samurai can set into motion a process that attracts Samuel L. Jackson to participate in an anime that travels the globe.

The emphasis on characters and worlds as opposed to stories is not unique to anime. In fact, it may be possible to imagine a palette of conceptual tools that differ in value and importance depending on the media form. Of course, an emphasis on characters does not eliminate, or even reduce, the importance of a story. Rather, it provides a different way to see how collaborative activities are organized. Arguably, feature films in the Hollywood style tend to emphasize the story, with all of the attendant curiosity and critical reflection on "how the story ends." In contrast, situation comedies on TV tend to emphasize the seriality of fluctuating relationships between the characters and the worlds they inhabit, as in the way the series *Seinfeld* was famously "about nothing." Soap operas, with their long-running and complex plots, perhaps lie somewhere in the middle. Videogames vary in terms of how empty characters, such as classes of warriors in *World of Warcraft*, might be, compared with a character in a videogame related to some externally driven, ongoing story, as in the videogame versions of the *Matrix* franchise. If one is a Night Elf in *World of Warcraft*, the personality (or *kyara*) of the character is constructed by how the player plays and the objects and skills gained as a player levels up. In a videogame based on a film or other external narrative, such as the *Matrix* videogame, some characters come with a personality already depicted and developed elsewhere.

In this chapter, I have tried to show how anime creators design new projects not in terms of the stories they tell but, rather, in terms of the distinctiveness of the characters and worlds that are then used as the basis for stories. The anime shows, ancillary licensed goods, and various fan activities extend anime worlds in diverse directions, and they are connected through characters. Nevertheless, I hope it is possible to see how the principle of creativity revolves around characters, which in turn encourages extensions by not limiting anime worlds to one particular story. Part of the value of widely popular anime series arises precisely from the flexibility in adapting characters and worlds across a wide range of media.

In today's world, media vehicles themselves remain a powerful organizing principle of industry, but they may be losing force as a logic of production. An ethnographic method that attends to the people and how they use media brings a focus away from media as an object to media as embedded in social practice. A critical theory of production can work from this starting point to trace how social relationships, both inside and outside industry, are energized, activated, and focused in ways that lead to the emergence of robust and vibrant media worlds.

THREE

Early Directions in Postwar Anime

✳ Why is Japan the source of the majority of television cartoons broadcast worldwide? What can the early days of Japan's postwar anime industry tell us about the emergence of success? To begin to answer these questions, I look at the complex interactions between domestic and international influences and consider in more detail what success means for a media form that depends on transmedia synergies. The development of the anime industry depended on diverse collaborative, creative networks that operated across media forms. To see how these networks emerged, we revisit spaces of contemporary anime production and consider some of the early history of anime studios in the 1950s and 1960s. I introduce divergent approaches to production, briefly considering Toei Animation's early emphasis on feature films and the innovations (some would say limitations) of Mushi Pro's *Astro Boy* TV series. We also consider some of the influence of Disney as a global model and the perspective of a Korean American animation director who works with studios in Seoul, Los Angeles, and Tokyo. The chapter closes with a look at the "democratic capitalism" of Japan's manga industry and what this suggests about success in media more generally. Thinking about anime as a generative platform of creativity allows us to see how different studios conceived of the platform to establish business models in particular ways. The choices studios made were neither uniform nor entirely consistent.

In addition, success in Japan does not always translate into success overseas. In fact, the longest running and most popular anime TV series in Japan, *Sazae-san*, is not even licensed in the United States and is basically ignored by fansubbers. Noriko Hasegawa created *Sazae-san* as a four-frame comic strip in 1947; it takes a humorous look at the family and domestic life surrounding the housewife for whom the strip is named (Lee 2000). The anime began airing in 1969 and continues today. Even in 2007, the series garnered the top ratings of any animated TV series, reaching more than 21 percent of households (Dentsu 2009: 96). For comparison, the ratings for *American Idol* in the United States peaked at 29 percent in 2007 (Nielsen 2008), but the show cannot claim the steadiness of *Sazae-san*'s audience. I was personally struck by the breadth of the *Sazae-san* fan base when a Japanese friend whose day job is to help manage a mixed martial arts gym in Tokyo, and who helps promote caged "ultimate fighting" matches throughout the year, said that he usually watches it on Sunday evenings. For him, it is similar to comfort food, and he's not alone. A Japanese rapper who calls himself Kohei Japan jokes in one of his songs, "Once *Sazae-san* is over, I start to feel a little blue" (because that means it's Sunday evening, and Monday is on the way). So even with the expansion of anime on the global scene, the examples available internationally represent a small fraction of the anime produced each year domestically. Japan boasts a huge range of television series. Generally, more than ninety series air each week and range from children's programming in primetime and on Saturday mornings to adult-oriented suspense and comedy shows that tend to air late in the evenings (Dentsu 2009: 96). Depending on where you look, the meaning of anime can vary dramatically.

This brings into focus another aspect of ethnographic research—namely, the challenges of coping with contradiction. Ethnography refers to an approach to analyzing culture that begins by portraying what the world looks like to those involved in a particular sphere of activity or in a certain community. The commitment to the "native's point of view" now encompasses a wide range of potential informants, from those at the upper echelons of society (Hamabata 1990) to homeless people sleeping in a park (Gill 2001). Cultural anthropologists emphasize participant-observation fieldwork as the basis for establishing findings, but ethnography is more than simply getting out among the people. At its best, ethnography is a collaborative process of doing research, a method whereby the questions we ask are shaped by the perspectives of those working in their worlds. Ethnography thus encourages a research agenda that begins with the views of active participants and unfolds from there to develop theory. By juxtaposing voices, we can recognize patterns in the ways people choose to act, and we get a sense of how people view their own range of control—or, to use academic phrasing, their agency amid structures of inequality. We can also observe how constraints and opportunities are experienced. Needless to say, the stories people tell and the perspectives they bring to larger projects are often contradictory. Despite their differences (or sometimes because of them), somehow the different actors—their competing perspectives and individual ranges of power—collaborate to produce the world as it is today.

The disjunctures between perspectives can produce a kind of "creative friction," as the anthropologist Anna Tsing calls it in her ethnography of global connection. She draws attention to the "systematic misunderstandings" between social groups and the "zones of awkward engagement, where words mean something different across a divide even as people agree to speak" (2005: x). In this respect, an ethnography allows us to approach questions of anime markets and cultural power from diverse angles. The values that guide production are part of what determines the potential of anime. What we discover is that there is no single definition of "anime" and that the fault lines in the debate about what matters hinge on different understandings of the sources of creativity, the desires of audiences, and the broader media contexts in which animation industries develop. The story of anime revolves around competing perspectives of what success even means.

Anime producers are accustomed to thinking of animation in terms of labor, and in terms of quality. In March 2005, I interviewed Toshio Suzuki, the head producer at Studio Ghibli, at the studio's main building in Koganei, on the outskirts of Tokyo. Behind him in a cabinet sat an Oscar for Best Animated Feature from the 2002 Academy Awards and a Golden Bear (from the Berlin Film Festival), both for *Spirited Away* (dir. Hayao Miyazaki, 2001). The film is a beautifully rendered story of a young girl trapped in a magical, otherworldly bathhouse, where she must unravel a mystery to save her parents. The film was Miyazaki's most successful overseas, and it serves as a prime example of anime that achieves critical acclaim and mainstream visibility.

Yet when I asked Suzuki what he thought about the success of anime, he frowned: "Do you want me to sit here and tell you sunny stories about the anime industry, or do you want to hear the truth?" He described problems that arise from outsourcing work to South Korea and the Philippines (sometimes with spotty results) and overproduction (too many series made with too little talent in Tokyo), and the enduring problems of low budgets and the hindrance that low wages pose for even devoted animators. He added other concerns, including unreasonable demands by sponsors and the challenges of dealing with overseas distributors. His litany of complaints gives pause to the notion that anime in Japan is by and large characterized by success.

Or, rather, perhaps we need a subtler definition of success to better understand the lessons of anime. The presence of anime on so many television screens around the world does not mean that every program in Japan is successful. On the contrary, the editor of an online anime magazine published by Oricon, the leading company for tracking media audiences in Japan, estimated that only one in four series can be counted as a success.[1] Even for Studio Ghibli, the sense of success is always qualified by uncertainty about what will happen in the future. This uncertainty is ubiquitous in media industries and means that we can gain something in our understanding by considering how different studios picture the unknown.

Toei Origins: Feature Films and the Joy of Movement

When I visited the Toei Animation studios in August 2006 in Oizumi, west of Tokyo, I was led to a small museum room with smartly displayed cels from some of the company's many hit TV series. Toei is Japan's foremost producer of children's animation, and it produced many of the most influential anime of the postwar period, including *Galaxy Express 999*, *Dragon Ball*, *Sailor Moon*, and *Digimon*. The museum also included a short documentary about how animation is made. The documentary was narrated by the voice actresses for the two characters from the magical schoolgirl duo Pretty Cure, who manage to balance ultra-cute girlishness with over-the-top, violent hand-to-hand combat against enormous supernatural monsters. At the time, *Pretty Cure* was one of Toei's leading properties aimed at young girls. But when the narrators comment on a scene in the documentary that features the people who design the show, they aptly exclaim, "What a lot of old men (*oyaji*)!" As mentioned earlier, anime production is dominated by men, although a growing number of women are finding spaces to work in it. The documentary goes on to show how digital technology is transforming the kind of work anime studios do, with flashy examples from *Pretty Cure* action sequences. Toei holds a solid position among animation studios, with prominent properties that also include *One Piece*, *Slam Dunk*, and *Fist of the North Star*. A brief look at some of Toei's early history gives a sense of the emergence of a studio with a particular combination of commitments.

Toei Animation began as a studio aimed at making feature films. It was established in 1956 under the name Toei Dōga (*dōga* means "moving images") as a wholly owned subsidiary of the film production studio Nichi Dō Eiga. According to a published history, the announcement at Toei's founding looked forward to the possibility of overcoming the "international inaccessibility" (*hikokusaisei*) of Japanese-language entertainment by using drawings and movements that can be readily grasped (Toei Animation 2006: 17). The company expressed confidence that it could "make productions rivaling Disney." The anime historian Yasuo Yamaguchi acknowledges that even though Toei did not have the budgets or the market to compete directly with Disney, it did aim to become the "Disney of the East" (Yamaguchi 2004: 67).

In 1956, Toei Dōga had thirty-five employees working in an empty classroom of a high school in Shinjuku (Toei Animation 2006: 17). By the following year, the company had moved to a studio in Oizumi, a suburb west of Tokyo, and began hiring animators to make feature films. Yasuo Ōtsuka was one of those animators, and in the years since, he has worked on many classic films and TV shows. He has also helped to train up-and-coming talent, including Hayao Miyazaki and Isao Takahata, who would later form the core of Studio Ghibli.

Animation can be defined as a form of production: the practice of creating filmic works one frame at a time. Hand-drawn character animation is the focus of my research, but it is important to keep in mind that animation in Japan includes claymation, puppet animation, digitally simulated paper-cut animation, full three-dimensional computer graphics (3D CG), and more, all of which is being made today. Even these distinctions can be complicated. When I went to the studio of the paper-cut animator who creates *Polta, from a Distant Country* for NHK, and who also created the wildly frenetic duo Bip and Bap, I discovered that his finely crafted, paper-thin characters are all constructed on computers *as if* they were made of small pieces of paper. And the doll animation of Kihachirō Kawamoto was much in the news in 2006, when his long-awaited film *Book of the Dead*, based on a tale from the Heian era (around AD 700), was released. What links these different styles is the challenge of creating the illusion of movement—the illusion of life, in fact—using a series of still images.

The Animator Test

For Yasuo Ōtsuka, animation is about the joy of movement—that is, the shock of delight at seeing one's drawings move. When Ōtsuka first applied for a job at Toei in 1956, he was given an illustration of a boy holding a sledgehammer. One of Toei's anime directors told him to draw five or six key frames to depict the boy using the sledgehammer to drive a stake into the ground. Ōtsuka thought, this will be easy. As the director started to leave the room, he stopped and added, "Oh, and by the way, the hammer is made of iron. It's so heavy the boy can barely lift it."[2] Ōtsuka says, "I realized, this was going to be harder than I thought" (Ōtsuka 2001: 21–23).

Ōtsuka stood up and acted out the movements. If the hammer was too heavy, the boy would have to lean over, grab one end of the handle near the head, bend his knees, lean back, and heave. In a documentary about his career in animation, Ōtsuka re-enacts his train of thought in figuring out that the boy could raise the hammer only to a vertical position or he'd fall backward. When the hammer hit the stake, the boy would almost stagger. Ōtsuka sat back down and, with pencil in hand, turned to the blank pages, each with holes at the top to align them in a metal holder called a "tap" (*tappu*). He got to work on the backlit desk and drew the key frames. The documentary film shows a key-frame animation challenge made more difficult by changing our view of the character, who is shown at an angle instead of directly from the side (see figure 15). The numbers between the key frames (*genga*) refer to the number of in-between frames (*dōga*) that would have to be filled in later to produce smooth movement. Calculating these numbers is part of the job of the director, animation director, and key-frame artists. Drawings like these would constitute about one and a half seconds of film. Making animation requires not only an immense amount of work but also special talent.

Ōtsuka's devotion to drawing, and especially to the art of drawing movement, gave him a role in Toei's success. He worked with the directors Hayao Miyazaki and Isao Takahata, although Ōtsuka acknowledges sadly in the course of the documentary that he did not have what it takes to be a director. Toei expanded in the postwar period thanks in part to synergies

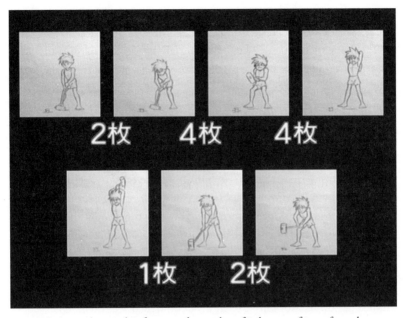

2枚　　4枚　　4枚

1枚　　2枚

15. Animator test showing key frames and a number of in-between frames from the documentary film *Ōtsuka Yasuo no Ugokasu Yorokobi* (2004).

across media and connections with other nations, and this in turn helps explain the particular directions pursued by other anime studios, too. To extend our discussion of the relationships between "niche" and "mass," which also relate to scales of analysis for crucibles of creativity, let's consider briefly the limitations of using a notion of national character as an explanation, in order to see how more proximate explanations better characterize anime's emergent success.

"The Japanese Have Always Liked Stories with Pictures"

Although some anime creators and scholars identify historical continuities in popular culture as a way to define national identity, these assertions should be interpreted with caution. Consider the anime director Isao Takahata, who is most famous perhaps for directing the stunning film *Grave of the Fireflies* (1988). The film portrays the horror of the Allies' fire-bombing of Japanese cities in 1945, a practice that killed far more people than the atomic bombs and that decimated more than sixty Japanese cities (Sayle 1995). (Two large cities were spared the firebombing: Kyoto, for its historical importance, and Hiroshima, which figured in other plans.) Takahata's film, which is based on a novel, depicts the firebombing from the perspective of two children caught in the horror and its aftermath.

Takahata spent many years working alongside the master animator Hayao Miyazaki. In a book he wrote proposing a theory for anime's success in Japan, he notes that there is no country where more anime and manga is produced and enjoyed. "What explains the extraordinary development of manga and anime in Japan?" he asks (Takahata 1999: 3). He reminds us that in the aftermath of the destruction of the Pacific war, manga, "requiring only pen and paper," were cheap to make and thus more easily produced than theater or films, and anyone, in cities or in the countryside, could enjoy them. He singles out the manga *kamisama* (god) Osamu Tezuka for pioneering emotionally moving dramas in his comics, generating large audiences and, in turn, opportunities for other artists. As the output of manga grew, anime producers had a large catalogue to draw from and an audience already devoted to many of the fictional characters. Moreover, as those audiences matured, so did the output of manga and anime creators as they strove to innovate in new directions.

But Takahata seeks a more fundamental explanation and in so doing uses what I view as too simplistic a model of cultural resonance. "The biggest cause (*saidai no gen'in*), which is not limited to the present," he writes, "is the fact that the Japanese people have enjoyed anime and manga-like things from long ago all the way until today and have also been good at making them" (Takahata 1999: 3). To illustrate this, he points to picture scrolls (*emakimono*) drawn in the twelfth century. What defines manga and anime, he says, is not the reliance on caricature but the techniques of telling stories with pictures that unfold (or in this case, unroll) over time. From this perspective, picture scrolls are in effect "twelfth-century animation," the title of his book. Takahata extends this idea of resonance historically by showing how scroll artists used "manga-like" drawings to portray movements of spinning wheels and flying arrows. His experience with anime also allows him to see picture scrolls in terms of filmic techniques. In the book, he diagrams how picture scrolls were unrolled to portray one scene at a time. The reader also could "zoom out" by unrolling both edges at once or "pan" across a scene (rolling up and rolling out simultaneously), producing camera-like effects almost a millennium ago. Takahata's book is a wonderful overview of the storytelling magic that ancient Japanese artists employed. But as an explanation for anime's cultural strength, it relies too heavily on the appearance of similarity, which, in turn, short-circuits history.

Takahata is not alone in finding resonance between contemporary animation and traditional art forms. The media studies scholar Takuji Okuno (2007) argues that the roots of today's "Cool Japan" products—anime, manga, J-Pop music, and videogames—are to be found in the aesthetics of early modern Japan. He contrasts the European arts, such as oil painting and classical music supported by aristocratic courts, with Japanese arts of the townspeople and merchants that flourished during the Edo period (1600–1868). He proposes that picture scrolls of the twelfth century led to the early comic-book-style *kibyōshi* of the Edo era, which became manga in the twentieth century. He identifies lavish kabuki performances as the precursors to anime. This effort to link today's Cool Japan forms to practices that emerged in the Edo period appears elsewhere, as well. The neo-pop artist Takashi Murakami (2000) relates some of the innovation of anime to so-called eccentric artists of the Edo period because both rely on a visual plane that eschews a 3D perspective in favor of a "superflat" merging of layers. The "special characteristic of [the animator Yoshinori Kanada's] style," he says, "lay in his ability to produce effects like those of [the wood-block artists] Sansetsu, Shohaku, and Hokusai in images of warships, tanks, robots, and girls" in, for example, the feature film *Galaxy Express 999* (Murakami 2000: 15). This is a common way to identify the continuities within cultural settings to characterize national identity through time.

Lest this tendency to make cultural generalizations seem especially Japanese, I would note that a kind of *Americajinron* (theory of American uniqueness) can be found in studies of U.S. animation. Such perspectives tend to maintain a national frame of reference and to make loose cultural connections between animated works and broader social trends. In pointing out contrasts between pure cinema and animation, the scholar Paul Wells puts it this way.

> The animated film clearly said something different about American culture and said it in a different voice. In many senses its emergence was grounded in what had become typically American grand narratives—pioneers creating a language of expression which explored new frontiers; apparently ordinary people applying their artisanal skills to achieve fulfillment as individuals and as progressive working communities; succeeding within the harsh conditions of industrial capitalism and the new machine age; expressing the desire for a liberal democratic consensus that embraced utopian values and ideals. (2002: 10)

While this depiction of the deep insights that cartoons can offer is elo-
quent and insightful, it risks trapping analysis in a mode of resonance with
larger trends that may be more metaphorical than not. To be fair, Wells's
goal is to show that "mere cartoons" can and should count as substantial
cultural texts in their own right, and he adds concrete details to the
metaphorical connections he proposes. But there is still a danger, it seems
to me, of oversimplifying through ideas of cultural resonance.

Neal Gabler's biography of Walt Disney also works within a national
frame of reference, at times showing how the narrative structure of Disney's films resonates with larger cultural realities. For Gabler, Disney's
success is America's success: "In both Disney's imagination and the American imagination, one could assert one's will on the world; one could,
through one's own power, or more accurately through the power of one's
innate goodness, achieve success. In a typically American formulation,
nothing but goodness and will mattered. Disney's best animations—*Snow
White and the Seven Dwarfs*, *Pinocchio*, *Bambi*, and *Dumbo*—were arche-
typal expressions of this idea" (2007: xvii). Gabler traces in great detail the
course of Walt Disney's life and the conditions of his studio as a way to
support these broad claims. The problem is not that Gabler is wrong in his
interpretation, but he doesn't take full advantage of what cultural analysis
has to offer. By characterizing Disney's best animation as "a typically American formulation," Gabler equates certain artistic works with national
identity, and culture becomes a dead specimen, studied as if pinned to a
board rather than fluttering chaotically in its natural environment.

Disney as Model and Rival

An alternative to associating Disney solely with America is to consider
how the company was perceived as both a model and a rival in the early
days of postwar Japanese animation. When Yasuo Ōtsuka was hired, Toei
aimed to create feature films with potential for export, but not primarily to
the United States. Toei's first release in 1958, *Hakujaden* (Legend of the
white serpent) is based on a Chinese folktale; with the help of a Hong
Kong movie company, it reached Hong Kong, Taiwan, the United States,
and Brazil. The next few years saw the release of three more Toei feature
films, a much faster rate than Disney's one release every two years. Toei
viewed itself as more rational in production. By 1961, the company had
three hundred workers, but there were labor problems, including the for-
mation of a labor union, strikes, and lockouts (Toei Animation 2006: 20–

21). Labor unions for animators never became a powerful force in Japan, whereas in the United States, the struggles and successes of the animators' union is a remarkable story (Sito 2006). One wonders, to what extent does this help explain the poor working conditions of Japan's animators today? In any case, labor issues remain a challenge for animators, and the arrival of computers has not eliminated those concerns. How, then, does animation get going as an industry? In Japan, manga was important.

The manga writer and critic Eiji Ōtsuka (no relation to the animator Yasuo Ōtsuka) tells the history of manga by beginning with the comics in American newspapers in the early twentieth century. Comic book characters such as the Yellow Kid and Little Nemo helped increase newspapers' circulation and kept consumers coming back (Ōtsuka and Ōsawa 2005). This use of characters was imported to Japanese comic strips. For example, the manga puppy character Norakuro was created in 1931 and had satirically depicted Japan's wartime efforts in Asia. The hapless Norakuro kept getting himself into trouble but eventually found ways out. As Thomas LaMarre (2008) points out, the use of animals in wartime animation conveyed a linkage between animal species and racial groups in ways that reinforced the imperialist logic of the day. Humorous comics can be serious business. Of course, the influences can be traced to domestic forms of popular culture, as well—for example, in the ways the street performance of storytelling through a series of pictures (*kamishibai*) was the rage in 1930s (Nash 2009). Some of the artists went on to produce manga, as did some of the children in the audience as they grew up.

For Toei, however, the standard for quality animation was set by Disney. The anime historian Yasuo Yamaguchi outlines a variety of innovations by Disney that influenced the development of anime, and styles of representation were not all that were borrowed (Yamaguchi 2004: 36–38). Toei sent a young film director, Taiji Yabushita, to Los Angeles to learn the production system directly from Disney (Yamaguchi 2004: 67). Some of the influences, which crossed categories of animation aesthetics, labor organization, and corporate branding, included the following:

* The use of exaggerated expressions—for example, the "squash and stretch system" of deforming characters to emphasize their personalities.
* The storyboard system, which allowed Disney to use a variety of sequential pictures to convey the story and the feeling of the scenes to the animators.
* A curriculum for training new talent, which was necessary because with

each hit production, animators would be hired away from Disney at higher salaries. Disney responded by developing a system to train new workers.

* The division-of-labor system, which allowed the Disney studio to work on animated shorts and feature-length films at the same time.

* Establishment of the Disney brand—for example, by describing all works as "Walt Disney presents" and polishing the brand image by having Disney himself personally introduce the works.

* The development of merchandising, whereby the licensor of animated characters would receive 3–7 percent of the sales price of goods related to those characters, which was necessary to offset the deficits incurred by animation production. (Yamaguchi 2004: 36–38)

In this list, we can see some of the ways the creative crucible of anime was born. The influences shade from aesthetic styles (squash and stretch) through techniques of dividing up the work. Yet Toei also took pride in viewing Disney as a rival it could top through "more rational" forms of production organization. Some of these practices remind us that "technological" decisions can have a dramatic impact on the kind of labor required of animators.

Peter Chung on National Differences

The cultural analysis of national style and international influence is complex. In Japan studies, a focus on processes of transnational adaption has been used as a critical wedge to counteract the ethnocentric view that the Japanese are either passive victims of outside influence or active only in the sense of choosing to imitate others. What are we to make of squid pizza, Tokyo Disneyland, and tango in Japan? Joseph Tobin (1992: 4) tackles these issues through the concept of "domestication" in an effort "to indicate a process that is active (unlike Westernization, modernization or postmodernism), morally neutral (unlike imitation or parasitism), and demystifying (there is nothing inherently strange, exotic, or uniquely Japanese going on here)." He aims to combat the ethnocentrism of analytical perspectives that view everything in terms of its Western or American origins. A drawback of this approach, however, lies in reinforcing the boundary rather than highlighting the dialogue between Japan and the rest.

How can one balance this mix of dialogue and divergence? We might consider some of the interactions between media and performance histories in the United States and Japan and consider how they relate to differences in styles of animation. The animation director Peter Chung offers some interesting insights. Chung was born in Seoul but lives primarily in Los Angeles. He works closely with American, Japanese, and Korean animation studios, so he has a perspective on some of the national differences while also being a living example of the collaborative work that crosses national boundaries. He wrote and directed the short animated film that appears on the compilation DVD *Animatrix*, a project overseen by Studio 4°C of Tokyo that aims at extending the *Matrix* franchise through short films by famous and up-and-coming directors. Chung's installment, *Matriculated*, was produced by the DNA animation studio in Korea. It features a female resistance fighter who lures two Sentinels (evil robots) into a trap in an effort to negotiate with those who control the Matrix. Chung gained fame in part for his *Aeon Flux* series of animated shorts that aired on MTV, which were set in a dystopic future ruled by a sadistic dictator. (He disavowed any involvement in—and any blame for—the live-action film version that starred Charlize Theron.) He draws in a style that can be perceived as "anime-like" in the sense that it contains pointed lines, spiky hair, and futuristic settings, but Chung dismisses the idea that a particular style of drawing distinguishes anime and animation.

In November 2006, I visited Chung at his home overlooking the city of Los Angeles. For him, what makes Japanese animation distinctive has less to do with the drawing style than with how it is produced. The most obvious difference, he said, is that "in American animation the dialogue is recorded first. Even though that may sound like a little technical, procedural issue, it actually affects how animation is used, the aesthetics, and the entire approach to the idea of animation as performance. This is a central difference between American animation and Japanese animation."[3] As Toei's history confirms, it is most common in Japanese animation for voices to be recorded after the animation is drawn—hence, the term *afu reko* (after recording). Sometimes exceptions are made, as in the case of Gonzo's *Red Garden*, for which the voices were recorded first (see chapter 4). *Zenmai Zamurai* used the after-recording method, and in the voice-recording session I observed, I was surprised by how little attention was given to closely matching the mouth movements that had been animated. The focus instead was on having the right emotion portrayed by the voice actors.

The differences that follow from recording voice actors first, however, can be profound. In the case of *Red Garden*, the producers viewed the prerecording as especially helpful for emphasizing the nuances of the particular actresses' performances. By having the animators respond to the voice actresses, rather than the other way around, the producers gave more weight to the actresses' work. This is precisely what Chung pointed to in explaining how recording the voices first means that a cascade of differences follow in how artistic decisions are made:

> American animators think of themselves as performers, as actors. They take very seriously their job of interpreting the voice performance and giving it the correct physical gestures. Also, usually for American feature films, an animator is cast for a particular character. For example, in Disney's *Aladdin*, one animator will work on the Aladdin character, another on Genie, and so on. In Japan, the animators each work on entire scenes. In Japan, they are more like illustrators. The term for animator is *"genga man,"* [or] "original drawing person." The [animator's] role is to make a drawing, not to perform. But this comes out of working from drawings, not from a voice track.[4]

This also means that, while making the drawings, the animator tends to work more closely with the storyboards produced by the anime director than with the actors' voices. I observed this firsthand at meetings between the director of *Red Garden* and the three *genga man* (two men and a woman) going through the storyboards he had drawn. Although the director emphasized the importance of matching mouth movements to the recorded voices, most of the discussion focused on other aspects of drawing particular scenes, such as how rain should be portrayed and the speed at which a character would fall.

According to Chung, the differences relate to the origins from which the respective traditions drew:

> American animators come out of vaudeville. The origin of animation as media was short films. When films first started being shown in theaters, they were preceded by vaudeville acts, out of which grew Bugs Bunny shorts and so on. All of these forms were born out of personalities—Bugs Bunny, Daffy Duck, Mickey Mouse, Goofy, Popeye. They are much less about the story.... [T]he character of Mickey Mouse was the equivalent of a Buster Keaton. That's the way that they functioned in the entertainment world. From the very beginning in American animation, animators saw themselves

as vaudeville performers. It affected everything. [For example,] their staging is much more proscenium-based.[5]

In Japan, animators drew inspiration from Disney and from the animated *Popeye* and *Betty Boop* shorts by the Fleischer brothers, among others. The emphasis on characters with personalities is not uniquely Japanese, therefore, but the linking of characters to particular actors and performances— such as Mickey Mouse's borrowing from Buster Keaton in *Steamboat Bill*—tends to be more common in U.S. animation. This can be taken to extremes when animated characters are inextricably linked—for example, Robin Williams as Genie in *Aladdin* or Eddie Murphy as Donkey in *Shrek*.

Yet the attention to physical movement as a way to portray personality necessarily introduces a localization dynamic based on what we observe daily. Yasuo Ōtsuka describes the mixed reaction in Toei's early days to a book showing animation techniques created by Preston Blair, an American. It was a time before copy machines, and one of Ōtsuka's supervisors had copied the book by hand. Blair depicts techniques such as the "take" (surprise), anticipation (the pose before moving), follow-through (body position after a movement), and so on (Blair 2003 [1949]). Some characters are animals (squirrels, dogs, rabbits); others are cartoonish people. Animation styles go global through this kind of observation and appropriation. At the same time, Ōtsuka (2001: 38–39) reports, the animators at Toei felt there was a bias and a lack in Blair's guide: "The textbook was born from analyzing actual movements, but these were still the exaggerated gestures of Europeans and Americans. . . . They portrayed 'Western (*batakusai*; lit., smelling of butter)' movements, like the way some Japanese who have lived abroad will spread their arms and shake their head when they say 'Oh no!'" This helps to clarify the challenges of defining anime in terms of "Japaneseness." There is a danger in defining "Japaneseness" as that which is not "Western," because outside influences are only "outside" in a limited sense. For Japanese animators, the skills and practices of Blair's guide were clearly recognizable, and Ōtsuka copied the entire book himself. "I have to do it with my hands or I can't learn it," he says in the documentary about his career. But the urgency to make something that spoke to them and their audiences also meant that Japanese animators adapted animation techniques through their own life experiences, including close observation of styles of physical movement among fellow Japanese.

Nevertheless, the emergence of Toei's approach to animation was less an exercise in defining a unique Japaneseness than an effort to secure a sustainable position in an evolving media market. After the success of its first feature film, released in only nine months ("several times faster than Disney," according to Toei [2006: 20]), the company worked on rationalizing the labor process with a "first key frame" group and a "second key frame" group dividing up the work. Three more feature films were produced in less than three years. Animation for TV began in 1963 with *Tetsuwan Atomu* (Mighty Atom, also known as Astro Boy), to be discussed later. Toei soon followed with *Ken, the Wolf Boy* (*Ookami shonen Ken*), which, like Astro Boy, was based on a manga and included a sponsorship tie to a confection company.

Toei hedged its bets by working on several different kinds of anime production aimed at slightly different markets. During the 1960s, Toei worked simultaneously on one TV series and two feature films each year. One of the features was designed for the export market (released in the spring); the other feature film was oriented more to the domestic market for release over the summer or winter vacation (Toei Animation 2006: 17). The success of the science-fiction adventure *Cyborg 009* (1966) as a feature film for the domestic market pushed Toei in new directions, partly because it was the company's first hit based on a manga (by Shotarō Ishinomori). After 1966, Toei shifted its emphasis toward TV series. *Maho Tsukai Sally* (Sally the little witch), from 1967, was the company's first TV series in color. It started the "girl witch" boom, a genre that benefited from the sale of toys that appeared as magical items in the show. *Gegege no Kitarō* (1968), based on a manga by Shigeru Mizuki, inaugurated horror anime on TV and got caught up in a monster boom in Japanese popular culture. *Taigā Masuku* (Tiger mask) of 1969 was a fighting anime, and it captured that era's popular *gekiga*, a reference to extreme drawing styles in manga, especially of fighting and action sequences. The feature film *Puss in Boots* (1969) was a remarkable hit for Toei; the animated cat Pero from the *Puss in Boots* series has since been the company's mascot (Toei Animation 2006: 34–35). It is this back-and-forth between the company and maturing audiences that led to the emergence of certain styles. Indeed, reading the history of Toei from the company's perspective makes clear that the competitors the company thought most about were other studios in Japan. For this reason, contrasts with the *Astro Boy* approach deserve a look.

Astro Boy, Tezuka, and Manga's Place in Anime

While Toei was working on feature films, Osamu Tezuka, rightly regarded as a "god of manga," aimed to move into the world of TV anime—or TV manga (*terebi manga*), as it was known at the time. Television broadcasting began in Japan in 1953, but few homes had sets. In the following year, some of the largest televised events were professional wrestling matches between Rikidozan and Masahiko Kimura versus the Sharpe brothers (Mike and Ben), who were then visiting Japan from the United States. At times, thousands of people would stand on the streets outside train stations to try to watch the TV screens inside the stations (Chun 2007). As the 1950s progressed, economic growth expanded consumer spending so that by 1958, TV sets, washing machines, and refrigerators became known as "three sacred treasures" (Yamaguchi 2004: 74). Tezuka established his animation studio Mushi Pro in 1961, but, as Yasuo Yamaguchi notes, "Production time and budgets [for TV animation] were simply unrealistic." Toei was taking about eighteen months and spending about 60 million yen (roughly $167,000 in 1961 dollars) to produce ninety-minute feature films with a staff of two hundred to three hundred people, comparable to the schedules and budgets of other studios working in the field, including Disney. At that rate, Yamaguchi points out, a single thirty-minute TV show would require about one hundred people, a production time of six months, and a budget of about 30 million yen ($80,000). But the market for a thirty-minute TV production was 500,000–600,000 yen (roughly $1,500), and that is what Tezuka agreed to. "Needless to say, this meant working at a loss," notes Yamaguchi (2004: 74–75).

Nevertheless, Tezuka benefited from an impressive catalogue of characters that were already popular. The outpouring of emotion that arose from his riveting stories could be viewed as a kind of untapped resource, a social energy that could be captured through both television animation and its connection to merchandising. In this respect, Tezuka made an enormous impact on the development of manga and anime. He was incredibly prolific from the time he began publishing in the late 1940s until his death in 1989. Disney's influence is noteworthy here, too. Tezuka reportedly watched *Snow White and the Seven Dwarfs*, which was first shown in Tokyo in 1950, more than eighty times and *Bambi*, which premiered in Tokyo in 1951, more than fifty times (Schodt 2007: 59). Tezuka even produced his own comic book versions of the Bambi and Pinocchio stories,

16. Tezuka's *Metropolis*, a metaphor for Disney? Courtesy of Dark Horse Comics.

which were published first without obtaining permission from Disney, only to be officially licensed years later. It is tempting to see a metaphorical portrayal of Tezuka's complex relationship with Disney in his manga *Metropolis* published in 1949. One of its heroes, Detective Ban, is imprisoned by bad guys in their underground fortress. The jail is overrun by enormous irradiated mice that closely resemble the famous Mickey. In trying to flee, Ban falls on a mouse and kills it. To make his escape, Ban slices open the dead mouse, sews himself inside, and runs off, terrifying those around him (see figure 16). Is this Tezuka taking on Disney and using it for his own purposes? Yes and no. Frederik Schodt and others make the important point that Disney was not Tezuka's only influence. He grew up enthralled by the all-women Takarazuka Revue in the neighborhood outside Osaka where he was raised, a study in complex gender dynamics (see Robertson 2008). Tezuka also linked *Astro Boy* to inspiration from Mighty Mouse (Schodt 2007).

Why the Big Eyes in Anime?

A recurring question in anime studies is, why the big eyes? So many of the characters "look Western" (i.e., white, Caucasian), I often hear. Does this mean that the Japanese want to be white? This is a complicated question and, frankly, difficult to prove one way or the other, once and for all. My own explanation, however, would lead through Disney and Tezuka and the early history of animation. I should note, however, that when I've asked Japanese friends and colleagues for their opinions on this issue, one of the interesting responses goes like this: "Why do you think anime characters are Western? They are speaking Japanese, so obviously they are Japanese." Some Westerners' interpretation of big eyes as "white" may be more a measure of Western prejudice than of Japanese yearning. Moreover, as the cartoonist Scott McCloud (1993) argues, greater abstraction in cartoon drawing also leaves more room for readers to insert their own interpretations. Perhaps it's human to see ourselves in abstractions of people, and that could be one explanation for the persistence of this thorny issue in discussions of anime.

More generally, however, I tend to see the large eyes as a style. Some explain it in terms of the expressiveness of eyes: Bigger eyes enable illustrators to play more with the nuances of communicating with one's eyes. But there is also the centrality of Tezuka in manga history in Japan and Tezuka's own obsession with Disney characters. Tezuka learned from Bambi and Snow White—not to mention Popeye and Betty Boop, who also have large eyes. Emulation can help explain a global style. Given that anime is now associated with "big eyes" more than Disney is, we can also see how generational differences in audiences (and productions) can obscure some of these historical connections. In the end, what makes the eyes in Tezuka's characters so influential was indeed his very success as a manga artist, even if this did not translate into success for his anime studio.

Tezuka's popularity also paved the way for other manga artists. Schodt provides a fascinating examination of *Astro Boy* in the context of Tezuka's life, noting that later stars of manga publishing, including Fujiko Fujio, Leiji Matsumoto, Shōtarō Ishinomori, Tarō Rin, and Yoshiyuki Tomino, gained training in his studio (Schodt 2007: 49; Yamaguchi 2004: 81). Yet Tezuka's success, especially in terms of anime, was mixed. Later in life, Tezuka joked that manga was his wife, while animation was his mistress. "He loved manga, [but] his passion for animation was almost beyond control," says Schodt (2007: 56). Despite the huge popularity of the TV series *Astro Boy*, Mushi Pro went out of business.

Can Failure Be a Kind of Success?

As mentioned, Tezuka proposed an extremely low budget for making *Astro Boy*. He planned to make up for the budget shortfall partly through merchandising and by using money from sales of his manga (Schodt 2007:

56). A central merchandising outlet turned out to be *Astro Boy* stickers bundled with Meiji chocolate bars. Marc Steinberg argues that this tie-in ignited a boom in character merchandising partly because media became ubiquitous and constant: The "anytime-anywhere potential of the stickers arguably led to the new communicational media environment and cross-media connections that characterize the anime system and the force which drives it: the character" (Steinberg 2008: 113). Steinberg gives a sense of the social dynamics of the classroom and playground, where having a sticker of a powerful boy robot transformed media into something attached to oneself (a pencil case, a backpack) at all times. Yet it might make more sense to consider the "anime system" as something that emerges from this circulating energy and that finds different expression depending on through whom and to where it passes. I see this social energy of the people who care as the force that drives whatever "system" (partial, unfinished, multidirectional) eventually emerges, a social energy that arises from people's commitments and shared interests. Characters are an organizing principle, and merchandise can be seen as physical extensions of our feelings for characters. Tezuka's *Astro Boy* led the way for TV animation, but the processes had been under way for some time.

Despite the challenges, Mushi Pro managed to make a weekly *Astro Boy* episode by radically reducing the number of frames that needed to be drawn (Yamaguchi 2004: 80). The weekly *Astro Boy*, which premiered on New Year's Day in 1963, was the first animated TV series to air regularly in Japan. Separate cels were used for arm and leg movements while the rest of the character was left unchanged. Only three mouth movements—open, closed, and middle—were used. Commonly used scenes, such as Astro Boy flying, were banked and reused. Cuts were kept short (only a few seconds) so the weaknesses in the animation would be less apparent. To show a car going by, one cel was moved across a background; for walking scenes, the background was slid (and legs were not shown). The Mushi team aimed to make half-hour episodes using only two thousand drawn frames. In feature films such as Toei's, it was common to use only one cel for two frames of film, but for *Astro Boy*, one cel for every three frames shot was the smoothest animation used, and often the animators tried to use only one drawn cel, with zooms and pans giving the illusion of movement. Despite the severely limited animation, *Astro Boy* was an enormous success, drawing audience ratings of 30 percent of all households.

This was not an entirely beneficial development for animation, however, at least, not from the perspective of those like Yasuo Ōtsuka, who viewed animated movement as the goal. Indeed, Ōtsuka (2004) discusses the enduring legacy of *Astro Boy* with a somewhat disappointed air. In the early days of Toei, the story and characters were all created within the company. But in the case of anime based on manga, the process of production and the sources of success are somewhat different: "The story and the characters were already worked out, and they aimed to get viewer ratings from the popularity of the magazine. It didn't just make it easy to get support for a program; it also made [the program] easier to produce" (Ōtsuka 2004: 29). This evenhanded assessment belies a great sense of loss for Ōtsuka. In the documentary about his life, he expresses frustration at what became of anime after *Astro Boy*: "Anime is mass production now. With TV shows and films based on already popular manga characters, sponsors know they can get a large audience that comes just to hear the voice actors and to see the story (which they already know). You can use pans and tricks, and the characters don't even have to move. I didn't think that an era would come where audiences would turn out because they wanted to hear a voice actor or because it was a particular story." He had hoped people would watch for the quality of the hand-drawn animation.

The conflict between those who love the art of drawing movement and those who worry about the cost of production is a basic one in animation, and Tezuka cannot be blamed for all of it. When I interviewed Hiroshi Yoshioka, a producer at Toei Animation, in 2006, he had been in the business for many decades. He dismissed the idea of "the curse of Tezuka," that is, blaming one person for the low budgets provided for anime production and the practices of limited animation. "We all had those problems," Yoshioka said. Indeed, as time went on, Toei began to rely more on manga-based animation, including, as mentioned earlier, *Cyborg 009*, a manga by Shōtarō Ishinomori.

Still, it is tempting to see in *Astro Boy* a split that continues to complicate the question of what matters in the art of animation. LaMarre points to the distinction between "drawing movement" (as in character animation) and moving drawings (as in sliding foreground and background cels) as two ways to understand the art of anime. To see full animation as the pinnacle of achievement and limited animation in terms of its lack is to downplay the aesthetics of sliding planes of images, which is precisely where LaMarre (2009) sees the distinctiveness of anime as a medium. For him, the relationships between these planes of drawings are a powerful tool for us to rethink our relationship to technology more generally. If cinematism arises from a "ballistic" view of a monocular camera—flying through space like a bullet or as if one were watching out the front of a train, for example—then "animetism," according to LaMarre, is to see the world from the side, looking out the window of a train, understanding scale and distance by observing how the trees and hills of the countryside slide by at different speeds. This is a very interesting insight, and it has made me see things in animation in ways I had never seen them before. I am familiar with animation picture albums that focus on "the art of . . ." (fill in the blank), which often emphasize the elaborate backgrounds and settings of various worlds. I also have come to expect anime books to begin with the characters and their biographies. But thinking of animation by beginning with the multiplane camera and in terms of sliding planes is taken further by LaMarre than by anyone else. By drawing attention to the divergent layers of animation, LaMarre draws inspiration from the multiplane camera, which facilitates the art of sliding planes of images and thus expands our sense of what can be observed in the world of anime. To follow this metaphor, we might also extend our thinking about anime by viewing it as a plane sliding against a background of manga and raising the possibility for new aspects of characters and worlds in other media forms. Or to put it another way, we might read the distinction between planes in terms of cross-media synergies, especially in the additive value of manga characters and in terms of their audiences.

"Democratic Capitalism" of Megahit Manga

About 60 percent of current anime programs are based on manga series. This continuing connection between manga and anime adds another dimension to thinking about who makes anime and what anime makes. To some extent, manga artists make anime in the sense that they play an important role in providing the characters, premises, and worlds on which the majority of anime TV series are based. But I would argue that not only the force of imagination of the artists but also some of the particular features of the manga industry strongly contribute to the health of the anime industry. Granted, the long hours and low wages for animators is a threat to the long-term sustainability of anime as a global media force. At the same time, the enormous back catalogue of manga—not to mention of other common sources of anime, including young adult fiction ("light novels" in Japan) and videogames—suggests that Japanese companies will remain well positioned for years to come. The catalogue has a certain social and cultural power precisely because a wide range of Japanese audiences are familiar with the visual storytelling styles and are devoted to particular characters. As audiences for manga grow in the United States and other countries, this should bode well for expanding anime audiences.

In the inaugural issue of *Kino*, a magazine devoted to manga analysis, the editors ask a provocative question: "Why is it that in manga, unlike in other media forms, the hit series are also the best series?" The magazine is published by Kyoto Seika University, the first college in Japan to have opened a department in manga. The editors offer this answer:

> Although it may sound like an exaggeration, manga represents the perfect combination of democracy and capitalism. Unlike films, music, and literature, which can turn lousy works (*dasaku*) into hits through the strategic use of marketing and reviews, in the world of manga this rarely happens. This is because manga readers pass around copies of magazines and read manga for free while standing in bookstores and convenience stores. Manga readers are less swayed by promoters and critics. That means that megahit manga are those that prompt people to say "I want to read this; and I want to get others to read it too." ("Megahitto no hōsoku" 2006: 3)

The editors draw attention to the intimate "call and response" between manga artists and readers. Unpacking some of the details of this process can help us understand vibrant crucibles of creativity beyond the studios themselves. This offers a useful contrast to Takahata's cultural analysis ("the Japanese like stories with pictures") by showing a more dynamic, interactive understanding of the process by which pop culture success emerges through specific dynamics related to marketing, pricing, access, and distribution, not to mention contrasts in terms of content.

Manga's success as a media form relies on the feedback loop between producers and audience. Manga is cheap to buy and can be accessed for free relatively easily. The full price for weekly magazines is roughly $3, and they contain about twenty different serials. Yet these can also be read for free while standing in convenience stories, a practice known as *tachiyomi* ("reading while standing"). For the editors of *Kino*, this is important because it reduces the influence of promoters and critics, not unlike imagining a democracy without lobbyists and pundits. Reading for oneself or hearing by word of mouth is the more likely mode for learning about new manga. Manga in print are also easily passed around, a kind of grassroots circulation where reading itself is part of a social relationship. This takes us further than Gladwell in thinking about crucibles of success as depending on audiences.

Publishers take advantage of audiences' passion by including postcards with the magazines, asking which stories were the readers' most and least favorite. One of the major publishers, Shogakukan, reports receiving three thousand to four thousand postcards every week. Unpopular series are quickly cut. Those that survive for years have prevailed against stiff competition, vying against old favorites and a constant stream of new artists attempting to break in. One can understand the tension as a professional manga artist in a country with an endless supply of semi-pro manga artists. The largest annual convention in Japan revolves around fan-made comics (dōjinshi). When I attended Comic Market in August 2006, I was stunned by the size and intensity of the event. Over three days, almost half a million people attend. Roughly thirty thousand dōjin circles (amateur groups) occupied small tables to sell their wares, generally for less than $5 each. Most of the tables sold fan-made comics, but a variety of things were for sale—buttons, T-shirts, information guides, character goods, videogames, and so on. Manga publishers are not enthusiastic about the practice of selling fanzines, which they feel cannibalizes their market. Yet in the larger scheme of things, it may be that the global success of manga arises in part from the widespread amateur production that also builds energy around this popular culture world.

Some large-scale contrasts between such media worlds can expand our notions of emergence and media success by pointing to alternative paths and different contexts. Today, Japanese manga is viewed as violent, sexually transgressive, and disturbing in its themes—at least, compared with American comics. But that has a very specific historical basis. As David Hajdu describes, the wild spaces of American comic book production in the 1930s and 1940s in the United States took a sharp turn in the early 1950s. Until then, he argues persuasively, comic book artists were "cultural insurgents," who helped instill "in their readers, a disregard for the niceties of proper society, a passion for wild ideas and fast action, a cynicism toward authority of all sorts, and a tolerance, if not an appetite, for images of prurience and violence" (2008: 330). Crime, horror, and lurid tales were the bread and butter of early American comic books. That all changed when outrage among some critics exploded, and a consortium of publishers established a Comics Code in 1954, a remarkable salvo of self-censorship in the realm of popular culture. The following were some of the rules of the new American code:

* Policemen, judges, government officials and respected institutions shall never be presented in such a way as to create disrespect for established authority.
* All scenes of horror, excessive bloodshed, gory or gruesome crimes, depravity, lust, sadism, masochism shall not be permitted.
* Profanity, obscenity, smut, vulgarity, or words or symbols which acquired undesirable meanings are forbidden.
* Suggestive and salacious illustration or suggestive posture is unacceptable.
* Females shall be drawn realistically without exaggeration of any physical qualities.
* The treatment of love-romance stories shall emphasize the value of the home and the sanctity of marriage. (Hajdu 2008: 290–91)

As Hajdu notes, when the comics industry recovered in the 1960s, it fell back on the formulas of superheroes. This helps explain the greater diversity and more extreme content of manga from Japan compared with the United States.

As the sociologist Sharon Kinsella (1998) explains in the case of adult manga, the extreme forms of storytelling that appeared in Japanese comics were also occasionally vilified, but the industry did not succumb to the same kind of self-regulation. Whether a new law passed in Tokyo in 2010 that aims to prevent some of the more disturbing aspects of child-related eroticism/pornography in cartoons will serve as a turning point remains to be seen. But at the least, we can observe that a greater openness in manga created a kind of space where adult themes could be portrayed and examined. This, too, helps to explain how anime gradually shifted from being primarily a children's form to one that spoke to teens and adults, a process I explore further in the next chapter.

Conclusion

The early postwar history of anime reveals a complicated process of emulation and learning from overseas, along with contrasting approaches within Japan itself. Disney animation served as both rival and model for a variety of anime that developed in Japan, not only in terms of style, but more broadly in terms of labor organization, branding, merchandising, and training new talent. Yet the democratic capitalism of manga in Japan also meant that the catalogue of original works to draw on encouraged a closer link between anime and manga, while also explaining a relative absence of variety in American comics after the Comics Code was established.

Anime offers the opportunity to explore the complex workings of value in today's transmedia environment, especially in how value arises through the social circulation of media objects, not just in terms of moments of commodification. The story of anime's "success" might be best understood as a cast of characters playing out their parts through shared dramatic premises in a world that changes as time goes on. From that perspective, it makes sense to understand that the success of the anime industry, for example, in dominating TV broadcasts worldwide, nevertheless does not ensure success for each individual anime studio. Success looks very different depending on where one stands. My effort to move the analysis from resonance to emergence is paralleled by a move from content industries to collaborative creativity. In the examples of Toei's feature films and Mushi Pro's interest in TV, however, we can see that the anime industry is characterized by a variety of cross-cutting commitments and approaches. My interest in collaborative creativity draws attention to the networks of cooperation and spheres of competition that produce today's worlds of anime.

The concept of collaborative creativity is meant to remind us that anime's influence cannot be gauged solely by examining what happens on-screen or only by how it is marketed by studios. More broadly, anime is illustrative of processes of cultural production that reach across media forms and across categories of producers. Thus, collaborative creativity can also provide new insights into the distribution of power in media, both in terms of top-down or bottom-up forces and in terms of Western hegemony versus local difference. Karl Marx proposed that those who control the means of production have the overriding power in social-economic relationships, but given that fans can powerfully influence the meanings and values of popular culture, who ultimately controls the "means of production"? The ordinary oppositions no longer hold once we acknowledge that fans and consumers are indispensable actors in generating the value of cultural goods. This brings us back to the energy around anime, which arises through its circulation and the combined efforts of large numbers of people, whose collaborative approaches to creativity built an industry through hard work, through synergies with other media, and by developing a fan base that has grown and matured over time. At each stage of the process, collaborative creativity arises from both a focus of attention and a circulatory movement that constantly reframes and redefines what anime is about. We might think of this collective energy as a kind of soul, the tendrils that run through media and connect us to others. This becomes even clearer as we turn to questions of robot, or mecha, anime and its relationship to toys in the next chapter.

FOUR

When Anime Robots Became Real

In June 2006, a colleague, Yuichi Washida, invited me to attend a brainstorming session in Toy Town. At the time, he was working at Hakuhodo, a leading marketing and research firm, and had been asked by Bandai, Japan's largest toy company, to organize a workshop to help think toward the future. The day-long meeting involved assessing trends, considering popular culture touchstones from the past, and imagining entirely new kinds of products, and not just toys. "Toys" proper face an uncertain future in Japan, where the size of the population is declining and its average age is rising—a graying that seems to bode ill for an industry premised on youthful play. But in some ways, Bandai's strength lies less in designing and selling material goods for children than in capitalizing on the emotional attachments people feel toward virtual characters. At first blush, this seems to be a process of taking what is virtual and making it real. A closer look at the "real" in anime, however, leads us more deeply into the varieties of the social in media.

The materialization of anime (and other media) speaks to broader challenges faced by entertainment businesses that depend on packaged forms. It is easy to imagine that before long CDs and DVDs will seem as quaint and outdated as eight-track tapes and player pianos. Anime-related media creators are responding in a number of ways—for example, by moving toward live, "you have to be there" experiences like musical concerts featuring voice actors and merchandise like holographic trading cards that cannot be digitized and downloaded. Both strategies can be seen as movements toward the "real," yet, arguably, they move in opposite directions. This is the landscape Washida aimed to explore, and he planned an entire day of team activities for the Boys' Toys (*boizu toizu*) division of Bandai. Knowing about my interest in anime and the licensed merchandise business, he included me.

The relationship between anime and toys builds on the previous chapters' movement between the cultural platform of anime and the social dynamics that bring the characters and worlds to life. As we observed in the last chapter, the success of anime in Japan depends partly on the characteristics of the manga world, a fiercely competitive realm with tight feedback loops between readers and publishers. Yet depending on the medium, the speed of production and logics of fandom can diverge. As we continue to consider the scales of analysis that can help clarify the crucibles of creativity that lead to success, it is clear that we need a nuanced sense of the broader network of production nodes. This contrasts with the more common approach to anime—and to media success more generally —which focuses on the auteur. I started with a version of this in discussing Mamoru Hosoda to highlight his craft at organizing studio work and his skill at marketing his films to a wider public, explaining their significance in terms of societal trends. In much popular media analysis, the story ends there: A great film resonates with a wide audience because of the vision of the auteur. But we've seen the importance of transmedia connections in developing and sustaining Japanese animation, so how do we grasp the interconnection between diverse "structures of creative action" (Graeber 2001), especially when they reach across industries and categories of producers? Sitting in on script meetings points to the value of seeing the emergence of new projects in terms of a "platform" of characters and worlds. Rather than viewing the media technology (television, Internet, DVD, multiplex theaters) as the platform, I argue the platform is better viewed in terms of characters and worlds—that is, both as free-floating ideas and as objects of emotional attachment. Looking at some examples of anime from the late 1950s through the 1960s, we saw how the emergence of different approaches to animation grows out of collaborative creativity. In this chapter, I focus on examples from the 1970s through the 1990s to explore further connections beyond anime studios themselves, including Toei Animation's success with robot anime, the unexpected turnaround from failure to success for the Gundam franchise, and the story of Gainax, which in some ways went from toys to anime. If an important part of the story of anime's success is the "democratic capitalism" of manga, then another aspect involves extensions of licensed merchandise. One could tell this story through a number of different kinds of examples, including "magical schoolgirl"–type anime, which capitalized on a desire for transforming (*henshin*) goods and appealed to girls. But my fieldwork yielded more information on giant robot, or "mecha," anime, and it is this example that I use to help make the connections to toys.

Brainstorming in Toy Town

The workshop was held in a place called Omocha no Machi (Toy Town), about an hour and a half from the Ueno Station in Tokyo, and which included one of Bandai's large complexes of buildings. The rural town was once the center of Japan's toy manufacturing industry, and as we took a taxi from the station, we passed enormous factory buildings that were now silent and mostly empty. As has occurred in many other industries, almost all of Bandai's manufacturing production had moved to China, Thailand, and other low-wage countries in Asia. Bandai was in the process of remaking their main building there as an archive and museum, and the giant foyer featured a selection of Namco arcade games from the past. The complex was also used for in-house company meetings and retreats. The exception to Bandai's overseas manufacturing is the Bandai Hobby Center in Shizuoka, about an hour from Tokyo on the bullet train, where automated machines churn out extremely finely detailed plastic model kits. Robot forklifts move the completed model sets into boxes for shipping, and only three people are required to keep the manufacturing process moving. Most of the Shizuoka plant is devoted to designing new products, essentially turning 2D cartoon images into 3D models for home hobbyists to assemble (see figure 17). My guide at the Hobby Center, who, like everyone else, was dressed in a costume inspired by the original *Gundam* series, said that the most complicated models ("Perfect Grade") took him about twenty hours to build. "And I'm pretty good at it," he added. Not everyone, we can agree, has that kind of time and inclination, but because enough people do, Bandai has become more interested in targeting these types of adult consumers.

The goal of Washida's meeting was to think five or ten years into the

17. GunPla anniversary "Real Grade" (intermediate level) *Gundam* plastic model.

future and to come up with new product ideas for the "high target" market. For the Boys' Toys division, this means men in their twenties and older: high age, high income. Bandai hoped the workshop could help in the development of expensive "toys" in a broad sense. The forty attendees were from Bandai, more than half in their late twenties and thirties, and although they were mostly men, as might be expected of the Boys' Toys division, about a fifth were women. They were also the cream of the educated crop. One Bandai executive told me Bandai received about twenty thousand applications for new management track hires each year and selected about thirty-five people.

After breaking up into small groups of about six people, we spent the morning discussing a packet of newspaper and magazine clippings about trends in Japanese society. Washida encouraged each group to come up with clusters of future developments and to think about how consumerism was changing. My group, Team B, identified several possible trends, including the coming of a new era of the individual (*ko no jidai*), with increasing numbers of divorces, fewer children, and generally greater concern for individual happiness. Here, again, we see the theme of greater personalization, introduced in relation to Hosoda's film *The Girl Who Leapt through Time* that seems to characterize media and consumer markets more widely. My team also proposed that men and women seemed to be coming closer or more similar in a variety of ways, such as an increase in "boys who are pretty" and "girls who are cool," while acknowledging that trends in popular culture were still largely guided by female consumers (note the implied theory that women drive the movement of consumer objects from niche to mass). Team B also noted that people's investments in their "fake lives" were leading to a growth in the gross domestic product —for example, when people paid money to have their online game characters improved. Among the new generation of adults, some would be interested in luxury toys and status brands, and others were more likely to be interested in renting than in owning consumer items (the "rental generation"). From these clusters of ideas from our group and the others, Washida ended the morning session by identifying a set of trends to consider in designing new products, the goal of the afternoon session. We ate our box lunches and went downstairs to see a small museum exhibit related to the inventions of Thomas Edison.

We reconvened after lunch to brainstorm ideas for new products, and things got interesting. While the morning was spent bringing together themes about changes in Japan's consumers, the afternoon began with a consideration of the popular culture trends that might be useful in designing products for grownups. Washida gave us each a handout that summarized in timeline format the hit television shows, feature films, manga, and other merchandise of note for each year of the 1980s and 1990s. As the members of Team B looked over the list of TV series and manga, they grew increasingly excited as they recalled their love of particular anime series and manga characters, such as the gag manga by Akira Toriyama called *Dr. Slump* and Rumiko Takahashi's series *Urusei Yatsura* (roughly, "those obnoxious aliens"). Some fondly recalled giant robot series, while others expressed a preference for sports dramas. What struck me was the intensity of the debates that followed about the best of each of the years. Although the designers were discussing shows that were a decade or two old, they expressed heartfelt devotion to their particular favorites. In addition, it was striking to see how a few years' difference in age among the team members meant very different favorites. A three-year difference in age would mean a different range of popular culture items that would be the source of extravagant nostalgia. The dynamics of niche and mass are complicated: a mass phenomenon, like a hit anime, is also part of the dynamics of personal distinction, especially in terms of age. This reinforces the idea that media objects are important for defining peer groups.

In the end, these touchstones of nostalgic excitement helped the various teams develop possible product ideas that were aimed at adults, few of which would be seen as "toys" in the traditional sense. Contemporary trends were viewed as guiding the ways in which such new products could be designed so that (1) Bandai should respond to the desire that things seem more "real" (*riaru*), yet this use of the term "real" should not conflict with the spread of interest in one's "fake" (*feeku*), or online, life; (2) Bandai should be designing things that were inaccessible before, either because they would have been too expensive or because it wasn't possible to create such things in the past; and, finally, (3) Bandai would have to respond to the growing desire among consumers to choose from a wider variety of options and to enable buyers to customize their things after purchase. For example, businesspeople may want to avoid carrying luggage and could have a wardrobe and shaving kit ready and waiting at foreign destinations. The Bandai design team recognized that their task depended on mediating between the wistful longing for characters they had come to care for in the past, and the challenge of making something new that would appeal to today's adults. Compared with anime studios trying to make original characters, however, Bandai has a distinct advantage: It can work from what is already a booming success. Yet even this advantage is not decisive. The brainstorming session aimed to anticipate how best to adapt to an as yet unrealized future.

Fragments of the Possible

One of the strangest keywords of Japanese animation might be the term "real" (*riaru*). Given that animation is made from drawn pictures that give an illusion of movement, one would expect animators to revel in the possibilities of representing things that are the most difficult to capture in real life—that is, those things that are furthest from the "real." Much of the theorizing of early animation in the United States stressed the ability to deform characters plastically in ways that produced unique cinematic effects (Wells 1998). The anime scholar Susan Napier (2005) views the styles of the fantasyscape of Japanese animation as one explanation for its global success, illustrative of a growing desire for fantasy worldwide, particularly as young people become increasingly disillusioned by politics and technology. The many examples of postwar Japanese anime featuring magical schoolgirls or young people who pilot giant robots point to genres that rely on fantasy and futurism. My interviews and discussions with anime fans also confirm that certain anime films and series are deemed attractive at least partly because they create imaginary worlds that go beyond what is really possible. One might think that the "real" in anime would be a moot issue. On the contrary, however, over the postwar period, questions of reality in anime have highlighted key faultlines in the collaborative creativity that led to defining new genres and reaching new audiences.

Scott Lash and Celia Lury propose that we have entered a new era in which media should no longer be viewed in terms of "representation," whereby media represents some other reality. Instead, they argue, media has become "real" in itself (a matter, in their words, of "the cultural superstructure . . . collapsing into the material base"). An example of this is the way flagship stores called Niketown aim to transform the immaterial Nike brand into a lived experience. In their view, the implications are far-reaching: "goods become informational, work becomes affective, property becomes intellectual and the economy more generally becomes cultural" (2007: 7). They call this process the "thingification of media." Although I admire the ambition of this approach, especially in attempting to show how cultural forms can in themselves become a kind of "infrastructure," I would argue that their notion of the "real" takes for granted a kind of fundamental materiality and a focus on the "biographies of cultural objects." They end their book by arguing for recognizing the importance of the movement toward "person to person"—that is, the intersubjectivity of meaning. But to me, that is where the real should begin—namely, with the social in media and the question of impact flowing from there—rather than from the objects themselves.

Thomas LaMarre highlights this dimension of media in the contrasts between digital and analog media. He explores the relationship between animation and cinema and notes that the real is often viewed as defining the boundary between old analog media and new digital media. He points out that "indexical media" such as photography and cinema "touch the real or impress it into images," thereby allowing for stable points of reference and thus, he adds, "for identity and history" (LaMarre 2006a: 168). In contrast, digital media seems to "generate realities rather than record them." Although some might see this as the end of cinema, LaMarre argues instead that the development of film has always been a process of reinventing the "perpetual potency of cinema" (2006a: 175). In his book *The Anime Machine*, LaMarre looks at "the technologies of the moving image and the angle of their force" (2009: x) to show how anime offers new ways to think about humans' relationship with technological realities.

An alternative formulation of the real comes from the cultural studies scholar Toshiya Ueno (1998), who focuses on depictions of war in mecha anime. He argues that anime straddles a desire for real representation, and yet, at the same time, it can succeed only because it is ultimately fictional. For Ueno, this success relates to providing a critical perspective on war's violence yet at a step removed because it is animation. Ueno gives the example of the anime director Mamoru Oshii, who uses lens flares (the distinctive spread of light that comes from looking through a camera lens) in his anime. "He doesn't do this to be faithful to reality. He does it to show straightforwardly that both anime and reality are simply fragments of the possible" (Ueno 1998: 183–84)—fragments of the possible, in other words, that must be assembled and put into action to be significant.

In these and other ways, we can view the history of animation as a variety of engagements that link the imagination with the real—or, at least, the social constructedness of what we call "the real," an ambiguous notion that runs the spectrum from physical solidity to meaningful experience. LaMarre points to the link between animation and the "real world" (as portrayed in live-action cinema), while Ueno draws attention to the historical backdrop of (real) war in Japan as a reality that adds an impact to robot anime. Indeed, Ueno makes the intriguing point that anime of the 1970s and 1980s was one of the few places in Japanese public culture to debate war and its consequences, a complex mix of trauma and capitalism. To these questions of photorealism and historical realism I would add another dimension of realism beyond the screen—namely, sustainable creative networks. In some ways, what ultimately constituted the real in anime were those examples that could garner a grownup audience and turn a profit.

Giant Robots and the Rise of Merchandising

Although some mecha anime is well known in the United States, even hard-core anime fans might be surprised to learn about the sheer volume of such anime that Japan has produced. A poster produced for an exhibit at the Tokyo Anime Fair, for example, provides a listing of more than 120 anime series since the 1970s, many lasting a year or more, that revolve around giant robots. Unlike the robots in *Astro Boy*, the giant robot (*kyōdai robotto*) genre tends toward robots piloted by people, often teenagers, who battle against various enemies. Some note that the "robots" more accurately are "metal suits," because they are not automated but, rather, are piloted from the inside. Many classic and influential anime series fall into this category, including *Macross, Patlabor, Gundam*, and *Neon Genesis Evangelion*, and more recently, *Eureka 7* and *Gurren Lagann*.

The authors of the published history of Toei Animation relate the emergence of giant robot anime to the boom in "transforming heroes" of a wide variety of television series (Toei Animation 2006: 49), the best known in the United States being *Power Rangers*. Prefiguring the idea of collaborative heroes of Mamoru Hosoda's film *Summer Wars*, the cultural anthropologist Anne Allison notes that a new genre of live-action superheroes began in 1973 with *Himitsu Sentai Gorenger* (Secret team force of five rangers). "Instead of a single hero, there was now a team," she writes; moreover, they constituted an "embodiment of post-Fordism and a postmodern aesthetics," because these TV heroes are "flexible transformers who move back and forth between a mix of modalities" (2006: 96–97). Like these shows, giant robots took up the themes and the settings of futuristic worlds consumed by battles, often with bizarre space monsters, and in need of heroic figures. One of the epoch-making robot shows was Toei Animation's hit *Mazinger Z* of 1972. Not only did the series draw viewership ratings of about 30 percent, according to Toei, but perhaps even more important, metal-alloy toys in the shape of Mazinger Z became big sellers. This helped launch a new interest in animated TV series about giant robots on the part of toy companies eager to capitalize on children's fascination with robot action figures.

Mazinger Z, based on a manga by Gō Nagai, became an anime TV series that operated in effect as a thirty-minute commercial for a slightly more upscale than average "super-alloy" (*chōgōkin*) toy (see figure 18). The success of *Mazinger Z* arose not only from the viewership ratings but also from the interest in the toys sold. As with the *Astro Boy* stickers included with Meiji chocolate and the later Pokémon phenomenon, which included trading cards and a logic of trading within the original videogame, there are ways in which commodity exchange shades into more sociable realms. Allison shows that the reality of toys and other forms of licensed

18. *Mazinger Z* "super-alloy" (*chōgōkin*) metal toy introduced in 1972.

merchandise arises not only from their materiality but also, and perhaps more importantly, from their grounding in social relationships: "In *Pokémon* one sees the principles of both gift exchange and commodity economy at work. Pocket Monsters, the currency of play here, are simultaneously traded and accumulated; they build capital for the player but also relationships with others" (2006: 217). Satoshi Tajiri designed the original *Pokémon* videogame. Inspired by his childhood hobby of collecting insects, he aimed to develop a game that integrated social exchange. The videogame requires a player to capture Pokémon (a Japanese abbreviation of Pocket Monsters) by exploring a variety of worlds. Part of the innovation of the game, which originally was designed for the handheld Nintendo Game Boy, is that it requires two people to connect their devices and to trade in order to acquire all of the Pokémon. The virtual is brought into the "real" world through the strengthening of relationships.

Real Robots and the Birth of the "Anime Fan"

If we think of the real in terms of toys and relationships, we can see that *Mazinger Z* in the early 1970s helped not only bring characters out of the pages of manga and the screens of anime into the hands of children; it also strengthened the relationships between anime producers and toy companies. As the children who watched *Astro Boy* grew up, a new generation of anime creators emerged. In the 1970s, Yoshiyuki Tomino was making a name for himself as an anime creator whose TV shows sold robot toys effectively. One of Tomino's early projects as a director, *Umi no Toriton* (Triton of the sea), was based on a manga by Osamu Tezuka. According to the critic Gō Sasakibara, when Tezuka released the collected volume of his serialized manga, he added a note disavowing his connection to the anime version (Ōtsuka and Sasakibara 2001: 192). Sasakibara interprets Tezuka's distancing himself from the anime as a reflection of his distaste for the ways Tomino altered Tezuka's original manga in order to attract a new kind of viewer. In 1972, Sasakibara points out, there was still no widespread concept of an "anime fan." In fact, the word for "anime" at the time was still "TV manga" (*terebi manga*) with the assumption that it was for children.[1] He also notes, however, that by the early 1970s, the kids who had grown up watching *Astro Boy* were reaching adolescence and growing tired of immature fare. "It was *Umi no Toriton* that found a technique to grab (*tsubo ni hamaru*) adolescent viewers" (Ōtsuka and Sasakibara 2001: 195). The hero of the series is a boy, the last of the Triton tribe, who must battle the Poseidon tribe. He is forced to become a man even though he is only on the verge of adulthood. Sasakibara sees this character's premise (*kyara settei*) as identical to the experience of the adolescent viewers, who feel deeply their own liminality, betwixt and between childhood and adulthood. This is another example of the logic of resonance, using ideas of audience identification with certain kinds of characters and worlds. More intriguing to me, however, is how this success created opportunities for Tomino to work in new directions. For, despite Tezuka's disavowals, Tomino's star began to rise.

A couple of years later, the hit TV series *Uchu Senkan Yamato* (Space battleship Yamato) (1974) contributed to a shift in understanding the anime audience, solidifying the idea that many anime viewers were becoming adults. The mainstream media caught on, as well, when huge lines formed outside cinemas for the release in 1977 of the theatrical version of

Yamato. The huge, global success of *Star Wars* (dir. George Lucas, 1977) further extended the interest in space battles. Meanwhile, Tomino also directed *Muteki Chōjin Zambot 3* (Invincible Superman Zambot 3), a giant robot anime that solidified his reputation as a director whose anime sold toys. Television stations increasingly made room for giant robot shows, and Tomino became a sought-after creator.

Toy manufacturers often designed the robots themselves, but they relied on anime companies to bring them to life in a way that would make children want to buy them. Interestingly, Sasakibara observes that although toy manufacturers generated rules about the kinds of robots they wanted to see in the TV shows, once the creators fulfilled those requirements, they were actually rather free to make the kinds of shows they wanted. "Like so-called 'pink films' [soft porn], if the artist cleared these 'peripheral' requests, then he could use the work as a stage for pursuing his own artistic vision" (Ōtsuka and Sasakibara 2001: 202). Such "peripheral requests" may explain why, in these anime programs, the appearance of a new robot is usually followed with a repetition of the name and a description of the new features. Again, we see that marketing requirements can in some ways offer greater creative freedom. Similarly, the director Shinichirō Watanabe (*Samurai Champloo*, *Cowboy Bebop*) has said that he began working in anime because he was told that it would be easier, and quicker, for him to become a director there than in live-action films. Nevertheless, in the case of Tomino and the first *Gundam* TV series, this freedom to explore an artistic vision led to ruin, at least that is how it appeared at first.

Gundam: Failure, Then Success

Today, *Gundam*, produced by Sunrise, is a leading brand in anime and a core business for Bandai. The franchise continues to develop. In 2006, I visited a new studio space that Sunrise had converted from a 7-Eleven convenience store, where the animators were working on *Gundam 00*. What makes that so remarkable is that the first season of *Gundam* in 1979 was deemed a failure, and the program was canceled. The turnabout hinged in part on the difficulties of making an anime that was more "real."

Masao Ueda, a producer I met through fieldwork on the *Zenmai Zamurai* TV series (see chapter 2), worked as a producer on the original *Mobile Suit Gundam* (*Kidō Senshi Gandamu*). He described the aims of the original creators who worked with Tomino: "We struggled to make a show that rid itself of the kinds of lies (*usoppoi*) that characterized hero programs up to that point. In *Gundam*, the robots do not have superpowers. They are just weapons of battle. In addition, most heroes that came before were unrealistically courageous, but in *Gundam* they had doubts, and they were scared. This seemed to us to have much more reality (*riariteii*)."[2] In the original *Gundam*, which started airing in 1979, this seriousness was conveyed through a setting in which overpopulation led humans to build space colonies. The gruesome destruction of war appears in the opening segment, as Zeon battle cruisers blast holes in other space colonies. We watch one of these enormous space-station colonies crash into a city on Earth and create a gigantic explosion. In the first episode, one of the lead female characters, Fraw Bow, watches helplessly as her mother is killed by a blast. The series unfolds by following the Earth Federation spaceship *White Base* as it tries to escape from rebel Zeon pursuers. The *White Base* has one Gundam, a prototype of a new, very powerful "mobile suit," or giant rideable robot, for which the teenage boy Amuro Rei turns out to be the ideal pilot. The *White Base* is chased by Amuro's rival, Char Aznable, who pilots a Zaku robot. A complex cat-and-mouse game plays out over the course of the series, with side stories and complex conspiracies developing alongside love affairs and family trauma. According to Ueda, the creators became increasingly engrossed in (*hamatta*) the world of Gundam, and their excitement and commitment to the project grew deeper and more intense. "We wanted to make a world that seemed like it could actually exist," he said.

Much to the disappointment of Clover, the sponsoring toy company, however, the Gundam toys did not sell. Ueda acknowledged that it was a difficult time for the creators (*yappari, taihen deshita*): "Clover complained in many ways. The show was too complex, too confusing. It was too dark. Children couldn't follow what was going on. Clover wanted all kinds of changes. But with animation, you have to plan episodes six months in advance to get them on air. It's not the kind of thing you can easily change in reaction to what audiences respond to."[3] What did Clover want? "It's a little harsh to put it this way, but they just wanted toys to sell. They didn't really care how we did it," said Ueda. Moreover, past examples seemed to clarify *Gundam*'s failure. In contrast to shows like *Astro Boy*, which generally reached a resolution at the end of each half-hour, *Gundam* wove complex story arcs, with storylines extending across many episodes. If you missed an episode, it would be difficult to catch up the following week.

This was before VCRs and video rental stores, not to mention TiVo and digital video recorders. When the toys didn't sell, Clover canceled the program early—after ten months instead of the one year that was originally planned.

But then something remarkable happened: Bandai, then a small toy company, approached Clover and asked to buy the rights to make plastic models of Gundam robots. Clover was not in the business of making plastic models, so it was happy to sell those particular rights. A representative at Bandai recognized that with *Yamato* and *Star Wars*, teenagers were eager to build such models, and he thought that Gundam plastic models would be similarly successful. Sure enough, sales of Gundam plastic models, which came to be known as GunPla, boomed. It is tempting to see this as a prophetic moment: Clover eventually went bankrupt, and Bandai is now Japan's largest toy company. New variations on the *Gundam* series are still being created.

Other synergies helped *Gundam*, especially as the broader media context around anime shifted (Ōtsuka and Sasakibara 2001). As fans matured, they founded new forms of fandom. Specialty anime magazines aimed at teenagers and older readers, such as *Animage*, had been launched with the *Yamato* boom. Anime fan clubs emerged around *Gundam* in high schools and colleges. Many of these fans were energized by the military and sci-fi elements of *Gundam*; in turn, "research" (*kenkyū*) into the show became an important fan activity. For example, one of the show's conceits was that "Minovsky particles" could be used as a kind of defense shield. Fans took this idea and developed detailed theories of "Minovsky physics" (*Minofusukii butsurigaku*), producing study guides and other fan-made materials. Significantly, the creators never objected to fans' interpretations of the Gundam world. According to Ueda, "When asked about these fan works, we always said, 'It's possible that's the way it is.'" This openness helped energize fans in the 1980s and beyond, an early example of how media could be a platform for participation as much as an object of consumption. In this regard, too, we see the precursors of today's social media and a kind of prehistory of media's shift from content to platform.

Collaborative creativity in *Gundam* draws attention to the synergies among anime, the toy companies, and fans. Clearly, we need to look beyond the content of the show and the marketing strategies to understand the feedback loops that led to the emergence of a popular movement, even after the series was deemed a failure. The eventual success of the *Gundam* series illustrates the power of fans as active participants in the production of the world around the series. But we also see that explaining the phenomenon in terms of "spreadable" or "drillable" media (Jenkins 2009b) risks pulling us into a critical reading inside the world of *Gundam* when we also need to be sensitive to changes in the "outside world," including the development of anime specialty magazines and high school and college fan circles. The emergence of anime's success comes from this wider dynamic.

Gundam also helped to solidify the idea that "real" anime was that which appealed to adults. This was a key moment in the history of television animation in Japan, highlighting a wider shift from an emphasis on children's shows toward the inclusion of more adult-oriented themes. The term "real" in "real robots" primarily indicated an emotional seriousness, but more broadly it indicated a dividing line in terms of the age of the audience, the kinds of toys produced, and in the style of the anime, particularly in terms of more brutal representations of war and fighting. "Super robot" anime tended to refer to shows aimed at elementary-school-age audiences; small robot toys were sold in association with those shows, and each episode was resolved at the end through the help of a bright, cheerful hero who avoided devastating destruction. In contrast, "real robot" anime aimed at adolescents and adults, featuring story arcs that continued over many episodes in which the heroes were often troubled figures and whose battles left ruin in their wake.

The ongoing *Gundam* franchise is also intriguing because what links the various series is not so much the characters themselves. Indeed, the starring roles shift, the eras change, and the settings are various as well. Rather, what links the series are the premises of powerful suits, warring parties, and space settings. The creators built up the "reality" of *Gundam* across the many episodes. I would add, however, that the reality of war that the *Gundam* creators espoused nevertheless portrayed some aspects of reality while ignoring others. For example, the drama of the TV series relied on what might be called an action-movie scale. The battles hinged on a limited number of heroes and rivals that hardly characterizes actual wars. It may be too much of a stretch in logic, but I wonder if this misrepresentation of war, which is common to so many action movies, helps explain some part of the unfortunate expectations of the American invasion and occupation of Iraq, which began in March 2003. In the early days of the insurgency, I was struck by how much hope the American military (or, perhaps, media coverage of the military) placed on capturing or killing leading figures. The attitude seemed to be, "If only we can catch Saddam Hussein, then things will get better"; the same went for the insurgent leader Abu Musab al-Zarqawi. Of course, Saddam was eventually captured and killed, but the insurgency did not end. Nor did killing insurgent leaders end the bloodshed. Why did so many people seem to think that it might? One reason might be our education in action films. When the hero of the *Die Hard* series finally kills the evil rival, the movie is over. Not so with actual wars.

Gundam also distorts with the idea that the better technology determines the victors. The examples from real wars can in some cases be used to support this idea, but one can point to many contrary cases, as well. Robot anime often reproduces the fallacy that powerful technology itself is decisive in battle. In fact, the technologies that may have been decisive in mecha anime's battle for ratings are the toys. Although "real" in *Gundam* indicates a connection between the content of the series and its fans, the series' revival depended on a specific type of toy. When Bandai recognized the untapped value of plastic models for teens, it was a fateful day for both Sunrise and the toy company. Indeed, this value emerged from a kind of hidden social energy. Fans experience a sense of accomplishment after completing a complex plastic model, and this also offers a means to interact with the Gundam world in a material way. This demonstrates an important aspect of the idea of social in media, namely that social relations need not directly include other people. In this regard, the idea of "social media" is flawed if it considers primarily online, digital spaces rather than the interstices between virtual and lived experiences. These connections can form various kinds of structures of creative action.

The Origins of Gainax

The anime studio Gainax, which is most famous for the TV series *Neon Genesis Evangelion* (dir. Hideaki Anno, 1995) and the films that followed, illustrates how fan communities sometimes developed into professional businesses. Yasuhiro Takeda, one of the founders of Gainax, tells the story of how the studio can be said to have originated from fans' activities related to science fiction (Takeda 2005). He relates other ways in which anime emerged not primarily because of economic forces but, rather, via the energy and commitment of people who wanted to impress their peers.

I am reminded of Winsor McCay's parlor bet with his cigar-smoking friends. Yet in the case of Gainax, the projects were transmedia from the start.

Takeda was born in Osaka in 1957. By the end of elementary school, he had become fascinated by science-fiction novels. When he was in junior high, he watched a live broadcast of the Apollo landing on the moon. "I was blown away," he writes. "All I could think was, *Right now, right this second, humans are standing on the moon!*" (Takeda 2005: 20). He stood in line for hours at the Osaka Expo in 1970 to touch a moon rock. In 1976, he entered Kinki University in the Engineering Department, but his discovery of the Sci Fi Club in his sophomore year introduced him to an alternative realm of learning, one that would lead him away from his official studies:

> I thought that I was extremely well read, but after joining, I was surprised to discover that the upperclassmen in the club had read a lot more than me.... Once I began talking to them, I discovered the incredible amount of information they actually knew. During the course of a single conversation they'd jump from one topic to another, go back to where they'd started, then take off in another direction altogether. It was nothing more than idle chit-chat, but it was incredibly entertaining, and I couldn't get enough of it. (Takeda 2005: 25)

This combination of admiration for others and a sense of a lack of confidence in oneself adds a level of complexity to the idea of participatory culture; status always seems a step away, even when we are allowed to participate.

Takeda spent "countless hours" at coffee shops because the Sci Fi Club was not officially recognized by the university. He was also very taken by the excitement of sci-fi conventions. At one of these conventions, a friend introduced Takeda to "someone just like you," namely, Toshio Okada who would later become a co-founder of Gainax. Takeda recounts his first impression of Okada: "*Here's a geek if I've ever seen one.* With his girly long hair and his freakishly excited way of speaking, all I could think was, *This guy is exactly like me?* I guess he was like me, in a way. But still, it wasn't exactly thrilling to be compared to a guy like that" (Takeda 2005: 31). As I know from my experience in the academic world, geek knowledge tends to impress only other geeks, and even there, first dates can be rocky. Things improved for Okada and Takeda when they met at another convention and found themselves bored. They skipped the official events, Takeda recalls, and started an energetic conversation near a bank of vending machines: "We started going off about things like, 'What if *Uchu Senkan Yamato* (Space battleship Yamato) had been made in China?' We were just making things up as we went along. . . . As we continued to entertain ourselves, a small crowd started to gather. . . . It was the first time I realized how enjoyable it was to perform for an audience" (Takeda 2005: 34). The crowd continued to grow. and the conversation continued from 10 PM till dawn. This caught the attention of some of the convention's organizers, who invited the two young men to perform on stage before the closing ceremonies. Although they were exhausted, Okada insisted that they take advantage of the opportunity, and in the end, it affected Takeda immensely: "Again, our audience ate it up. 'Sci fi standup,' they called it. . . . We were dubbed the 'Kansai Entertainers,' and we would be alighting a number of different stages over the next several years. . . . I couldn't help feeling that my future would be all about sci fi. Or maybe it was just that I learned how great it felt to be accepted by an audience" (Takeda 2005: 35). Before long, Takeda, Okada, and the other key members of what was to become Gainax decided to try their hand at organizing their own conventions. This turned out to be a fateful move.

The Blurry Line between Fan and Professional

In the process of helping to organize a sci-fi convention for the first time, Takeda met more people who would affect his life and the development of Gainax. At first, he and others worked to organize an event called the Japan Sci Fi Show, and this whetted their appetites for something bigger. They set their sights on the Japan Sci Fi Convention, which, when held in Osaka, was known as Daicon (the *dai* is a reference to the first character in Osaka, and *con* is the abbreviation for "convention"). The result was Daicon III.

Daicon III was held in 1981 in Osaka, and preparations for the event moved the group closer to becoming a film studio. The organizers wanted an impressive opening film. They met Hideaki Anno and Hiroyuki Yamaga, two students from Osaka University of the Arts, who were able to make animation. When Anno reportedly drew a powered robot suit and made it run using a few pages of paper at the coffee shop, it was decided that they would make their own animation. They couldn't afford the regular animation cels, so they bought a roll of vinyl and cut it into pieces. "This was homemade anime, after all," writes Takeda (2005: 51). In the end, the organizers lost money on the convention, so they decided to sell videos and reels of the 8-mm film. This ultimately made a profit, and the money was put back into preparations for Daicon IV and the Daicon film series.

Despite its limitations, the animated film that opened Daicon III impressed viewers at the convention and was even reported on in the magazine *Animec*. According to Takeda, unlike major anime magazines that were leaning toward "reviews" that read like advertisements, *Animec* was popular among hard-core fans for its in-depth analyses and large proportion of work contributed by readers (Takeda 2005: 105). Again, we see the importance of specialized media for the "emergent" aspects of anime's development and the role of feedback loops in amplification. The dynamics of "user-generated media" were evident in activities that preceded the Internet.

An innovation of Daicon III was the addition of a room for dealers to sell merchandise, a feature brought to Japan after some of the conference's organizers attended the Worldcon science-fiction convention in Boston (Takeda 2005: 56–57). After the Daicon III executive committee made all kinds of items to sell as official goods, and quickly sold out, Okada spearheaded the development of a store that he called General Products. It specialized in making polyresin models of characters and robots (later known as garage kits), a part of Gainax's history described in an original video animation (OVA) titled *Otaku no Video*. It is worth noting that General Products was able to develop its business despite serious skepticism on the part of major toy companies that garage kits could become an industry. General Products also began organizing a convention for people who designed their own toys, which became known as Wonder Fest. The excitement around that convention is renewed annually partly because the convention places the power of creativity in the hands of fans and acknowledges the legitimacy of their desire to create.[4]

With the success of Daicon III, the organizers set a goal to make Daicon IV in 1983 Japan's largest and most successful convention. As part of the planning, Takeda established Daicon Films to create a production process where he and the staff "grow and learn to work as a team," he explained (Takeda 2005: 69). This was a further step from fan and homemade to professional and industrial, but where exactly should we place the boundary? It seems that collaborative creativity rather than "producer versus consumer" makes the most sense for analysis. Meanwhile, the success of Daicon III's opening animation drew the attention of Studio Nue, which hired Anno and Yamaga to help produce the *Macross* series. At the same time, the General Products store, which Okada had incorporated as a subsidiary of his parents' embroidery business, was open for business and operated both as a hangout and a place to find potential recruits for projects. In 1982, the core group that would form Gainax was largely assembled. The first Daicon Films productions—*Aikoku Sentai Dai-Nippon*, *Kaettekita Urutoraman*, and *Kaiketsu Nōtenki*—were live-action parodies of special effects (*tokusatsu*) hero dramas along the "five rangers" line.

Daicon Film's opening animation for Daicon IV in 1983 was longer and more elaborate than the opening anime for Daicon III in 1981. It lasted almost six minutes and used a song by the British rock band Electric Light Orchestra as background music. Professional animators were impressed by the quality of the techniques used to create the animated film, which included guided missiles, explosions, and careful touches in the mecha and the illustrations of the spaceship. In the end, Daicon IV met the organizers' goal of four thousand attendees, becoming the largest science-fiction convention of its time in Japan.

A Desire to Make Original Characters Leads to *Evangelion*

In the years following the Daicon IV convention, General Products continued to make money by selling garage kits and organizing the Wonder Fest, but some in the group set their sights on full-fledged animation production. Okada, Yamaga, and Hiroaki Inoue secured funding from Bandai to produce *The Wings of Honneamise*, which was released in theaters in 1987. Takeda argues that the film was a success in the sense that "not a single theater canceled its run, and at some locations, it actually had a longer run than initially planned" (Takeda 2005: 97). Although he acknowledges that the film did not make money, it did provide name recognition and a track record on which Gainax could build. One of the next projects was *Toppu o Nerae* (lit., "aim for the top" but titled *Gunbusters* in English), a three-part OVA in which each part featured two episodes. The new technology of videocassette recording proved a boon for intense-fan anime because the productions did not need to have the wide appeal demanded of TV broadcasts; thus, VHS tapes created a new outlet for selling niche-oriented productions.

Okada, Yamaga, and Inoue also produced *Fushigi no Umi no Nadia* (Nadia of the mysterious sea). Although it did not make money (and

Gainax did not retain any of the rights), it was broadcast for a year on Japan's public television station, NHK, once again increasing the anime studio's visibility. Gainax achieved more solid financial success by producing computer games such as *Dragon Quest* and *Princess Maker*, the latter based on an unusual premise in which the player nurtures a young princess. According to Takeda, *Princess Maker* spawned a new genre of "nurturing games," an element of the *moe* phenomenon discussed in chapter 7.

Gainax's history with anime is a story of continual commercial failure, yet the company built enough of a reputation that it was asked to help on a variety of projects. Although Gainax's games and garage kits were doing OK financially, the group members decided in 1992 to close General Products in the hope that they could develop characters of their own rather than always license characters from other companies. Yet Takeda also notes, "We learned we were unable to take on projects for which the sole aim was profit. There had to be more to it than that" (2005: 135). More important than economic motivations were the friendships and the sense of peer competition that motivate many kinds of creative activities.

The director Hideaki Anno secured funding for the *Evangelion* project from the major record label King Records. When the TV program began airing in 1995, it became such a hit that it was deemed a "social phenomenon" (*shakai genshō*). The following summer, *Evangelion* made news when hard-core fans lined up overnight to see the feature-film version. Takeda reports that record numbers of *Evangelion* laser discs were sold in Japan, and the DVD continues to sell well today. Gainax finally had its own hit anime, with its own characters to use for games and licensed merchandise. A decade later, in 2006, Anno directed a rerelease for the theaters, and there has been talk that a live-action version is in the works.

The toys associated with *Evangelion* also continue to evolve. For example, Bandai released a figurine of several of the characters that comes on a stand that has recordings of the *real* actresses who perform the voices in the series. The ad copy on the box reads (in English) that the figures each come with ten "signature lines with the VOICES of real voice actresses providing high realistic sensation. These dramatic scenes and striking phrases of your favorite story are coming back vividly." We might wonder here, too: In what sense is this "real"? The recordings are by the actual voice actresses, but those actresses are channeling something else—a character that exists but was born from a collaborative multitude. So while this may be a dubious assertion of reality, the ad copy brings home something

19. The Asuka figure says classic lines, such as "Are you stupid?" and "Shinji, wanna kiss?"

else: It acknowledges that the goal is to evoke nostalgia for "your favorite story" by giving you the chance to experience something of the character, on demand. Truth be told, however, I only saw this feature of the figurine used to make jokes or to try to guess which classic phrase was associated with each button (see figure 19).

The Gainax story shows how a group of devoted fans managed to turn their fan activities—notably, science-fiction conventions and the contacts and networks they developed through them—into a business enterprise that, although it did not make much money, managed to sustain itself through the force of the personalities of those involved. In contrast to LaMarre's focus on anime's relationship with technology and Ueno's emphasis on the relationship between imagined futures of anime and real history, I would draw attention to the ways that the group that created Gainax brought anime and science fiction into the real world through fan activities that eventually morphed into businesses based on sustained social relations. This is neither the "thingification of media" nor the reality of representation, but the reality of production in a social realm. It also illustrates that the boundary between fan and producer is fluid and that many of the same motivations operate in both worlds. The success of *Evangelion* demonstrates that niche fandoms can find an outlet (e.g., with home videocassette players) and promoters (e.g., in the expansion of anime-related specialty magazines). The crucible of creativity for anime in Japan thus developed outward, generating new spaces for production, discussion, and distribution.

Conclusion

The interactions among businesses, sponsors, fan cultures, and genre conventions reveal the limitations of more common explanations for anime's success, such as underlying Japanese cultural foundations, the vision of individual auteurs, or economic determinism. The networked connections among these forces, and some serendipity, seem to provide the best explanation for anime's success. Yet *Gundam* and *Evangelion* also showed something else: that original animation not based on famous comic book characters could succeed. At the same time, however, they illustrate that the success of these shows depended on fan cultures outside the limited world of anime itself. By examining anime in terms of the keyword "real," we can see that much of the impact of anime, and many features of its production, depend on the world outside of what is depicted on the screen. When Bandai gathered its Boys Toys' division in Toy Town, the brainstorming took for granted that these understandings of nostalgia, the real in anime, and the social dynamics of today's world were the premises on which they had to build. The examples in this chapter reveal a widening sensibility of media as something that is open, accessible, and participatory —or, at least, they reveal that those dynamics working in tandem can lead to success. In sum, anime's development in the 1980s and 1990s pointed to more vibrant niche worlds becoming advanced enough to allow groups of creators to branch out into new areas. In some ways, this remains a model for anime studios today, as I examine in the next chapter.

FIVE

Making a Cutting-Edge Anime Studio

THE VALUE OF THE GUTTER

> We have a particular starting point. We begin with
> the creators, and we only develop projects that they
> really want to make themselves.
> —EIKO TANAKA, chief executive, Studio 4°C

⁕ What makes an anime studio cutting edge? There are
as many answers to that question as there are anime
studios. Every leading studio sees itself as constantly
breaking new ground, creating innovative works, and nurturing
new audiences by pushing forward some kind of leading edge. In
the previous two chapters, I examined some aspects of the emergence of anime in Japan and a particular nexus around manga,
toys, magazines, and audiences. Now I turn to the 2000s to see
what can be learned about anime from a look at some of the ways
producers and directors explain their ideas for generating progress. How do they design their structures of creative action? What
values guide decision making and what ultimately gets produced?

While the question of what constitutes "success" tends to look
backward at previous accomplishments—highlighting the good,
glossing over the bad—the question of the cutting edge points
forward, imagining directions toward as-yet-unrealized possibilities. By considering differences between studios in their focus and
commitment, we gain a perspective more broadly on the contexts

in which anime creativity unfolds and on the ideas that help guide new approaches. How do producers articulate a vision of what it means for a studio to be creative, forward looking, and cutting edge? We find that specific approaches to openness are central in guiding the intersections between top-down design and bottom-up elaborations.

In this chapter, I begin with fieldwork on the making of *Red Garden*, a TV series produced by Gonzo and aimed at a late-night, grownup audience. I had access to the show thanks to Shin Ishikawa, the chief executive at Gonzo, who suggested *Red Garden* because it was at a stage of production at which, he said, "You can see everything." I spent July and August 2006 attending production meetings, and the first episode debuted in October of that year. The opening episodes were in the final stages of production, while the later episodes were still being developed, even at the level of plot and story. A look at this clutch of creators' activities grounds the more abstract discussions of other producers that follow, including those of Studio Ghibli and Studio 4°C. The studios I discuss are by no means comprehensive, but they offer a range of contrasting perspectives, from film to TV, and contrast with Aniplex and NHK's *Zenmai Zamurai* series for children (see chapter 2) and Hosoda's films for teens and young adults for Madhouse (see chapter 1). Given these examples, it is tempting to see the contexts of manga and licensed merchandise as forcing the styles of anime productions in particular directions, but anime studios are designed to take advantage of their levels of freedom of expression as well.

The cutting edge evokes a forward boundary, a shedding of the old in favor of the new. Still, innovation is meaningless if it leaves nothing behind. In the mercurial transmedia worlds that anime inhabits, producers must somehow wrestle with the questions of what that something substantial might be and how it might become something more than what appears on the screen. How can they design something that can live on? As a concept for thinking about this combination of "cutting edge" and "substance," I like the term "avantcore," from the Los Angeles rapper Busdriver. In his song "Avantcore," on the album *Fear of a Black Tangent* (Mush Records, 2005), Busdriver ridicules market-based notions of success in the rap business. He also needles those fans fascinated by gems of popular culture hidden in obscure places. The song is a reminder of the space between the creators and the work, between the work and the audience, and between the audience and the market. What I found interesting about the perspectives of anime producers is how they viewed making a space for creativity as a central part of their efforts. In fact, a useful way to imagine a crucible of creativity is to see it as an open space that people can fill with their energy, commitment, and skill. It's like the open space between the frames of a comic strip, known as the "gutter," where the reader must fill in the missing steps. Yet in addition to making a space, anime studios must finish the tasks at hand, generally with an air of uncertainty and anxiety about how it will all work out. Yet when anime studios succeed, they create an avantcore—a cutting edge with substance—that creates possibilities for others to revolve around, build on, and extend.

Red Garden Studio Ethnography

When I first met the director Kou Matsuo in the summer of 2006, he was busy preparing a new TV series called *Red Garden*. The twenty-two-episode series (plus a short original video animation [OVA]) was created as an original Gonzo production, with the character designs and story produced in-house rather than being taken from an already successful manga or other work. Although risky for Gonzo and its parent company, GDH, the potential returns were much higher if the show became a hit. In the case of *Red Garden*, Gonzo was striving to create the "original work" (*gensaku*) itself rather than making "a work based on an original" (*gensakumono*). Gonzo has since fallen on harder times, shedding staff and reducing its number of projects, highlighting again the difficulties of working in animation.

Red Garden is set in contemporary New York City at a fictional wealthy high school on Roosevelt Island. The story revolves around the struggles of five female students who share a dark secret and must fight mysterious enemies to survive. The setting is a reminder that part of Gonzo's business strategy is to make globally oriented anime, according to Ishikawa, an effort we discussed in the context of the *Afro Samurai* project (see chapter 2).[1] For *Red Garden*, Ishikawa sent the director and a producer to New York City to shoot thousands of location photographs. Gonzo enlisted the character designer Jun Fuji (a.k.a. Fujijun) to develop the five girls as independent entities, each stylish in a particular way. The scriptwriter Tomohiro Yamashita worked closely with the director to write the story. Matsuo's job as the director was to bring the whole operation together.

In a promotional video on the Gonzo website, Matsuo explains the concept of *Red Garden* in terms of the characters and the world of the series: "It's not really a story of beautiful girls who are cool fighters. It's a question of what happens when teenagers find themselves in a unique situation. How would they respond to finding themselves in trouble? Where would they turn, and what would they do? That was really the theme and the concept."[2] The struggles between the characters, in their collaborations and conflicts as they face a violent enemy, constitute the main action that drives the story forward. During one script meeting, a person new to the project asked where the story was leading. Matsuo said they were working toward a scene in which Roosevelt Island becomes entirely covered in red flowers—hence, the red garden of the title. Beyond that, Matsuo showed little interest in the ending and even acknowledged that he wasn't entirely sure how it was going to work out. Instead, the relationships between the characters grounded the dramatic tension of the series.

In the same video, Matsuo emphasized aspects of the world in which the girls moved. He said New York City is generally regarded by Japanese as an exciting but dangerous place. By choosing Roosevelt Island as the site for the girls' private school, the creators wanted to juxtapose the island as a place of safety and quiet against the threatening noise of the city just across the river. Yet the school had its own conspiracy and element of danger, and the girls were forced to cope with the gap (*gyappu*), Matsuo explained, between their expectations and their reality. This tension—the space between expectation and reality—enlivens the characters' struggles.

In the spring of 2005, Matsuo and a producer traveled to New York City and took the location photos, filling giant notebooks that were periodically brought out and consulted in meetings. In July and August 2006, I observed many layers of production for the show. The first episode was set to air in October, and the work was operating on all levels. For example, one day for Matsuo included a script meeting (for episodes 14–16), drawing storyboards (episode 12), checking the key frames (episode 3), and meeting with the animation director (episode 6). Script meetings were weekly (at least), along with numerous voice-recording sessions. I also attended a session for recording the orchestral music and meetings with freelance key-frame artists in Tokyo, whose work, once approved, was sent online to South Korea, where the in-between frames were drawn. One evening I observed the director editing episode 1, which was still missing a few cuts and did not yet have the sound added. He usually worked late into the evening, but that night was likely to be an all-nighter (I headed home at 3 AM, when the editing was completed).

Some meetings were stressful. In one, a half-dozen producers, all men and most of them appearing to be in their mid-twenties, were awaiting the arrival of their superior, one of the head producers at Gonzo. When I walked into the room, I wasn't entirely clear what the meeting was for, and when I asked, one of the young producers said, "It's *ijime*" (bullying). Others nodded in a dark-humored way. Since much of the key-frame work is hired out to animators in Tokyo, part of a producer's job is to cajole and harass the freelancers until the work is completed. The meeting centered on progress reports on the scenes for which the producers were responsible. Sure enough, when the head producer arrived, he demanded to know why work was proceeding so slowly on certain projects. He raised his voice, ridiculed some of them, and cut others off in mid-sentence. The young producers looked at their pages and pages of checklists, explaining who was doing what and when it was due. Still, the head producer browbeat them and complained that they weren't pulling their weight. Toward the end of the meeting, one of the younger producers stood up to say, "This will be the last day of [another young producer in the room] as he will go off to explore other challenges." The head producer failed to stifle a laugh at this. "We will have a going away party [at such-and-such date and place]." I didn't have to ask whether slow progress means producers actually get fired sometimes.

I don't think the harshness of this producers' meeting is unique, yet it was also different from the world of the animators. The people who work on the drawings, background paintings, colors, and computer graphics tend to be referred to as "creators" (*kurieetaa*). Their work and their workspaces are different. Producers sit in what I view as "normal salaryman" style—that is, in an open space with desks facing each other and no walls or cubicles between the desks. The creators sit back to back in two rows, usually in carrels with small cardboard walls between the desks, presumably to avoid distraction. I had a chance to spend a couple of days sitting in the cramped space where the main in-house team of creators worked, which offered a revealing perspective on anime making. Above all, I was struck by the social energy and the comfortable camaraderie among the key staff members, a contrast to the bullying of the producers.

The meetings for hammering out the script were sleek and corporate, conveying an air of professionalism without ostentation. When I did fieldwork at Gonzo, the offices were in a fancy corporate building overlooking a park in Shinjuku. (The studio has since moved to the less upscale neighborhood of Nerima.) Entering Gonzo on the fourth floor, one was greeted by a futuristic brushed-aluminum foyer (see figure 20) with posters advertising the studio's recent releases, such as *Samurai 7* and *Brave Story*, a summer blockbuster sci-fi/fantasy movie based on a novel by Miyuki Miyabe. The script meetings were held in a brightly lit, shiny white meeting room (see figure 21). Matsuo and the lead writer Tomohiro Yamashita hammered out plot and script ideas while two producers sat by and joined in the discussion periodically. Meetings with sponsors and media representatives were held in these kinds of spaces, too. Yet when the creators walked back to their individual desks, they entered a world of paper-based clutter that reminded me of a certain style of academic office. Indeed, when Matsuo led me to the back area where his team members spent their days, we had to wind our way past large shelves of blank paper for drawing (see figure 22).

There, in a back corner of the office building's floor, the six key staff members had desks. Matsuo worked on storyboards and checking key frames while three men next to him worked side by side in what seemed in studios to be a common division of labor: one painted backgrounds (tempura paint on paper), one created computer graphics on a souped-up PC, and one colored the frames by clicking on a computer screen in a dark, curtained-off space. Behind Matsuo sat two women: the animation director (*sakuga kantoku* or *sakkan*) and the character designer Fujijun. Because the character designer's work was largely finished, she showed up only to work on the so-called eye catch (*ai kyacchi*)—that is, illustrations shown briefly between the show proper and the commercials. I sat at her desk surrounded by the clippings from Japanese fashion magazines that helped inspire her designs.

These sections of anime studios are strikingly quiet. Except for the hum of air conditioners or fans and the tiny, distant sound of music on someone else's earbud headphones, all I hear is the scratch of pencils and the whoosh of paper being flipped (as animators check the movement of characters between pages), the click of a mouse, and the occasional buzz of a vibrating *keitai* (cellphone). The section of Gonzo for the creators of the *Red Garden* TV series had the feel of a library, where talk is permitted but should be done quietly and kept brief. There were no office phones on the desks, though most people had two cellphones: one for business and one personal. The creative staff members sat together in the same space, but they worked mostly alone, with their backs to each other in their carrels.

20. Entryway of Gonzo with the director Kou Matsuo (left) and the assistant producer Rie Shimasue in August 2006.

21. Script meeting for *Red Garden* at Gonzo in August 2006.

22. Stacks of paper as part of Gonzo's digital work, with Matsuo walking to the desk.

23. Gonzo studio folders for each cut, *Red Garden*, August 2006.

At the Cartoon Network studio in Burbank, California, directors, writers, and designers had their own wood-paneled, head-high cubicles. Several animators I spoke with in Burbank commented on the dreary working conditions in Japan, and one wonders how much this has to do with the successful efforts of American animators to unionize, a fascinating story told by Tom Sito (2006), an animator who was on the front lines, compared with the largely unsuccessful attempts in Japan, notably in the 1960s at Toei.

At Gonzo, six creators for *Red Garden* were the core group around which an international network of workers revolved. Each person faced checklists of deadlines for his or her section of the project. The background artist would take six hours to paint a landscape that would likely appear for about six seconds of the show. "And that's pretty long," he said. The animation director would spend day after day checking the work of the freelance key-frame artists, going through manila folder after manila folder, each labeled with the episode and cut number, and a series of checkboxes for the people who had to sign off on the work (see figure 23). The director focused on turning the scripts into storyboards and coordinating the other direction that was required to turn his storyboards into the final product. The work was complexly layered, unfolding in stages, with more than a year of preparation before the show began. The long working hours of a deeply committed workforce, laboring in an environment that mixes 1950s-era pencil, paper, and erasers with today's computer technology, are part of the story of anime's success.

Learning by Watching

The challenge of doing fieldwork in anime production was eased in part by the common practice of "learning while watching" (*kengaku*). As I attended more meetings over the course of the summer, I often found I wasn't the only stranger in the room. The producer Junichi Takagi was kind of enough to keep me informed about meeting times and locations. When he introduced me in new settings, he never said I was a cultural anthropologist doing fieldwork research on the making of anime. Rather, he said I was in the room for *kengaku*, and that usually was that. I had been invited, which implied that enough people higher up had agreed. At the same time, *kengaku* was common throughout the process. At some script meetings, an artist-management guy who worked with the voice actors would sit and take notes. Like me, if someone was new to the meeting, he or she would introduce himself or herself, identify the company he or she was from, and say that he or she was there to observe. Done.

One example of this stands out. At one of the *Red Garden* voice-recording sessions, a budding voice actress sat in the director's area. About ten of us were sitting silently on a room-length couch in the back while the sound director ordered people around with a confident warmth and Matsuo, the director, chimed in periodically. Unlike most Japanese animation series, where the voices are added after the drawings are completed, *Red Garden* was produced by recording the voices first. The reason given echoes what Peter Chung says about putting the actors first: This would emphasize the emotion of the young women who performed the five main characters and, Gonzo hoped, add a special extra something to help the series catch on. The actresses would work with a script booklet, reading their lines while watching a screen that showed stills from the storyboards. It was somewhat disconcerting to me, and some of the voice actors said the same thing, because no one had a complete picture of how the series was going to look and sound. The show was being built as they went along, and this uncertainty brought both anxiety and excitement.

Fieldwork reinforced that feeling that there is something about learning by watching that makes one want to participate. With thirty-nine people focused on the project at hand (twenty-nine voice actors and the ten of us in the control room), an interesting buzz arose that helps to explain the value of working and watching in a group. We see the people in charge; their authority is being respected, and that is attractive. We see the star voice actors, their status reinforced by a collective focus of attention. A certain social dynamic pulls you in, makes you feel the energy in the room, and—for some people, at least—helps amplify a desire to be part of the action. I felt it while listening to the directors. I saw it in the eyes of the young voice actress reading along with the script likely imagining herself in front of the microphone. Of course, she, like me, was sitting utterly silent. Yet the energized dynamic was there in the room.

Toward the end of my fieldwork, I had a chance to leap from "learning while watching" to learning by doing. While I was observing a voice-recording session, the voice acting director turned to Matsuo and asked what he should do about an extra required for the scene. Matsuo said, "Let's get Ian to do it." Before I knew it, I was in the recording booth, facing a microphone and a "puff screen" (to prevent pops from percussive pronunciation) with a script in my hand. The scene appears in episode 11, when two of the main characters are wandering lost in New York City. At one point, they knock on a door, and a sketchy man leans out the window and says, "Yes, what is it?" When he sees the young women, he says, a bit lecherously, "Why not come on upstairs?" It was simple enough, but I found myself shaking with nervousness, stumbling over my two short lines in Japanese. Although the director praised me for my ability to sound lascivious, we had to record the lines several times before getting a usable version. Then my moment at the center of attention was gone. It is easy to imagine how experiences such as this can motivate one to seek out more and more opportunities. The excitement, combined with a sense that one could do better if given another chance, brings to the fore the insights of ethnography, not only in capturing the detailed experience of the media-making processes, but in showing how social factors help motivate and direct the kinds of things that get produced. It's not that the social factors override the broader market and cultural logics, but that the communication between people might be seen as what conveys the realities of those logics.

Gonzo thought explicitly about overseas markets, especially the United

States but also more globally. The studio's *Afro Samurai* used American voice actors. *Red Garden* was set in New York City and eventually aired on U.S. television. When I spoke with Matsuo about growing overseas interest in anime, I was surprised by his response: "I can't really welcome the attention (*kangei dekinai*)." Despite Gonzo's enthusiasm for building overseas connections, Matsuo said he was partly worried that his works could be taken the wrong way. "We make these things for a Japanese audience," he said. The production process I observed focused on Japanese artists aiming for a Japanese audience. In the course of observing a half-dozen script meetings, it became clear that questions of whether the series was "Japanese" or "global" played a modest role in the design. Matsuo and Yamashita, the lead writer, worked around manipulating the tension between the different characters. They thought more about genre conventions (zombies, monster fighters, school conspiracies) and how to transform them than about "American audiences," a somewhat abstract and oversimplified idea to begin with. Matsuo's concerns made sense in light of his experience. He had worked as an assistant director (*enshutsu*) on *Millennium Actress* (dir. Satoshi Kon, 2001) and had directed the TV series *Rozen Maiden*. He has demonstrated that he knows his audience and how to get the job done. When I asked him whether there were surprises in the making of *Red Garden*, he said there really weren't. He'd seen everything (so far) before.

The creators traveled to New York City, but they were adapting reality in relation to a variety of genre conventions and in terms of their own interpretations. Initially, I thought I could be helpful in bringing elements of realism to the portrayal of America and, specifically, New York City. When questions arose, however, I often found I had no useful answer. For example, during one script meeting, Matsuo was discussing a rainy scene with the main writer when he turned to me and asked, "Why don't Americans use umbrellas?" When he had visited New York City the year before, he explained, he was struck by how few people used umbrellas, even though the weather was terrible. I fumbled for what turned out to be a non-answer, only realizing later that I could have posed the counterpoint question to him: Why are you Japanese so umbrella-centric? Having lived in Japan for about five years altogether, I am fully accustomed to the presence of umbrella lockers at Japanese hotels and theaters. I know what to do when faced with an umbrella condom (a long skinny bag to prevent drips on the floor) at department store entrances on rainy days. I have experienced the sinking feeling of returning to an umbrella bucket at the entrance to a restaurant and finding my umbrella gone. Yet I had never considered why I hadn't missed these things in the United States. In other words, the basic assumptions—that is, where the creators began in their development of images and ideas—were generally at a far deeper, less accessible level than I was expecting. Matsuo's question also reflected the very practical challenges that animators faced every day—namely, that filling up a blank page requires answering dozens of these kinds of questions. This gap between the day-to-day concerns of anime creators and the ways anime is spoken about by leading producers can be seen in a similar light. Ideally, it's a productive gap.

A View from the Head Office

The New York setting of *Red Garden* makes sense in light of one of the goals envisioned by Gonzo's chief executive officer, Shin Ishikawa: to make anime that can compete on the global scene. When I interviewed Ishikawa, he described a particular strategy for pushing his company into a leading role. Because Gonzo was a relative newcomer to the anime world, he acknowledged that the company would have difficulty if it tried to mimic the more seasoned styles of Studio Ghibli: "For us to compete, we had to find new technology and new areas, where everyone is starting from scratch. That way we could compete at the same level. We chose digital animation. When we started, in 1995, animation was still analog. That was the time of *Lion King* and Hayao Miyazaki. It was, if you will, cel animation's last shining moment before Pixar came in. So we saw the digital as a new opportunity."[3] Ishikawa hoped that digital technology would enable Gonzo to catapult over more established anime competitors. He acknowledged that the studio's first attempt, *Blue Submarine No. 6*, was not entirely an artistic success. "We were still learning the techniques," he said. But over time, Gonzo was able to work on both TV series and what he called high-quality "flagship OVA," which included *Samurai 7* (2005) and *Gankutsuoh* (2004). A surreal, futuristic adaptation of *The Count of Monte Cristo*, *Gankutsuoh* offers stunning visuals highlighting the digitally constructed layers of anime. As the characters move, their clothes are filled with background textures, as if the clothing is transparent, revealing a flat mosaic behind them.

For Ishikawa, the goal was not simply to catch the wave of a new production method for animation. His strategy was also intertwined with his predictions for what would happen with media in an Internet age. He noted, for example, that when he was an astrophysics major at the University of Tokyo in the late 1980s, the Internet was used to move large amounts of scientific data around. By the mid-1990s, he was working for the Boston Consulting Group, and one of his projects was to forecast what the next fifteen years would bring for telecommunications. He says he recognized that the Internet would move into the broadband era and that this would have profound consequences for global media: "Once broadband becomes widespread, that means that all content becomes more global. So any content that is suitable for a digital platform must be the world leader in order to compete. Only that content will survive, or will have a high value. In Japan, we have anime, karaoke, and videogames. In the U.S., you have several sports (except soccer), live-action feature films, TV series. So that's why I came into the animation business: to become a global leader."[4] In other words, being able to reach global audiences also means global competition. So Ishikawa's view of the cutting edge is conceived partly through Gonzo's works but also in relation to that of other studios and to larger shifts in the world of media. Moreover, with the Internet, the spheres of competition become increasingly global and less defined by the wishes of domestic broadcasters. Ishikawa also envisioned new possibilities for selling through micropayments (i.e., directly to consumers for small fees as opposed to distributors for large fees) and other alternative distribution channels. Nevertheless, in 2008, Gonzo faced difficult times and reportedly asked 20 percent of its staff to "voluntarily retire." After the restructuring, however, Gonzo is striking out in new directions again, working on a 3D computer graphics animation series (for standard televisions). Although the company is still looking for an enormous breakthrough success, it continues to make works and to push in new directions.

Studio Ghibli

Studio Ghibli offers a different kind of vision of the cutting edge, as explained by the producer Toshio Suzuki. He excels at making connections between the intricately detailed work of the star director Hayao Miyazaki and a much broader animation industry that has always struggled to press forward. If we were to identify Ghibli's "avantcore," we might point to an emphasis on feature films for mass audiences, a commitment to visual virtuosity, and a concern with setting that is perhaps more central than that with storytelling. Miyazaki is Ghibli's most prominent director, and he has become a national icon as his movies continue to make a mark globally. Susan Napier (2005: 152) underscores the uses of enchantment in his films, discussing "his richly realized fantasy worlds and his memorable female characters," including Nausicaa, Satsuki and Mei, Kiki, San of *Princess Mononoke*, and Sen/Chihiro, among others. Helen McCarthy surveys Miyazaki's works up to *Princess Mononoke* (1997) and says that he "stands at the pinnacle of Japanese artistic achievement" (1999: 48). Colin Odell and Michelle Le Blanc offer celebration, saying Studio Ghibli's films "can enrapture and delight everyone from toddlers to pensioners" (2009: 14). My approach is based less on reading the films as texts than on working from interviews with Suzuki in an effort to continue developing a critical theory of production that gauges the structuring aspects of studios and the creativity that emerges from viewing anime as a platform.

I visited Studio Ghibli on a rainy, cool afternoon in March 2005. It is about a half-hour's walk from the nearest train station in a largely residential neighborhood. We sat in a conference room with a U.S. Academy Award and a Golden Bear from the Berlin Film Festival, both for *Spirited Away*. Suzuki explained Miyazaki's current success in relation to his long career in the business. In the 1970s, when other studios were making science-fiction anime with robotic suits, the director Isao Takahata and Miyazaki became involved in a project with a very different kind of approach—namely, the TV series *Heidi: Girl of the Alps*, which began airing in 1974. The series is based on a Swiss novel by Johanna Spyri, and, as Suzuki tells it, Takahata resisted the idea of turning it into an anime program. How would it be possible to make a fifty-episode series based on this story? The solution, they discovered, was to make a series based not on the story but on showing the lifestyle and customs of a girl in that world. The series achieved 30 percent ratings, said Suzuki, because Japanese children across the country tuned in to see how children on the other side of the world lived. The TV series was "cultural anthropology as entertainment," Suzuki said.

Suzuki identified another key moment in anime innovation in the baseball-themed TV drama *Kyojin no Hoshi* (Star of the giants, which aired in 1968–71). He used the series as an example of how Japanese animation went to extremes in terms of deforming time and space. In the drama, he explained, one pitch could take up an entire thirty-minute episode, as the mind of the pitcher wandered during the ball's flight from hand to home plate. Suzuki also recalled with fondness how the portrayal of family members seated around a low table in their four-and-a-half-mat apartment (a very small, ten-by-ten-foot flat) in which, when they quarreled, both the room and the table expanded so the family members were all sitting far apart. Experiments like this showed what animation can do, not only with the squash and stretch of characters to portray their personalities, but also in deforming the shape of the worlds in which the characters move.

The animator Yasuo Ōtsuka was among those who helped train Hayao Miyazaki and Isao Takahata, and both remember him in the documentary about Ōtsuka's life (see chapter 3). But in his ability to oversee projects as a director, Miyazaki surpassed his mentor. We can observe some of Miyazaki's directorial sense for the layout of scenes from a comparison in Ōtsuka's *Sakuga Asemamire* (Drawing pictures soaked with sweat), which offers a comparison of different approaches to storyboards. In explaining the art of storyboards, Ōtsuka uses an example from the TV series *Lupin III*, on which both he and Miyazaki worked. He notes that the script read, "Lupin and Jigen watch as the thieves come ashore. Jigen starts to light a cigarette. Lupin stops him, and they notice a boat coming into the harbor" (Ōtsuka 2001: 149). Then Ōtsuka shows two examples of storyboards drawn for the same scene. The one on the left was drawn by an animator still in training; the one on the right, by Miyazaki (figure 24). Ōtsuka notes that the young animator portrayed Lupin and Jigen standing bolt upright and always head-on. In contrast, Miyazaki used dramatic shading, poses, and camera angles. He also approached the action differently: Rather than having Lupin yell to stop Jigen from smoking, he drew Lupin reaching in from off-screen, with a pan over to Lupin's face (Ōtsuka 2001: 149). There is more energy and vitality in the Ghibli master's early storyboards.

At the time of the interview, Studio Ghibli was deeply involved in promoting its new feature-film release *Howl's Moving Castle*, directed by Miyazaki. "For Miyazaki, the key was the premise (*settei*)," Suzuki said. Miyazaki liked two things: the moving castle and the idea of an eighty-year-old girl (*shōjo*). As for the story, "Really, anything would've been fine (*sutorii wa dō de mo ii*)," Suzuki said. He also argued that there was something distinctly Japanese about how Miyazaki had approached drawing the moving castle: "Miyazaki didn't start with the overall plan but

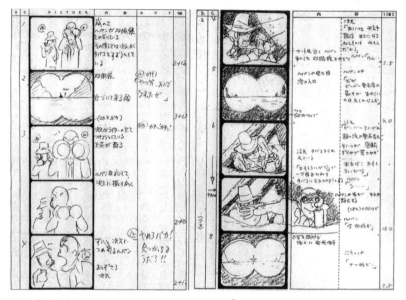

24. Which is better? Same script, two storyboards (Ōtsuka 2001: 149).

instead began with one feature." As he said this, Suzuki walked over to the movie poster in the room and pointed to a protruding section of the castle's face. "Then he worked his way out from there." Suzuki likened this to the construction of old Japanese homes that would be built up over time, room by room. Suzuki waxed on about Miyazaki's artistry, as well as his contradictions (e.g., "He's a pacifist but loves drawing weapons and gunships").

Suzuki clearly viewed himself as playing an important role in moving the Ghibli project forward. "Miya-san asks me, can't we just do without the merchandising?" Suzuki said, laughing. "Of course, we can't do that." At the same time, Suzuki bristled at the idea that what Studio Ghibli does should be seen as instructive for pushing the "content industry" forward. Asked by Masakazu Kubo, a producer of the mass-commercial Pokémon phenomenon, what he thought his studio would do to advance the world of content businesses, Suzuki replied, "I'm not really sure what to say about the content business. . . . I feel there are two sides to films. One is its quality as a work. Up until a certain time, films were 'works (*sakuhin*).' At some point, the element of 'merchandise (*shōhin*)' got added to films. When I hear 'content,' I feel you're talking about merchandise. From

Ghibli's standpoint, fundamentally we want to move forward by making works. Sometimes they become content—at least, that's Ghibli's stance" (quoted in Hatakeyama and Kubo 2005: 19). This brings home a central point: Even if great works become models for both artistic achievement and business potential, Suzuki (like most producers) emphasizes that a certain quality of work should be the overarching measure of value.

Suzuki also measured Miyazaki's greatness partly in terms of his unwillingness to give up the old ways. Although Studio Ghibli's films increasingly incorporate digital production methods, Miyazaki strives for a cel-type aesthetic. Can there be a cutting edge that pushes toward nostalgia? "Films have always progressed along with new technology, but I think there's something different about the shift to digital," Suzuki said. "Early on, talkies were the big innovation, then it was color, and now it is digital. It was Charlie Chaplin who resisted talkies to the end. One could say Akira Kurosawa resisted color to the end as well. When it comes to digital animation, I think Hayao Miyazaki will oppose it to the end. He'll keep drawing by hand" (quoted in Hatakeyama and Kubo 2005: 19–20). Thomas LaMarre describes this aspect of Miyazaki's films as a "critical minimization of animation technologies." Despite Suzuki's efforts to keep merchandising as part of the picture, Studio Ghibli does poorly in the emerging communication networks that operate across media. The result, LaMarre (2009: 315) says, is "an insistence on authority and the brand," which means that Studio Ghibli's association with a single creator is both a blessing and a curse. Miyazaki's signature styles continue to draw huge audiences in Japan. But as Suzuki noted, in a wistful moment, "Sometimes I think when Miyazaki dies, that will be the end of anime."[5] When I mentioned this idea to another creator, he quipped, "Anime won't die, but Ghibli might." LaMarre (2009: 315) says the studio's approach is simple: "Ghibli serializes *auteurs*." If the branding of Studio Ghibli can be transferred to new auteurs, there's good reason to think it will build on a prolific and remarkable past. Studio Ghibli created an avantcore that consists of high-quality family fare, with a touch of mystery and a deep artistic vision.

But what kind of success is Studio Ghibli? Again, it is perhaps more of a cultural success than an economic one. The manga critic Eiji Ōtsuka argues that it is a mistake for Japanese government officials to look at Miyazaki as a model for other animation studios to emulate, because his works are better viewed as a subcategory of national cinema than as exemplary of anime per se. Even Studio Ghibli's biggest overseas success, *Spirited Away*,

Table 1. The 2002 Academy Award Nominees for Best Animated Feature

	SPIRITED AWAY	ICE AGE	TREASURE PLANET	LILO AND STITCH	SPIRIT
Distributor	Disney	Fox	Disney	Disney	DreamWorks
No. of theaters	151	3,345	3,227	3,222	3,362
U.S. box office	6	176	38	146	73
Production cost	16.7 (¥2 billion)	59	140	80	80
Marketing costs (est.)	N / A	35	40	40	35

Note: All box-office revenue and costs are in millions of U.S. dollars, unless noted otherwise; $1 = ¥120.

Source: Ōtsuka (2005: 203), citing data from Box Office Mojo, March 22, 2003.

ended up a small player in the U.S. animated film market, grossing only $6 million at the box office and appearing on 151 screens. *Spirited Away* won an Academy Award for Best Animated Feature. The losers in that category were four U.S. films. Two of them, *Ice Age* and *Lilo and Stitch*, were box-office successes, and two, *Treasure Planet* and *Spirit*, were failures. Eiji Ōtsuka points out that even the "failures" reached twenty times the number of theaters, and the worst box-office performance of the failure was still six times greater than the success of *Spirited Away*. He views this as an indictment of government policies premised on the idea that anime is hugely successful overseas. What we can also see is that the scale of success can vary widely, and Studio Ghibli's value may not be measured best in terms of U.S. box-office returns. Instead, the avantcore offered by Studio Ghibli arises from making hugely popular "Miyazaki anime," with sometimes unrivaled visual achievements. As a cross-over phenomenon, Miyazaki fills a role akin to that of Akira Kurosawa, representing a national style. Studio Ghibli stands as a national icon, and its influence is likely to continue for years to come.

Studio 4°C

What makes Studio 4°C stand out in part is the commitment of its chief executive, Eiko Tanaka, one of the few (possibly only) female heads of an anime studio. With her hipster glasses, stylish outfits, and warm, if abrupt, manner, she strives to create a space that values the visions of her leading creators (see figure 25). The director Kōji Morimoto is also part of the

25. Chief Executive Eiko Tanaka and the director Michael Arias standing in front of posters for *Tekkon Kinkreet* at Studio 4°C.

studio's center of gravity at the studio, helping attract others. His works include "Extra," a striking music video for the techno musician Ken Ishii, and "Beyond," an animated short for the *Animatrix* compilation. In an interview, Tanaka said she had worked for years as a line producer at Studio Ghibli but became frustrated with the limitations imposed by having to follow the vision of Hayao Miyazaki. She wanted instead to form a studio that would allow creators to choose the projects that they really cared about rather than beginning with what a toy company wanted to sell or with a manga that was already hugely popular. The studio's name, 4°C, refers to the temperature at which water is its most dense. Tanaka wanted to capture this density of activity in the films she produced.

A good example of Studio 4°C's idiosyncratic style of anime filmmaking is the film *Mind Game* (dir. Masaaki Yuasa, 2004), with a mixture of styles that incorporates flat, simple characters, photographs, and elaborate 3D modeling (as in the surprise appearance of a large animal). *Mind Game* began as a comic book by Robin Nishi and was adapted to film by Yuasa with a captivating soundtrack coordinated by Shinichirō Watanabe (who directed *Samurai Champloo*). The film opens and closes with a rapid-fire montage that surveys the history of the film's characters, then moves into a violent chase and an unlikely turn of events that frees the three main characters from the threat of pursuing gang members but introduces a very different setting and challenge. Visually, the film has an edgy style, stretching the boundaries of character animation. One of my favorite scenes is the portrayal of God as an endlessly transforming character accompanied by countless voice changes.

Studio 4°C is a model of trying to create an open space into which others can step. A good example is the circuitous career of Michael Arias, an American expatriate who has lived in Tokyo since about 1995, although he had visited before then. Arias got involved in the animation industry through his work on programming digital effects, especially where cameras fly through 3D space. Some of his early work involved creating the animation for amusement park rides in simulated spaceships. Arias also developed the software Toon Shaders, which facilitates the integration of digital computer graphics with cel-style animation. When he moved to Tokyo, he became fascinated with the manga *Tekkon Kinkreet* (an unusual title explained below) by Taiyō Matsumoto:

> It was around 1995—a weird time in Tokyo, just after the Kobe quakes, right in the midst of the Aum Shinrikyo gas attacks. Helicopters flying over the city, police patrolling the streets in force. And my friend and I, both unemployed at the time, were spending hours and hours on his balcony watching the streets below. All of that weird pre-apocalyptic tension—two guys sitting up high and looking down on the streets—that felt so much like *Tekkon*'s first panels of Black and White, crouched on top of the telephone poles looking down, guarding the streets. (quoted in Matsumoto 2006: 5)

Arias also recalled an enormous construction project in his neighborhood: "The city had finally decided to demolish the old Doujinkai apartments of Daikanyama. An entire neighborhood—a beautiful gem in the city, with tons of street life, artists ensconced there, covered with ivy—got leveled as we watched and then gradually transformed into a skyrise. Anyways, seeing a big chunk of my world evolve like that was very influential in the end" (quoted in Matsumoto 2006: 5). The story of *Tekkon Kinkreet* revolves around questions of urban development and the social energy of neighborhoods.

Arias wanted to see *Tekkon* created as an anime. In the late 1990s, he lined up investors and worked with Kōji Morimoto to make a pilot film, but the project never got off the ground. Eight years later, Eiko Tanaka

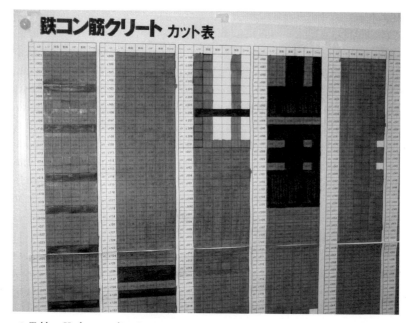

鉄コン筋クリート カット表

26. *Tekkon Kinkreet* cut list, August 2006.

told Arias that if the film was ever going to be made, he would have to make it himself. "I got tired of hearing him talk about it," Tanaka said.[6] Arias worked with the screenwriter Anthony Weintraub and the sound designer Mitch Osias, along with the animation staff at Studio 4°C, and they all created a visually stunning work.

When I met Arias in late summer of 2006, he was in the final stages of production, looking a bit ragged but also energized. On a wall of the studio hung a chart that showed the status of the overall project (figure 26). Squares colored red (gray in the black-and-white photo included here) indicated cuts that were completed; white blocks indicated work that remained to be done. The black blocks? Arias explained the special emotion attached to those scenes, which had been eliminated from the film. "I sometimes go out drinking with [the anime director] Mamoru Oshii, and he put it best," said Arias. "He said you spend years working on a project, it becomes like your child. Then in the final stages, there is too much to be done, and you have to decide: do you want to cut off a leg or an arm?"[7] Perhaps there inevitably will be a space between one's vision and what can be accomplished.

The Gutter and a Partner in Crime

This brief overview of some of the variety in approaches of different studios points to a way of thinking about media creativity as occurring in structured, open spaces. Although anime studies is a multidisciplinary field, there is a tendency to think of anime primarily in terms of representational content. Just as different creative modes within animation refuse to yield a singular magisterial solution, so do the varieties of anime studies offer tests for cultural exploration, creating worlds and characters and, ideally, generating platforms for others to build within, on, and beyond. In other words, collaborative creativity depends on conversation. In the world of comics, there's an interesting perspective on the openness that engenders dialogue.

How do comics differ from anime? Arias said something interesting in an interview: as the director of a film, one controls the timeline, the pace at which the scenes and the story unfold; as a manga artist, one controls the frame. A key aspect of comics is that the frames themselves are in dialogue. In *Understanding Comics*, Scott McCloud points out that comic artists not only control the frame but they also have a potent tool in the space between the frames. He uses the example shown in figure 27. The space between the panels, "what comics aficionados have named 'the gutter,'" he writes, "plays host to much of the magic and mystery that are at the very heart of comics" (McCloud 1993: 66). This magic and mystery also depends on someone else. "Every act committed to paper by the comics artist is aided and abetted by a silent accomplice, an equal partner in crime known as the reader," McCloud (1993: 66) writes. "I may have drawn the axe being raised in this example, but I'm not the one who let it drop or decided how hard the blow, or who screamed or why. That, dear reader, was your special crime, each of you committing it in your own style." This observation is only partly true. We, the audience, are not equal partners in crime, but we do have a role. The gutter draws attention to that role as the negative space that creates a vacuum, pulling the reader in and encouraging us to finish the thought.

In another example of this, we might consider a way in which the manga artist Taiyō Matsumoto works with the frame and the gutter to create his distinctive work *Tekkon Kinkreet* (*Tekkon kinkuriito*), an odd title that mashes together the two words "*tekkin* (steel-reinforced)" and "*konkuriito* (concrete)" and that can be seen as a reference to the not-

27. Scott McCloud (1993) shows how the gutter makes readers "partners in crime."

always-positive community remix that happens with urban development. The manga was serialized in thirty-three episodes that appeared in the *Big Spirits* comic weekly in 1994–95. In the manga, Matsumoto experiments with dramatic framing techniques. Sometimes the frames show contrasts between the characters and the city, and sometimes they are used to shape the pacing of the scenes. For example, figure 28 shows the end of episode 13, as the boy Shiro (White) is being pursued by two other boys who want to claim control of territory in Treasure Town. The sound effects are limited to the noise of sneakers scraping across the asphalt. We can note the diagonal lines used to divide some of the frames, as in the upper left with the two boys chasing, Shiro looking back, and a closeup of Shiro's shoe before he takes flight. To watch the opening scene in the film and compare it with the scene in Matsumoto's manga is to understand what Arias means when he says that the anime director controls the timeline, but the manga artist controls the frame.

We can also observe how the gutter can be conceived of more broadly in terms of storytelling. The manga *Tekkon Kinkreet* is set in Treasure Town, portrayed as a rundown but intricately networked social space that repre-

28. *Tekkon Kinkreet* manga, with Shiro leaping while being chased by two others in episode 13.

29. Minimalist approach to a battle at a clock tower in *Tekkon Kinkreet* (Matsumoto 2006: 259).

sents both nostalgia and the pressure of urban renewal. Part of the drama revolves around the appearance of a developer whose newly opened downtown amusement park, "Kiddie Castle" (*Kodomo no shiro*), seems to bring broader changes to the neighborhood. Much of the manga revolves around two orphan boys, Shiro and Kuro (White and Black), who are endowed with unusual strength and a penchant for resolving disputes with bloody violence. In episode 14 of the manga, the two outsider boys are still chasing White when they arrive at the top of a building with an enormous mechanical clock. Although the two interlopers think they have White cornered, White's ally Black suddenly appears, riding an enormous mechanical elephant that rolls out from under the clock as the clock's bell rings five times. Then the four boys battle. All we see of the fight is the image shown in figure 29. Again, the contrast between this approach and that of the opening scene of the film version is striking.

In an intriguing use of the gutter, the next frame shows the boys talking together after their fight. In that panel, one of the interlopers explains why they attempted to move into Black and White's territory: He and his companion were driven out of their neighborhood by adult assassins. In this case, the gutter is used in a way that differs from the example given by McCloud. Matsumoto, like McCloud, leaves the details of the violence off-screen—or, rather, out of the frame—but instead of portraying violence through a scream, he shows the boys coming together after the fight with mutual respect. There are a variety of ways in which Matsumoto uses remarkable framing to portray the ultraviolent world of rival yakuza gangs, ineffectual police, foreign assassins, and street-tough youth. The anime creators faced challenges of interpretation due to the different mediums. Arias and the creative staff he worked with at Studio 4°C added color and refrained from changing the drawing style of each of the characters, as Matsumoto did. They reorganized the plot as well, fitting a much longer and more complex story into an hour-and-forty-minute film.

Conclusion

The empty spaces in creative production therefore can take many forms. The gutter, combined with the participation of the audience required to make something of it, gives us a sense of how storytelling in anime and manga must be understood partly in terms of what is not portrayed—what is left open, in the blank spaces, that must be filled up not only by the creators, but also by the audience. As we will see, a kind of openness can help us understand the energy of overseas fans as well.

The perspectives brought to light in this chapter point to a diversity of approaches to creating cutting-edge crucibles for production at various anime studios. Intriguingly, there is a common recognition across all of opening up an empty space to allow certain kinds of creativity to occur. Emptiness exerts a kind of gravitational pull on the mind. To be cutting edge is to fill that emptiness in a way that keeps pulling the story and audience forward. To define a cutting edge is also to acknowledge that part of the premise of anime—indeed, of media generally—is its capacity to leave things untold in order to force the audience to connect the dots and, in effect, to articulate the premises that guide the world. Like the idea of a media success story, the idea of a cutting edge depends very much on the context and audience that one has in mind. Any definition of "cutting edge" resides primarily in the eye of the beholder. But as a concept that helps organize the activities of animators, anime studios, distributors, and fans, the idea of cutting-edge anime orients our consideration of this media form in certain directions. Something "cutting edge" is leading forward, breaking new ground. But for whom? Partly, the cutting edge is the work of the studios, but it also depends on pulling audiences forward. It is this latter work, especially on the part of overseas fans, that I turn to next.

Dark Energy

What can we learn from overseas fans and their participation in expanding the worlds of anime? If openness is important for collaborative creativity, how can that help us understand the space between Japanese producers and fans abroad? In this chapter, I focus on fansubbing—the translation and dissemination of anime online by fans—a controversial practice that illuminates debates about culture, economy, and intellectual property in the digital era. Fansubbing refers to the practice whereby hundreds of fan groups digitize the latest anime broadcasts, translate them, add subtitles, and make the media available online. Fans add subtitles—hence, "fansubs." Such online sharing of media is perceived as a dire threat to industries that have relied on packaged objects such as CDs and DVDs. But to see the world of fansubs simply in terms of copyright infringement is to ignore the significance of debates within the fansub community about what should be valued in a digital era and how. Given the ineffectiveness to date of both technological and legal counter-measures to reduce online sharing, I would argue that the path forward depends on a social solution, one that works from the understandings and practices of both fans and producers.

Fansubbers view their work as contributing to anime culture by providing timely, high-quality translations of Japanese releases for free to fellow fans. The anime fans who participate in this world by making, downloading, or watching fansubs widely acknowledge that the practice breaks copyright law. Nevertheless, many of these fans view the sharing of media files online as justified—and, indeed, they believe that doing so can support anime businesses, provided that certain ethical principles are maintained. Not everyone agrees, even among fans, and the ferocity of the debate provides a way to interrogate emergent politics at the intersections of Japan's content industries, new digital technologies, and transnational youth cultures. I argue that the politics of fansubbing can be best understood if we consider the energy that drives the interest of fans, a kind of "dark energy" that is largely unseen when the focus of debate hinges on questions of property, piracy, and law.

What are these fan-based ethics? A conflict in 2003 between groups of anime fans is representative of important aspects of the debate as a whole. On one side, an editorial writer for the online news source Anime News Network (ANN) offered this criticism of the fansub group Anime Junkies: "For the most part, ethical fansubbers have long adhered to the rule that you do not distribute a title that has a North American licensor. But *most* isn't *all*. There are some fansubbers that give the activity a very bad name. One of those groups is Anime Junkies."[1] The next day a person who described himself (herself?) as the webmaster for Anime Junkies posted the following response, challenging the notion that his group had acted unethically: "We are an open group and we stand by our actions. . . . We leave it to the general populace to decide what they feel is right and wrong. Remember, the law is not our moral guide. The day people begin to stop living by their ethics is the day our society loses its humanity."[2] Intriguingly, neither side views the law as the measure of ethics, referring instead to other principles and assuming that a transnational community of fans, an intriguing networked public, is the appropriate citizenry for making judgments. Fansubbing is interesting because, although fans feel little compunction about breaking copyright law, they (or for some readers, perhaps, we) tend to maintain a deference toward ideas of promoting the anime industry. This deference has limits, however, because fansubbers also aim to make up for shortcomings in international markets for anime, particularly the slow pace at which broadcasts and DVD releases from Japan are made available overseas.

Fansubs clearly challenge dominant ideas of copyright, offering an alternative regime of value that contrasts with the tenets of global free-market capitalism—that is, the ideologies of neoliberalism.[3] As the cultural geographer David Harvey describes it, a central tenet of neoliberalism is that the "market is presumed to work as an appropriate guide—an ethic—for all human action" (2005: 165). Markets depend on commodification and respect for private property, and the sharing/piracy of media online challenges this ethic. As Harvey points out, however, "Commodification presumes the existence of property rights over processes, things, social relations, that a price can be put on them, and that they can be traded subject to legal contract. . . . In practice, of course, every society sets some bounds on where commodification begins and ends. Where the boundaries lie is a matter of contention" (165). Fansubbing points to the contentiousness of these boundaries and to the need to theorize a "society" that crosses national boundaries, as the community of anime fans does. Of course, due to mutual copyright-protection treaties between Japan and the United States, the law is unambiguous in its protection of all anime titles, whether they are licensed in the United States or not. So the controversy between the editorial writer and Anime Junkies is not about law. Rather, it is about the ethics of social practice. This reminds us that commodifying content depends on a complex mixture of technologies, practices, and beliefs.

With the spread of online video-sharing sites such YouTube, Nico Nico Douga, and peer-to-peer networks, fan practices pose not only challenges to commodification but also opportunities for promotion, remixing, and distribution. Most media companies themselves tend to look favorably on independent blogging and viral marketing, which is driven by motivations that are quite similar (if not identical) to those that lead to "online piracy." An ethnographic perspective on fansubbing clarifies the value of the energy that circulates through peer-to-peer sharing. This is what I call "dark energy," a reference to the hidden cosmological force pushing apart the galaxies of our universe; the effects are observable, but the source is poorly explained by current theory. Similarly, the dark energy of fandom is measurable but poorly explained by theories of economic motivation.

We might think of fandom's dark energy as a collection of social forces that enlivens the connections between content and desire, which in turn helps drive the circulation of media products. I say "dark" not because anime can be gloomy or horrifying, but because a strict focus on piracy versus commodification tends to dismiss the productive capacity of this power (i.e., by making it unseen). Also, some of these social forces operate through the murky world of peer-to-peer file-sharing networks. Dark energy is not unique to anime fandom; nor is it simply characteristic of online file sharing. More broadly, it provides a way to conceptualize the fluid links among fans, media content, technology, and producers. In this regard, fansubbers provide insight into the forces that drive transnational flows of anime and that reframe our understanding of "Japaneseness" to include the activities of non-Japanese fans. Rather than emphasizing the contrasts between producers and fans, we may benefit from closer consideration of the feedback loops between them, which at times reinforce and at times undermine the existing business structures and social practices of global media.

Popularity is enlivened by network effects. Dark energy draws attention to the flows that precede and follow moments of commodification, like a river that draws together many sources, passes through a dam, then flows on. The dam represents the moment of commodification, the place where the energy of the river is turned into commodifiable electricity. Dark energy evokes the larger, flowing system, not just the element that can be packaged and sold.

The Market and Globalization

We should note that official producers understand the value of giving away content for free. They just want to be in control. When I met with a director of overseas sales at Toei Animation's business offices in Shinjuku and asked what the company charges an overseas broadcaster to air a TV series, he had a surprising answer: Prices vary widely, and sometimes "we charge nothing. . . . If the series catches on, we start charging for the second season on."[4] The "freemium" business model, now in vogue, has had its precursors (Anderson 2009). Japanese studios are accustomed to making low-budget animation and using overseas animators, both of which help keep costs down. As we saw in the discussion of the competitiveness of the manga market in Japan (see chapter 3), low prices and easy access facilitate a kind of democratization of popularity such that growing excitement can become a kind of social platform in its own right. With the costs relatively low, anime was understandably attractive to overseas media buyers. But this is only part of the explanation for how anime went global; there is more to it.

Consider *Pokémon*, which began as a videogame for Nintendo's handheld devices and has become one the most widespread T V anime in history, airing in more than sixty countries. Why? Joseph Tobin's edited volume on Pokémon's global adventure begins with two scenarios, contrasting, on the one hand, a top-down corporate push led by the Nintendo game and subsequent television series and, on the other hand, a bottom-up pull by overseas children who adapted the pop culture forms of Pokémon to use with peer friendships in their own worlds. Tobin finds that "the truth is somewhere in the middle" and that Pokémon's strength arises partly from a "multidimensionality" that was "more emergent than planned" (2004: 10). The anthropologists David Buckingham and Julian Sefton-Green, writing in the same volume, say that participation by consumers was vital to success but argue that styles of participation are severely constrained. In their words, echoing a common thread through the book, Pokémon operates less as a "text" than as a "cultural practice"—that is, something you *do* rather than something you watch or consume (Tobin 2004: 12). They also see danger: "Yet while this 'doing' clearly requires active participation on the part of the 'doers,' the terms on which it is performed are predominantly dictated by forces or structures beyond their control," structures that are determined, they argue, "by the work of their designers—and, indeed, by the operations of the market, which made these commodities available in particular ways in the first place" (12). These two scholars may be giving too much credit to the operations of the market. As we have seen with *Gundam*, failure can lead to success through fans' activities. Fan participation also operates at times outside authorized markets, as in the case of fansubs, cosplay, anime music videos, and other remixes, such as playful "abridged" versions of popular anime. Tobin concludes his volume on Pokémon by arguing for a more expansive understanding of media: "Perhaps what's needed is to view Pikachu's global adventure, as Einstein taught us to view light, as both particle and wave, matter and energy; that is, both as physical commodities that get shipped to specific sites around the globe and also as a wave of interest and awareness that began in Japan" and spread to the world (291).

In *Japanamerica* (2006), Roland Kelts offers a different portrait of "how Japanese pop culture has invaded" the United States by focusing on a kind of cultural consonance among forward-thinking entrepreneurs who developed anime businesses both in Japan and the United States. He views the cultural connections between the United States and Japan as forming two sides of a "Möbius strip," seemingly different but in fact wedded together.[5] I agree in the sense that theorizing culture is more about understanding contexts than identifying boundaries. Because Japan and America share much in terms of global forces and influences, it makes sense that our contexts are in many ways similar. But ultimately, this is a limited explanation of how Japanese pop culture invades the United States. If our societies are two sides of the same Möbius strip, then why don't all aspects of Japanese culture become integrated into American ways of life (and vice versa)? Why the divergences? Ryotarō Mihara (2010), an anthropologist, argues that the distinctions between Japanese fans' and American fans' readings of anime are so great that the relationship between the two sets of fans is best viewed as a pair of "Orobouros strips"—that is, the mythical creature that eats its own tail. In Mihara's study of the unusual series *The Melancholy of Haruhi Suzumiya*, he finds the differences between U.S. and Japanese fans as analogous to parallel, closed circles, universes unto themselves (2010). Both Kelts and Mihara work from models of culture that emphasize resonance rather than the productive capacities of fans. Still, I find inspiration from Kelts's portraits of the creators and the businesspeople who devoted themselves to bringing anime and associated merchandise to the United States. That energized commitment, which often grew out of the businesspeople's personal fan interests, may have been decisive. Similarly, Sean Leonard, a past president of the MIT Anime Club, explains anime's global success in terms of the role of fans, specifically how fan conventions and the sharing of media, first by videocassette and later digitally, generated a kind of "proselytization commons" whereby fans could convert others to the cult of anime (2005: 282). I'm skeptical of the proselytization metaphor (religion differs from fandom in important ways), but his point is well taken in that shared resources are always integrated into commercial situations in complex ways. This is also true of the varieties of tools for distributing media these days.

Some programmers of peer-to-peer file-sharing software view their work as a much needed challenge to the money politics that guide so much contemporary media distribution. The file-sharing software BitTorrent is a case in point. While entertainment industries tend to regard unauthorized file sharing as piracy, pure and simple, the makers of BitTorrent argue, to the contrary, that the software is above all "a free speech tool [that] gives you the same freedom to publish previously enjoyed by only a select few with special equipment and lots of money."[6] From this standpoint, new digital technologies can reconstitute the power of media, which in the broadcast era was (and, to a large extent, still is) dominated by wealthy elites and powerful corporations. The makers of BitTorrent hope their technology can help produce a more democratic public sphere by mitigating such distortions of wealth. BitTorrent also encourages "seeders" (those with a whole file being shared) to keep their sharing open and not simply be "leechers" (those on the network only to download files). Seeders are necessary to keep active the circulation of a given file. In very practical terms, the distinction between "broadcaster" and "consumer" is blurred by users of BitTorrent. Bram Cohen, the creator of BitTorrent, even adopted a motto for his software: "give and ye shall receive." There is a democratic element of participation that makes BitTorrent particularly attractive to those who are interested in progressive politics. Fansubbing, however, brings to the fore a somewhat different range of issues in that BitTorrent can be used in legal or illegal ways, but fansubbing's ethics depend on reformulating traditional notions of intellectual property and rethinking fans' relationship to markets as something beyond simple consumerism.

Some recent developments around digital media are worth mentioning, including the consolidation of those who create content and those who distribute it, as in the merger of NBC Universal with the Internet service provider Comcast. In July 2011, the *New York Times* reported that this convergence adds pressure on Internet service providers to step up their fight against piracy by threatening those who download unauthorized media with a range of punishments, including radically curtailed bandwidth. "The effect on consumers, the companies hope, will be more of a deterrent-by-annoyance—rather than the random lightning bolt of litigation that was once the preferred method of enforcement by the Recording Industry Association [of America]" (Sisario 2011). Others are less sure that this would be a solution. Eric Garland of the company BigChampagne, which tracks file sharing online, is among the doubters: "The challenge is that consumers will continue to do whatever they wish on the Internet, and find clever ways to *not* attract the attention of the content companies or [Internet service providers]. . . . It will never end" (quoted in Sisario 2011). The way forward, I would argue, depends on sensitivity to the social dynamics of piracy and sharing, as well as recognizing that popular culture forms depend on access, buzz, and circulation to succeed. Fans' contribution to collaborative creativity hinges on multiple structures of creative action and hybrid systems of value. Part of the problem is that entertainment companies want to have it both ways: They want to benefit from the feedback amplification that happens through participatory fan activities while trying to maintain the false premise that markets are constituted by corporate institutions responding to individuals making personal, rational decisions. Fansubbers, in contrast, provide an intriguing example of how amateur cultural mediators add value to anime through collective action, which is characteristic of a broader range of noncommercial information production (Benkler 2011).

The Craftsmanship of Fansubbing

Today, the sharing of fansubs has exploded online. One popular website, AnimeSuki.com, lists thousands of shows available for download using BitTorrent. In October 2005, for example, AnimeSuki.com provided links drawn from 288 different fansub groups. Each day, ten to twenty new links to TV episodes and films are added to the site. Judging from nostalgic postings on online discussion forums, the number of fansub groups has grown dramatically in recent years. Fansubs of popular shows often appear within days of the shows' initial broadcast in Japan and once downloaded can be watched on a computer or TV at close-to-broadcast quality. Increasingly, some TV shows and films are distributed in high-definition formats with 5.1 surround sound (i.e., six audio channels compared with stereo's two). At the time of this writing, in July 2012, websites such as DownloadAnime.org and AnimeSuki.com were available to help users find fansubs of Japanese anime. Fansubs are produced not only in English but also in Chinese, French, Spanish, Italian, Brazilian Portuguese, and more. Although fansubbers receive no money for the work they do, they do accept donations to offset the costs of bandwidth.

Fansubs are posted at higher resolutions than YouTube videos and are managed directly by the fansub groups themselves. In some cases, it is possible to download entire seasons of a TV program, such as twenty-six half-hour episodes in a 6-GB pack. How long it takes to download a file depends on a number of factors—not simply the speed of one's broadband connection but also, and more important, the number of people sharing the file. (In general, the more people sharing, the faster the download.) Download times can vary dramatically, depending, for example, on seeder-to-leecher ratios; nevertheless, they can be much faster than iTunes downloads in my experience. A central aspect of fansubbing is not simply providing access to anime shows but also offering detailed, accurate, and timely translations.

In terms of quality and attentiveness to detail, the works of fansubbers illustrate the craftsmanship of translation and provide a concrete example of how fans amplify the meaningfulness of anime. What is interesting is how such attention to detail can lead viewers to interpret anime in a direction quite different from what the creators had intended. The anime television series *Samurai Champloo*, discussed in chapter 2, offers intriguing examples.

The opening page of the official Japanese website for *Samurai Champloo* includes this message (in English): "This work of fiction is not an accurate historical portrayal. LIKE WE CARE. NOW SHUT UP AND ENJOY THE SHOW."[7] Fansub groups, however, tend to be especially sensitive to portraying the cultural nuances of the shows they translate. Despite the *Samurai Champloo* creators' disavowals of actual history, some fansubbers went to significant lengths to share their insights on the show's historical settings. When the English-language fansub group Shinsen-Subs provided the translation for episode 24, its members went to great lengths to explain the context of the show in terms of history. The translation note began: "The Shimabara no Ran was an uprising by predominantly Christian peasants during the Tokugawa Shogunate in 1637–1638, when they were mainly persecuted for their religious beliefs. Sixteen year old Shiro Amakusa led peasants, including women and ronins from Shimabara and the nearby Amakusa Islands, in sieges at Shimabara castle and Hara fortress."[8] Two more screens provided additional background information, then the show proper begins. Such elaborate notes and on-screen explanations point to an effort to achieve accuracy and authenticity—that is, to link anime to the rich history of "real Japan." Japanese viewers are likely to know the historical references and to see *Samurai Champloo* as a playful work of fiction. Here, too, we see the working of the gutter, a space between viewer and content that can be filled with an expansionary dark energy.

In contrast, the effort to provide historical depth on the part of fansubbers indicates the different sources of pleasure that can arise from watching anime as a foreigner—namely, getting a small sense of Japan's rich history. While the official website points up the difference with history, the fansub products draw attention to the relevance of that history. In this we see how the flows of Japanese popular culture depend not only on what happens on-screen but also on how such content appeals to audiences in different ways. All of these examples are elements of the desire that drives dark energy, an energy that arises in the space between the viewer and the content.

Fansub translation notes sometimes reveal a deep knowledge of popular culture. Episode 8 of *Samurai Champloo*, which notably features a "beat boxer" (a person who makes DJ rhythms and scratch sounds using his voice) who backs up the rap of a big-talking braggart, opens with translation notes by AnimeForever describing obscure references to live-action samurai TV shows from several decades ago. Why go to all this trouble? Status seems to be part of the story. In February 2005, the website Baka-Updates.com listed five fansub groups—Anime-Kraze, Anime-Station, Aoi-Anime, AnimeForever, and AnimeOne—that were working on the first season's episodes of *Samurai Champloo*.[9] Clearly, the groups were competing with each other at some level. This characteristic of competitive teams helps clarify why people "do work for free." Artists, amateur athletes, and academics similarly show devotion to honing their skills and exemplify noneconomic motivations.

Fansub translations are often more detailed and provide more linguistic and cultural depth than the commercial releases. The fansubs for *Samurai Champloo* include on-screen explanations of food such as *dango* (rice dumplings) and *monjayaki* (savory pancakes). In episode 1, a fansub clarified that "Edo is the old name for Tokyo," whereas the DVD release leaves "Edo" untranslated. Translation notes are often added to fansubs to explain esoteric references. Consider episode 18, "War of Words," which reimagines what competition between members of a martial arts dojo would look like if, instead of competing in martial arts, the groups competed by "tagging" graffiti in the most outrageous places. The fansub group AnimeForever included an image with explanations at the beginning of the show, including notes on uses of *hiragana*, a Japanese syllabary (see figure 30). In the official DVD release by Geneon, the subtitles are only in English, in the Roman alphabet; they do not include the *hiragana*. Fansub groups clearly recognize that part of the interest of fans who prefer subs to dubs is that they want to learn the Japanese language. Thus, it is important to explain double meanings, such as the use of numbers to represent words. In the show, the graffiti artists write "4-6-4-9," which can be read as "yo-ro-shi-ku (roughly, 'Nice to meet you')."

Graffiti art has interesting parallels with fansubbing. As with other artistic pursuits that are deemed illegal, the participants must hide their legal names in favor of pen names or screen names that become associated with the work, so that only a small inner circle (if anyone) knows the person's actual identity. Fansubbers and graffiti artists are motivated not

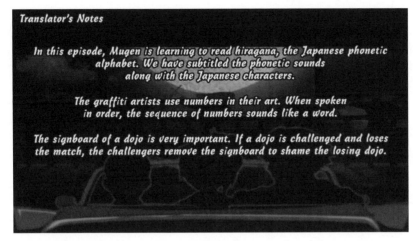

Translator's Notes

In this episode, Mugen is learning to read hiragana, the Japanese phonetic alphabet. We have subtitled the phonetic sounds along with the Japanese characters.

The graffiti artists use numbers in their art. When spoken in order, the sequence of numbers sounds like a word.

The signboard of a dojo is very important. If a dojo is challenged and loses the match, the challengers remove the signboard to shame the losing dojo.

30. AnimeForever translator's notes to episode 18 of *Samurai Champloo*.

by money but by a social energy that arises in part from public recognition among people in the know. Graffiti artists are valued because of the quality of their painting and the audacity of the locations of their pieces; fansubbers compete in an online realm to provide the timeliest, most accurate, and most detailed translations of shows. Interestingly, though, this doesn't mean that fansubbers always love their own fans.

Voices of Fansubbers

In reading through many online forums to examine the debates among fans about fansubbing, I was struck by how fansubbers themselves often expressed ambivalence toward their own viewers. Fans are not a mono-lithic category (Hills 2002). As sites such as "Fan Wank" make clear, fans can be harsh critics of other fans (Dunlap and Wolf 2010). In the voices of fansubbers online, one hears an undercurrent of anxiety that today's anime fans are not sensitive enough to the subtle differences in quality between different groups' translations, which is more evidence that important ele-ments of the fansubbers' motivations lie in a commitment to craftsman-ship and a desire to have viewers recognize it. Some anime fans express devotion to particular fansub groups, as in, "I will only watch *Ghost in the Shell: Stand Alone Complex* if it is the Laughing Man Fansubs translation." Other fans use particular fansub groups as a guide to the important anime to download: "I always try to follow what Shinsen-Subs is up to." But some fansubbers express frustration with what they see as trends in fansubbing. Consider this online exchange:

> BAOYAOB: Please . . . someone remind me why we fansub. . . .
>
> SACCHUN: Good that you see the truth bay. . . . At the end of the day, your majority leecher populations (ie, 90%) will say this: WE DON'T CARE WHOSE FUCKING SUB WE GET—end of story. It's the annoying vocal minority that need to shut up. Besides, all the fansubs these days are crap and are done with maximum overkill, ie, We want to be the stupidest and most over-the-top-with-stupid-effects idiots. And to think . . . that paid people working for companies get PAID and don't even touch this level of overzealous eyecandy that UNPAID people waste massive amounts of time on.[10]

This angry interchange criticizes the (assumed) failure of some fans to make aesthetic judgments about the quality of anime fansubs and the tendency of some fansub groups to include fancy visuals with their translations in ways that make the translations difficult to read. An interesting aspect of this discussion, and others like it, is that the fansubbers never complain that they are not getting paid. They view their work as a hobby, a labor of love, but they hope for a reward in aesthetic appreciation from their audience.

Sometimes fansubbers do receive the kind of feedback they desire. Consider this posting from someone who worked with the fansub group Anime-Empire. I quote at length to give a sense of the fansubber's multi-layered ambivalence:

> For some reason or another, I had disappeared from Anime-Empire, and subsequently the fansubbing business, for a good while and came back only recently, sometime near the beginning of summer. I guess I can say that I was somewhat relieved that my home didn't get up and move anywhere . . . but from that day, it has been nothing but more and more work, as I had decided to accept more responsibilities (in the form of work!). "Work" doesn't really seem to be a fitting word, as I actually enjoyed doing most of it . . . although for a few of the projects I forced myself to stay up past 3–4 AM in order to follow the strict schedule (I blame you for shortening my life, Koro!!).
>
> Despite the things I had to endure (and the few times I didn't wake up in

time, and held up the whole team . . . gomen [sorry]), it all worked out in the end when I can finally sit back, relax, and look at the result of all that hard work. I actually had a friend approach me and say, "You should check out this great anime by Anime-Empire called 'Midori no Hibi'! It's simply amazing!" Although the anime itself was what did it for her, it made me very happy to know that I, along with the great people I worked with on that project, have helped this person enjoy anime the way it was meant to be enjoyed.[11]

We can see the tension that drives what I'm calling dark energy emerging from the pressure within the fansub group to keep to deadlines and produce high-quality work—"work that is not really work"—and from the chance encounters with outside anime fans who appreciate having their eyes opened to a new title. We can also observe the sense of pride in completing a project and how that pride is connected with "the great people [the fansubber] worked with." I'm also struck by the boundary between fansubbers and fans: the fansubber quoted here, by my reading, doesn't reveal her or his involvement in the Anime-Empire group to the friend.

We can also see the power of commitment to the group, even in the absence of economic payback, and aspects of hierarchy ("I blame you . . . Koro"). Given the large amount of labor involved, and the various kinds of expertise required, most fansub groups divide up the work among their members. There is often a leader or group of leaders that organizes the entire operation, and within fansub groups, there is an array of roles. The "raw provider" acquires the "raw," unsubtitled version of a show, with commercials deleted, though sometimes the names of main sponsors are shown, presumably because the image behind the sponsors' names is deemed important. One can tell the raws are often taken from TV broadcasts because they occasionally contain emergency warnings related to earthquakes. Using the raw version, a "translator" translates the dialogue from Japanese to another language. The "editor" checks the translation for grammar and typos. The "timer" places subtitles in the correct locations (e.g., using software such as Sub Station Alpha). The "encoder" combines the subtitles and the raw video into one file. The "QC" (quality control) person checks everything. One or two people also specialize in providing the elaborate "karaoke" versions of opening and ending theme songs, which usually involves adding the lyrics in three forms: *kanji/kana, romaji* versions in Japanese, and English translations. The *kanji* and *romaji* subtitles are usually animated by some kind of "follow the bouncing ball" format that shows when to sing the words of the lyrics. Each worker gets his or her screen name added to the credits.

This forces us to reconsider how hegemonic market forces actually are. Not only do fansubbers deny, through their unrepentant participation in file sharing, that market relations are the appropriate guide for ethical behavior, but they argue that value arises from group craftsmanship, aesthetic quality, and appreciation by fans. All of this reminds us that such "virtual" groups operate through deeply felt social dynamics. The ethnomusicologist Rene Lysloff (2003) describes the complex systems of exchange involved in the amateur online music scene surrounding "mods," whereby musicians share and collaborate on musical works online. In his words, the "Internet provides a place for individuals to gather and, as a collective, to generate emergent (sub)cultures, complex prestige systems, elaborate commodity exchange networks, and structured governing bureaucracies" (2003: 258–59). What we can add is that the fansub world is driven not only by a desire to participate in a collective project of promoting anime culture but also by a desire to compete, sometimes to the point of fierce animosity, to make the best translations possible.

Are Fansubs Ethical?

Like AnimeMusicVideo.org, fansub groups make a distinction between legal and ethical, and some of this depends on how money enters the picture. As mentioned above, although some fansub groups accept "donations" to offset the costs of bandwidth, they often distribute their translations with an on-screen stipulation that the fansub is "not for sale, rent or eBay." In some of the online forums I've read, users who admit to buying fansubs on eBay face harsh flames. The explicitly noncommercial aspect of fansubbing keeps it in the realm of a "hobby" and in that sense provides some grounds for the defense that fansubbers are not profiting from the work of others. Between the black market for bootleg sales and the white market of official distributors lies the gray zone where dark energy operates to drive different kinds of groups. There is nevertheless a moral economy at work within this gray zone.

Participants in the subtitling and sharing scene make moral distinctions depending on whether a show is licensed in the translated language's market and whether a show has been released on DVD. It might help to consider four categories of unauthorized digital media of anime in a sequence of "most ethical" to "least ethical": fansubs of unlicensed shows; fansubs of shows licensed but not yet released on DVD in the United States; fansubs of shows licensed and released as DVDs; and rips (i.e., direct copies) of released DVDs. We can see in this logic a desire to support companies that are trying to bring anime into overseas markets. All of these media forms are circulated without money changing hands; therefore, this sharing differs from the black market of commercial bootlegging. Websites such as AnimeSuki.com and DownloadAnime.org list only shows that are unlicensed in North America. The editorial writer for ANN identified these kinds of fan groups as the ethical ones. If shows are licensed but have not yet been released (the situation with *Samurai Champloo* in the fall of 2004), some would argue that it is still OK to translate and distribute but that the fansub group should remove links to the shows once the DVDs for those episodes have been released. The justification here is that distributors sometimes license shows but don't release them promptly. These fans want to encourage distributors to release their beloved shows quickly, at which point the fansubbers will take their works out of circulation. (Shinsen-Subs, for example, followed this rule.)

The issue with Anime Junkies, introduced at the beginning of this chapter, arose because after the TV series *Ninja Scroll* began airing in Japan, the U.S. company Urban Vision licensed the title. Anime Junkies' webmaster explained his group's reaction to this announcement and subsequent communications: "With the announcement by Urban Vision that the series was licensed for American release, Anime Junkies was contacted by Urban Vision and politely asked to cease all distribution of the title. Anime Junkies chose to comply in a manner we felt was ethical. We stopped continued translations of the series a week ago in compliance with the request issued by Urban Vision. We did not however, immediately stop distributing the first five episodes we had already translated and released."[12] The webmaster noted that there is a range of ethical stances regarding fansubs. At one end of the spectrum, all fansubs are wrong. At the other end of the spectrum, some fansubbers will continue distributing titles even after DVDs have been released in North America. The Anime Junkies webmaster then added, "Anime Junkies has opted to assume a position in the middle of these two extremes. We view each scenario individually and simply choose to do what we feel is right in each instance.

We do not however, distribute any title once it has become available to buy and regularly stop MONTHS ahead of such time." Moreover, the webmaster said, it is disingenuous to claim that the fansub group does not support anime. To me, this gives the clearest portrait of why fansubbers view their piracy as pro-industry—or, at least, pro-anime-culture. "Finally, I would like to stress that [the] Anime Junkies stance can be summed up to this. We do not wish to harm the industry in America. We are a group of loyal and dedicated anime fans that annually put thousands of dollars into the industry straight from our own pockets. We only wish to help the growth of anime in America and around the world. I would also like to illuminate the fact that Anime Junkies regularly complies with requests from license holders to stop all distribution." In my estimation, the Anime Junkies decision to seek a "middle ground" reflects an effort to balance the group's commitment to "do no harm to the industry" with a desire to be appreciated for the work its members had already done. This logic makes sense only if we calculate the value of community admiration as part of the payoff for fansub groups. Because some American distributors fail to live up to these standards of prompt, high-quality, detailed, and aesthetically pleasing translations, some fansubbers feel justified in continuing to distribute titles because that is in the interest of expanding anime culture. Here, too, we can see ethics as something that emerges from a contested collaborative creativity.

What Do Anime Studios Think about Fansubs?

Judging from postings in online discussion forums, some fans believe that fansubbers' work is tacitly approved by anime companies. Few anime distributors actually voice that opinion. One American businessperson I spoke to, the founder of a company that licenses and sells anime and manga in the United States, said she viewed fansubbers as "legit" if they do in fact stop distributing work once it is licensed.[13] Notably, however, she asked that her name and the name of her company not be used because she feared that her opinion might sour the company's relationship with Japanese distributors. In March 2005, I met with several anime producers in Tokyo and asked each about fansubbing. Masakazu Kubo, a *Pokémon* producer, was unequivocal: "[Fansubbers] think they are supporting anime, but not a penny goes to the creators. It's stealing." Chihiro Kameyama, a movie producer at Fuji TV, was more open-minded. He viewed the Internet as an important promotional tool and said he could imagine giving away the first few minutes of a film to draw people to theaters, though he stopped short of supporting fansubbing. Perhaps the most interesting response, however, came from Toshio Suzuki, the producer at Studio Ghibli. Twice I asked him for his opinion of fansubbers, but both times he veered off and answered another question. When I asked a third time, "But do you think fansubbing is good or bad?" he looked me directly in the eye and smiled. To me, this captures the ways that producers themselves recognize their difficult position. Even if fans cannot be controlled, they can be angered. For Suzuki, the best response was no response.[14]

Not all of the studios have responded with silence, however. In December 2004, a letter from a Tokyo law firm was delivered to several fansub groups and websites warning them to stop facilitating the distribution of *Rahxephon*, *Genshiken*, and other anime produced by Media Factory Inc. The contents of that letter have been widely discussed in online anime forums. Several people noted that the law firm misrepresents (or misunderstands) how anime files are distributed—for example, in the sense that the media files shared through BitTorrent are never posted to a "website"; only the files that connect to "trackers" are, and they, in turn, set up small networks of computers sharing a particular file. Nevertheless, the general consensus among fans was that if a company asks, the websites and fansub groups should respect their wishes. It is this response that offers such a sharp contrast to research on music downloading among U.S. college students, who, when faced with arguments about the unfairness of downloading music for free, usually respond by pointing to the unfair practices and prices of the recording industry (Condry 2004).

In August 2006, I was asked to give a talk to a group of entertainment company executives organized by Keidanren, a large business organization in Japan. I told them about fansubs and the ethics guiding them. I argued that if they want to combat fansubs, they should at least try to understand what the fans were thinking so they could engage in a dialogue rather than simply speaking past them. The comments afterward, however, suggested that they were not convinced. The head of a videogame company put it this way. "I bet my life (*inochi o kakeru*) on the works we make. It pains me to think that some people are simply distributing our works for free." Another chief executive wanted to know about the differences between fansubs and YouTube, which the company clearly was more aware of and potentially more concerned about. In the fall of 2007, anime studios and creators seem to be increasingly vocal in criticizing fansubs, with artists like

Nabeshin (an anime director) speaking out at an anime convention and a spokesman for the anime studio GDH lashing out as well. It will be interesting to see what kind of effect, if any, this will have on fans' attitudes toward fansubs. It may be that new online experiments in distribution through Crunchy Roll and Hulu will succeed and perhaps even replace most fansubs. But debates about fair value and ethics are likely to continue.

Do Fansubs Hurt or Help the Market?

Might the producers' opposition to fansubs be based on a misconceived notion about their effect on the market? We may never know. Granted, the public debate about copyright usually hinges on whether the sharing of media online ultimately helps or hurts the market for music, television, and film. Posing the question in this way, however, too narrowly frames the debate, particularly by basing one's decision on speculations about the effects of file sharing. Some empirical analyses have attempted to assess the impact of peer-to-peer file sharing with regard to music sales. Felix Oberholzer-Gee and Koleman Strumpf (2007) argue that file sharing has a statistically insignificant effect on record sales. The economist Stan Leibowitz (2006) is among those who dispute their findings, but a range of other papers support the idea that file sharing may not be as damaging as the entertainment industry claims.[15] Indeed, a study funded by the Canadian government found that downloads have a positive impact on sales (Andersen and Frenz 2007). Even so, such analyses may sound hollow to creators within content industries who are watching steady declines in the sale of packaged media such as CDs and DVDs.

Ultimately, I would argue, it will be impossible to determine once and for all whether free sharing helps or hinders the market. The reason is simple. Any assertion of harm or benefit hinges on comparing the market that exists now, a hybrid one with both sharing and buying, with a market (without file sharing) that does not exist. In addition, like others, Rufus Pollock, the founder of the Open Knowledge Foundation (a nonprofit committed to openness in data sharing), makes an apt criticism regarding questions of the "economic loss" associated with pirated media. His argument is posted in a blog in response to a BBC article claiming that the United Kingdom "loses tens of billions of pounds in lost revenue" due to illegal downloads of music and film. Pollock (2009) notes that these figures are suspect and presumably assume that one download is equal to one lost sale. "Furthermore," he continues, "looking at revenues in a single industry is dangerous here: we've got to look at the overall impact on the economy (and that's still ignoring the welfare/income distinction). For example, if someone makes an unauthorized download rather than buying a CD, they spend the money they would have spent on the CD on something else, be that a haircut, a meal, or going to a concert. If we want to count that as a loss to the music industry we need to count the gain it generates elsewhere" (Pollack 2009). This adds another twist to the notion of "economic loss" due to file sharing online—namely, the recognition that one industry's loss is another's gain, a simple and obvious point yet seldom part of the debate. If it is impossible to judge the effect of file sharing on (hypothetical) markets, then focusing on energy and alternative approaches to commodification (or even noncommercial production) makes much more sense.

The anthropologist Chris Kelty (2008) offers a useful approach for thinking about the value of collaborative networks of people who are motivated for reasons other than profit. He explores the logic and practices of people who participate in the free software movement—for example, those who work on the Linux operating system. Kelty argues that they have been part of an ongoing "cultural reorientation" in the "governance and control of the creation and dissemination of knowledge." His main point is that they create "recursive publics," which he defines as "publics concerned with the ability to build, control, modify, and maintain the infrastructure that allows them to come into being in the first place and which, in turn, constitutes their everyday practical commitments and the identities of the participants as creative and autonomous individuals" (2008: 6–7). In other words, if markets set up certain approaches to value and success, Kelty shows how other forms of organizing one's labor can produce emergent systems with a different kind of cultural significance. He also notes, however, that recursive publics' "independence from power is not absolute; it is provisional and structured in response to the historically constituted layering of power and control within the infrastructures of computing and communication" (2008: 9). In other words, we live in a time of hybrid systems of exchange, contextualized by received understandings of how markets work while also shot through with the pressures of immediate (and distant) social relations, a point made by Ted Bestor (2004) in his analysis of the cultural dimensions of the Tsukiji fish market.

What we find with fansubs is not a "copyleft" utopia but, rather, a conflicted world that sometimes ignores industry and sometimes defers to it. A broader historical perspective, however, reveals that these conflicts are common to new media industries. Ironically, Japan was seen as one of the most egregious contributors to piracy, according to Jack Valenti, the U.S. film industry lobbyist, when the videocassette recorder was viewed as the Pirate Bay of its time.

Historical Examples of "Media Piracy"

Some historical context can help us see that charges of piracy have been endemic to emerging media throughout the twentieth century. Indeed, as the legal scholar Lawrence Lessig discusses, what we now call big media was in many cases born out of piracy. Because new media business models and charges of piracy go hand in hand, dark energy provides a way to conceptualize the interconnectedness between the excitement surrounding new uses of media technologies, even if some of those new uses fall outside traditional forms of commodification.

In *Free Culture* (2004), Lessig points out that the debate about media piracy often turns on the principle that "if something has value, then someone must have a right to that value." He underscores, however, that this is not the principle that guides copyright law. Rather, copyright was originally designed in the United States to offer a limited monopoly to inventors and creators as a means to "promote progress in science and the useful arts." There is a widespread assumption that protecting intellectual property from unauthorized use will necessarily improve markets. But, as Lessig shows, such efforts to define rights in terms of value belies the history of big media whereby new media became successful often by ignoring the "if value, then right" principle. As others have argued in many contexts, we do harm to emerging ways of doing things by protecting old ways. Indeed, among the industry sectors that are fighting piracy today are several that developed in part by ignoring copyright protections as they were then defined. Lessig writes: "If 'piracy' means using the creative property of others without their permission—if 'if value, then right' is true—then the history of the content industry is the history of piracy. Every important sector of 'big media' today—film, records, radio, and cable TV—was born of a kind of piracy so defined" (2004: 53). A brief look at some aspects of these historical battles in the United States offers lessons for contextualizing today's fansubbing practices.

The history of the film industry in the early twentieth century is one place to begin (Aberdeen 2000; Lessig 2004). After Thomas Edison invented the technology for filmmaking, he formed a monopoly trust called the Motion Picture Patents Company to exercise the rights to his patents. This trust set a deadline of January 1909 for all companies to comply with Edison's licenses. Some film companies that referred to themselves as "independents" rejected the trust's demands and carried on business without submitting to the Edison monopoly. This occurred during a tremendous expansion in the number of nickelodeons. The trust responded with strong-arm tactics that included confiscating equipment, stealing machinery, and even physical violence. Some independents, most prominently Fox, fled to California, where they could pirate Edison's inventions without fear of the law. By the time California came under more effective law enforcement, Edison's patents had expired. Thus, even the term "Hollywood" to stand for the film industry evokes a history of what was viewed at the time as piracy. In some ways, the migration of users of online file sharing from one software system to another (e.g., Napster to Kazaa to BitTorrent) mirrors this geographical flight away from control a century ago.

Recorded music, radio, and cable TV provide other examples of how new technologies threatened old business models. In each case, charges of piracy gave way to a rapprochement between content providers and media distributors in ways that ultimately grew both sides of the market. In several cases, such truces were brokered by the U.S. Congress. Television broadcasters, for example, objected to cable companies that sold their content without giving money to the broadcasters. Congress struck a balance by setting licensing rates and rules in ways that took away some of the control of publishers and creators while ensuring that they would get paid something for the use of their work. After a song is recorded, for example, anyone may record a cover version and sell it, provided that the original author is paid a rate set by statute. Radio stations do not need permission to broadcast recorded music; they simply have to pay a set fee to air individual songs. Interestingly, webcasts are treated differently from radio broadcasts in part because webcasting is viewed as performance *and* making a copy (which requires an additional fee), because streaming on the web involves making a copy in a computer's memory cache. One could imagine a statutory solution of some sort guiding the future of peer-to-peer uses, but as yet nothing appears imminent on the legislative agenda in the United States. On the contrary: New proposals demanding further action against online piracy seem to be on the rise. As long as the use of peer-to-peer software is viewed primarily as "stealing," then it seems unlikely that members of Congress will rise to the technology's defense.

Japan figured prominently in one of the most interesting historical examples of "media piracy," namely, involving the videocassette recorder. It is interesting because initial fears that it would destroy the movie industry turned out to be wrong. By the late 1990s, income from videos and DVDs constituted almost two-thirds of the revenue that movie studios received, far more than box-office income (Vogel 2001). But in the early 1980s, Valenti, who was then the head of the Motion Picture Association of America, gave testimony to Congress about the threat posed by the VCR. Most famously, he argued, "The VCR is to the American film producer and the American public as the Boston strangler is to the woman home alone" (Valenti 1982). As a moment in the history of Japan's cultural-technological relations with the United States, the language Valenti used in his testimony is striking:

> But now we are facing a very new and a very troubling assault on our fiscal security, on our very economic life and we are facing it from a thing called the video cassette recorder and its necessary companion called the blank tape. And it is like a great tidal wave just off the shore. . . . The U.S. film and television production industry is a huge and valuable American asset. In 1981, it returned to this country almost $1 billion in surplus balance of trade. And I might add, Mr. Chairman, it is the single one American-made product that the Japanese, skilled beyond all comparison in their conquest of world trade, are unable to duplicate or to displace or to compete with or to clone. . . . It is a piece of sardonic irony that this asset, which unlike steel or silicon chips or motor cars or electronics of all kinds—a piece of sardonic irony that while the Japanese are unable to duplicate the American films by a flank assault, they can destroy it by this video cassette recorder. (Valenti 1982)

This hyperbolic language of annihilation is being repeated today in assertions about the dangers of online piracy.

Charges of piracy have frequently gone hand in hand with the emergence of new media forms. In every case, the solution was not "stamping out piracy" but finding a means to develop a compromise that could move the industries forward. In this regard, the dark energy that drives fansubbing and the moral economy that is developing around these practices highlight some common ground between fans and content industries that could guide policy. The conflicts surrounding piracy are necessarily about more than whether stealing is good or bad. What dark energy shows is that the key is finding new ways to build on the interest in media forms—radio, cable TV, videos, DVDs, online digital media files—not in preserving the old business models.

Conclusion

If we look at spaces between the official rules of markets and the laws governing them, then we can see more clearly why we should attend to the forms of energy that fill that openness and, in the process, create structures of creative action amid diverse understandings of value. Fansubs, like other forms of fan creation, illustrate that, in some contexts, official markets impose less control than other social pressures. In this regard, social energies can become platforms in their own right, something others can build on, generating a dark energy that expands the universe of anime. Lessig (2008) might call contemporary anime markets a mixture of two economic logics—commercial and sharing—but to me it makes more sense to speak of this hybrid market in which we currently live as *the* market. This should enable us to think more broadly about varieties of approaches to commodification, production, and consumption. For me, this would offer a way out of the circular debates around sharing and piracy.

This is important because uses of media that operate outside the realm of commercial exchange contribute to the excitement around different media products. In some ways, this is obvious and commonsensical, yet it bears repeating because too often the public debate about online piracy focuses exclusively on securing that moment of commodification as the primary moving force of cultural production. Kelty's "recursive public" describes a social imaginary specific to the Internet that "draws together technical practices of coding and designing with social and philosophical concepts of publics." He highlights that concepts of social and moral order often take the form of "argument-by-technology" rather than deliberative spoken or written discussion (Kelty 2005: 186). The principle of openness operates as a foundational concept that organizes both practices and ideas of this community of programmers. There are intriguing echoes of this idea of "openness" in the fansub world. Fansubbers want *access* to programs that have aired in Japan yet may take years to be officially released in the United States. Fansubbers reject the artificial scarcity produced by closed national media markets. And, yet, because fansubbers are committed to the content itself, questions of access and fair use of other people's work take on a cast that is somewhat different from that in open source programming. We can recognize the originality of open source code, but can creating translations be seen as sufficient originality to justify sharing illegally? Doesn't this simply cannibalize markets for translations before they have a chance to mature? The answer depends on how we imagine our market futures—or, perhaps, how we operate within our current diverse range of possibilities.

A paper published in 2000 by four workers for Microsoft (which did not endorse their position) argued, among other things, that file sharing online via the "darknet" was likely to continue indefinitely, partly because "users will copy objects as long as it is possible and interesting to do so" (Biddle 2000: 2). I agree. So the solution will have to be a form of social engineering in which people agree with the ethical value of whatever rules ultimately emerge. This is largely how official laws work anyway.

Fansubbers in effect theorize an alternative approach to fair use that hinges on the recognition that the industry often fails to serve the public. Factoring in these networked fans' desires can help us understand the mechanisms of the globalization of anime by navigating between theories of cultural resonance and economic determinism. Something is missing from these formulations, because they tend to focus on the content or on the one-to-one relationship between content and the viewer or consumer.

The example of the gutter in comic strips points to the importance of understanding the potential of open spaces and how audience energy helps make connections. If we extend this concept of social energy to think about how anime moves across national borders, we can see a similar dynamic at work: a kind of dark energy that is largely invisible when viewed through the lens of economic globalization. We can easily imagine the excitement (and, perhaps, anxiety) a cosplayer who has made a costume of a favorite character to wear to an anime convention might feel about the chance to display his or her craft and performance to others who care. Of course, this passion is not the whole explanation of anime's globalization, as studios, manga creators, merchandisers, and sponsors have all played a role. It is tempting to dismiss Joseph Tobin's discussion of whether it is a top-down, entrepreneurial, market-driven process or a bottom-up movement driven by the passion of devoted fans, because clearly it was some combination of both. But the distinction remains important because the ongoing debate about what kind of labor and value is legitimate hinges precisely on the proper boundaries of markets and consumerism.

SEVEN

Love Revolution

OTAKU FANS IN JAPAN

✱ We use many words to discuss smaller cultural worlds in relation to larger cultural worlds—"subculture" versus "mainstream"; "fanatic" versus "popular"; "subaltern" versus "dominant"; "local" versus "global"; "niche" versus "mass"; "otaku (*otakii*)" versus "pop (*poppu*)"—and each binary brings its own associations, its distinctive advantages and pitfalls. What these different oppositions share, however, is the thorny analytical question of the relationship between the small and the large, which for the discussion here, I will consider in terms of the niche and the mass. The notion of "media success" often hinges on a movement from something small-scale that expands to become large-scale, but as we examine the crucibles of creativity that give rise to these creations, we often find that they center on very niche-oriented obsessions, something we can observe in studios, among fan groups, with merchandisers, and so on. Somehow, an outward-facing expansionary "dark energy" seems to depend on an intensely inward-focused energy.

As we have seen, anime went global in part by working from rather niche-oriented settings—for example, in the development of Gainax and in the thinking of cutting-edge studios. In this chapter, I examine the question of a niche cultural world's relation to mainstream Japan in terms of an unusual "love revolution"—namely, people who express love for virtual 2D characters. The debates about this phenomenon offer insight into how deeply personal emotional responses, often defended in terms of individual idiosyncrasies, nevertheless construct ideas about larger society. Some argue that this kind of love means that niche fandoms can become islands unto themselves, contributing too little to our collective social worlds. But I wonder: Do people's uniquely personal attachments to characters in 2D worlds necessarily mean a rejection of society?

The relationship between fans and their beloved anime characters took an unusual turn in the fall of 2008. On October 22 of that year, a Japanese man by the name of Taichi Takashita set up an online petition to call for legal recognition of the right to marry an anime character. He offered the following explanation: "Nowadays, we have no interest in the three-dimensional world. If it were possible, I think I'd rather live in a two-dimensional world. But this doesn't seem likely with today's technology. So can't we at least have marriage to a two-dimensional character legally recognized? If that happens, my plan is to marry Mikuru Asahina."[1] Within a week, roughly a thousand people had signed on, expressing their support for this unlikely project, and more than three thousand had signed on some two months later. Many signers mentioned the characters they would marry. Other signers took it as a curious joke. "I'd like to meet you distributing this petition in person," said one. A number of journalists and bloggers outside Japan picked up the story, mostly with a tone of joking about "those wacky Japanese," but also with a hint of sociological wonderment. Given the tendency for young Japanese nowadays to delay marriage, doesn't this signify more trouble in the future? One online commentator even speculated on possible legal ramifications: "Will Mr. Takashita be paying royalties to comic book creators? Or does he consider copyright protection a form of 2D slavery?"[2]

The idea of developing relationships, or even falling in love, with fictional characters is not especially new, nor is it unique to anime. Yet the debates surrounding Japan's obsessive fans, often identified as *otaku*, and their self-involved attachments are interesting for how they constitute a particular kind of argument about the future of masculinity and love and, in turn, the mutual imbrication of niche and mass. This provides another dimension for considering issues surrounding the control and circulation of value—in this case, the value of private, inconspicuous consumption as a legitimate expression of manhood.

Part of what gives the debate about Japanese men and anime characters a certain cultural specificity is not only the strange category of men known as otaku but also the notion of *moe* ("moh-ay"), which is loosely a term for affectionate longing for 2D characters or, more accurately, a reference to an internalized emotional response to something, generally with no hope for a reciprocal emotional payback.[3] In discussions about the cultural significance of anime in Japan, the idea of *moe* is also associated with larger questions about how fans relate to virtual characters and worlds and, in turn, about the power of media producers vis-à-vis consumers. For some writers, *moe* constitutes a "love revolution"—that is, an example of pure love and a logical extension of the shift from analog to digital technology. For another theorist, *moe* symbolizes a postmodern, "database" form of consumption, whereby today's otaku reject the experience of the larger stories of anime and favor instead the piecemeal sampling of elements of 2D characters.

What I find most provocative about the notion of *moe* is the assertion of the value of an internalized consumption. In chapter 6, I considered the expansionary force of overseas fans, a dark energy poorly captured by a commodity market view of media content. Here I would like to map some of the ways an internalized value is described as a means to point toward a new kind of politics. At least, *moe* offers an intriguing alternative to a focus on productivity as the measure of a man. Otaku raise this question: What kind of value arises from consumption, especially if that consumption is immaterial, a kind of affective attachment—simply, in a word, love?

Otaku versus the Salaryman

In some ways, the image of a Japanese otaku as an obsessive, socially inept, technologically fluent nerd represents a type of manhood that is a polar opposite to that of the gregarious, socializing, breadwinning salaryman. If the salaryman is measured by his productivity, then the loner otaku, with his comic book collections, expensive figurines, and encyclopedic knowledge of trivia, can be viewed as a puzzle of rampant asocial consumerism. The anthropologists James Roberson and Nobue Suzuki argue that, until recently, the dominant image of men and masculinity has been the "middle-class, heterosexual, married salaryman considered as responsible for and representative of 'Japan'" (2003: 1). Their edited volume aims to dislocate the taken-for-granted salaryman image of manhood by providing instead a variety of "ethnographically-based understandings which are sensitive to the reflexivities of the lived, constructed and embedded . . . diversity of masculinities in contemporary Japan" (2003: 5). Arguably, otaku represent part of that diversity, all the more so with their widening presence as a stock figure in Japanese popular culture, as portrayed, for example, in the film *Otaku no Video* (dir. Takeshi Mori, 1991), in the TV series *Paranoia Agent* (dir. Satoshi Kon, 2004), and in the Densha Otoko (Train Man) phenomenon, discussed later in this chapter. Yet the discourses around *moe* and otaku aim not only to illustrate variety, but also to establish different grounds for evaluating masculinity and, in turn, the value of anime.

In the United States, "otaku" is often used simply to mean "serious anime fan" (with a fairly positive connotation), but in Japan the term carries a more complex range of meanings. In general, the word indicates people with an obsessiveness toward "geeky" realms of knowledge and activity, such as cult anime, manga, computer games, military trivia, and so on. Images of the otaku in Japan tend to oscillate between negative portrayals focusing on antisocial behavior and potentially dangerous habits, on one hand, and, on the other, positive portrayals of future-oriented, postindustrial sensibilities that contribute to the global strength of Japanese products in popular culture. Of course, delving below the surface reveals that the debates surrounding otaku for the past twenty years complicate such a simple binary opposition. Scholars in Japan distinguish sharp generational differences among otaku-type cultures; there are gender differences as well. Indeed, even the word "otaku" is a slight misnomer in the sense that people who identify as these kinds of devoted fans today tend to use the shortened version "*ota*" (katakana "*wo*" and "*ta*"), in part as a way to distinguish themselves from older generations of otaku. Moreover, although otaku stereotypically tend to be male, there are female otaku, who are sometimes called *fujoshi* (lit., "rotten girls"), a term commonly used for the young female devotees of "boys' love" comic books, which portray beautiful boys in romantic relationships with each other. The science-fiction writer Mari Kotani, who organizes a club event for women obsessed with eyeglasses (*megane moe*), has noted that she is too old to be a rotten girl, so she prefers the term "*kifujin*," a pun on "aristocratic lady," with the kanji character for "woman" (*fu*) replaced with "rotten." Given these variations, Thomas LaMarre (2006b: 360) cautions against looking at otaku as a "bounded culture, psychology, or identity," and proposes instead that it makes the most sense to look at otaku activities in terms of labor. The question for him is not who is or is not an otaku but, rather, what do otaku-type activities do and do they constitute a kind of labor that can subvert, or provide an alternative to, capitalist control? In an analogous way, my look at discourses surrounding otaku is not meant to describe a bounded culture, identity, or psychology but, rather, aims to explore the meanings of consuming the virtual and how the social energy of collaborative creativity is found even here.

Many interpretations of otaku masculinity share an assumption with salaryman masculinity—namely, that value (a man's worth) tends to be grounded in productivity. If we consider some examples of "bad otaku" and "good otaku," we can see that they are deemed significant because of what they produce. Some "bad otaku" are notable for producing violence or disturbing, sexualized media. In 1988, the term "otaku" gained notoriety after the arrest of a serial killer named Tsutomu Miyazaki, who was accused of being an avid consumer of slasher kiddie porn manga (though in fact very little of this manga was found in his room). Less extreme but more widespread are those fans who produce their own comic books (*dōjinshi*), many of which explore varieties of playfully transgressive eroticism, as discussed by the sociologist Sharon Kinsella (1998), among others. More recently, in June 2008, a deranged twenty-five-year-old man attacked random people in the Akihabara section of Tokyo, killing seventeen, an act that, according to one commentator, "condenses the whole of the present" as a representative incident in part because the murderer declared his intentions online prior to committing the act (Ōzawa 2008: v).

In contrast, "good otaku" have been recuperated as leaders in the new information society, again because of what they produce. The game designer Satoshi Tajiri, for example, developed the *Pokémon* handheld video-game that eventually led to a global media bonanza. As Anne Allison (2006) describes, Tajiri's desire to use virtual worlds as a way to reconnect with other (living) people was part of what drove fascination with the *Pokémon* game, where players could not complete their collections unless they communicated with others. Susan Napier (2011) discusses the Train Man phenomenon, which shows how otaku can also be portrayed as sensitive diamonds in the rough, whose nerdiness can disguise a more generous manhood than that of drunken and emotionally distant salarymen. In each case, however, the measure of the man is his productivity: making a video-game, producing animated films, or, in the case of the Train Man, remaking himself. "Bad otaku" also are evaluated based on what they make, whether it is violence or homemade media. Although a focus on otaku-type masculinities can help complicate the too simple equation of manhood in Japan with the salaryman, we still remain wedded to a notion of manhood centered on productivity and heteronormative sexuality. Patrick Galbraith (2009) notes, "The *moe* man is actually very conservative in rejecting casual or paid sex and advocating imaginary marriage emblazoned in pet names for favorite characters such as *ore no yome* (my bride) or *nounai tsuma* (imaginary wife)." However we define "otaku," we might learn the most by considering the distinctiveness of their approaches to consumption. A powerful image of the so-called otaku is their attraction to virtual characters.

Character *Moe*

The debates surrounding anime and otaku often revolve around the elusive concept of the "character" as something that exists beyond its particular media instantiations. Takashita, the petitioner above, for example, does not say he wishes to marry "anime characters" per se, but rather 2D (*nijigen*) characters. This is partly because many of these characters move fluidly across media, including the character he mentions, Mikuru Asahina. She was introduced in 2003 in the serialized "light novel" (i.e., young adult fiction) *The Melancholy of Haruhi Suzumiya*, by Nagaru Tanigawa, as a *moe* character wearing outfits associated with otaku culture, such as a maid's uniform or bunny ears. The novel was made into a very successful anime TV series in 2006 by Kyoto Animation (see Condry 2011b). As we have seen, characters not only move across media, but they help explain the logic of a variety of activities related to anime. At anime conventions, many fans dress as their favorite characters in the practice known as cosplay. Fanzine artists reimagine their favorite characters in new, at times erotic, situations in their homemade works. As mentioned earlier, Tokyo's fan-made manga convention Comic Market is the largest annual event held in all of Japan, drawing almost a half-million visitors over three days each August. Toy companies take advantage of fans' love for characters by marketing all manner of figurines and other licensed merchandise. Characters move across media and even beyond media, and in this circulation they tend to develop an internal coherence despite being fictional and virtual. In some ways, the concept of *moe* can be seen as an attempt to substantiate the reality of the virtual in terms of an internalized emotional response.

Moe is the noun form of the verb *moeru* (to burst into sprout, to bud), as in a ripening green plant just developing into maturity. The kanji is written with the grass (*kusa*) radical on top and the character for "bright, cheerful" (i.e., the sun and moon together) underneath. The kanji character thus acts as a visual reference to the fact that the *moe* attraction is often bestowed on 2D characters who are on the verge of maturing into young women. *Moe* does not refer to girls per se but to the yearning desire to care for, or nurture, them. In this sense it is also a pun on *moeru* (to boil, to burn), which is with a different kanji and can also be viewed as a reference to a heated sensual desire. The term *moe* is troubling to some people in Japan because it apparently centers on an inappropriate desire by relatively grown men for (imaginary) immature girls.[4]

Yet others argue that *moe* should be seen in terms of purity and that the youthful aspect of the characters evokes innocence, not depravity. As one Japanese college student explained to me, *moe* isn't about sex; rather, it's a light, warm, pleasant emotion. "Feeling strawberry," he proposed, using pseudo-English. Takuji Okuno offers a similar perspective:

> Originally, *moe* referred to the affectionate feelings (*renjō*) that today's otaku held for female manga and anime characters. The objects of that affection were generally *bishōjo* (beautiful young girls), but the roots were in sister-like characters—for example, Maetel in *Galaxy Express 999* or Fujiko Mine from Monkey Punch's *Lupin III*. Although these characters were always intimates, their positions were quite separate, which meant that affection could not be expressed directly. *Moe*, then, was that hazy (*moya-moya*) feeling. Now, men with that *moe* feeling collect posters and doll figures as the object of their affection. In other words, they take that 2D desire for the opposite sex and bring it into the 3D world (or, sometimes, they confuse the two worlds). (2007: 168)

Okuno points to the complexity of yearnings even within the virtual worlds, such that attraction was often balanced with a sense that the characters needed to be protected and cared for. We might recall that the founders of the anime studio Gainax also produced a videogame with precisely this theme of nurturing: the goal of the game was to raise a young princess to maturity (Takeda 2005). Yet I would argue that the *moe* feeling should be seen not as a confusion of the virtual worlds and real worlds but, rather, as a questioning of the relationship between the two—or, perhaps, as a question of whether there really is a distinction between virtual and real.

The book *Ken Otaku Ryu* (Hating the otaku wave [Nakahara et al. 2006]) is a published conversation between defenders and detractors of otaku and extends the discussion of *moe* and love. In one section, the editors debate the idea that what *moe* offers is "pure love" (*jun'ai*) that exceeds what can be had with real women. One skeptic notes when one types "*moe*" into an Internet search engine, most of the hits are pornographic. Doesn't that mean that *moe* is mostly a euphemism for pornography? The otaku writer Melon Uminekozawa says no: "Even within pure love, can't there be an element of eroticism? . . . It's absolutely possible to feel pure love for a 2D character. I've had 2D characters that I'd think about, and like so much, that I couldn't escape from their spell. . . . Inside me, that character was a god. I really believe that's true *moe*. I might even be considered a *moe* fundamentalist. . . . The feeling of *moe* is exactly the same as love (*koi*)" (quoted in Nakahara et al. 2006: 61–63). Uminekozawa justifies the legitimacy of this kind of love in terms of a deep, inner feeling.

In many ways, this echoes a statement the anime director Hayao Miyazaki made while recalling the anime feature film *Legend of the White Serpent* (*Hakujaden*), which he saw as a high school senior in 1958: "I have to make an embarrassing confession. I fell in love with the heroine of a cartoon movie. My soul was moved. . . . Maybe I was in a depressed state of mind because of the [university] entrance exams, or [maybe the cause was] my undeveloped adolescence, or cheap melodrama—it's easy to analyze and dismiss it, but the meeting with *Legend of the White Serpent* left a strong impression on my immature self" (quoted in McCarthy 1999). Put this way, to desire an animated character seems quite reasonable. The anime scholar Helen McCarthy, who translated Miyazaki's statement, argues that this moment was instrumental in shifting his attention away from manga and more toward anime. Yet we can also hear in Miyazaki's words an element of embarrassment. He fears he was "immature," that his feeling might have been a symptom of a larger distress (depression), or perhaps his feeling was simply something "cheap" and superficial. Nevertheless, the feeling made a deep impression on him.

If one's relationship with virtual characters is deeply moving, and if it can influence the course of people's careers, why should there be any prejudice against this kind of attachment? One reason is that it seems to propose a rejection of society and more traditional measures of manhood.

Denpa Otoko (Radiowave Man)

A writer who uses the pen name Tōru Honda takes the idea of *moe* farther than most. He proclaims that *moe* represents nothing less than the dawning of a love revolution. Calling himself Denpa Otoko (Radiowave Man), he deliberately positions himself in contrast to the cultural phenomenon of Densha Otoko (Train Man), another popular image of contemporary otaku manhood. "Train Man" refers to a phenomenon that began on 2.chan ("two channel," or *nichan* in Japanese), an online message board that facilitates anonymous discussions. In the Train Man story, an otaku is on a train returning from shopping in Akihabara when he witnesses a drunken salaryman harassing a woman. The otaku man intervenes. Later, when the woman sends him a note thanking him for what he did, the otaku man realizes that this is his chance to ask a woman out on a date, something he has never done before. He goes to 2.chan for advice and over the next weeks and months, an online community coaches him about dating and women and things go pretty well (Nakano 2004). There is some debate about whether the events actually happened (maybe I'm a romantic, but I think they did), but in any case, the story captured the Japanese public's imagination. There are books, a TV series, and a decent film dramatizing this contemporary love affair. In this portrayal, the otaku becomes a man by shedding his awkwardness and getting the girl in real life. This is absolutely unacceptable for Radiowave Man (Honda 2005). To him, Train Man is a travesty.

According to Honda, otaku should not be ashamed of their alternative values. An otaku should be proud of his masculinity, even if he is enamored only of fictional 2D characters with big eyes, beribboned hair, and short skirts. Indeed, Honda views young men's fascination with 2D characters as the natural evolution of mankind. He even declares it a revolution comparable to that of the Meiji Restoration in 1868, when America's "black ships" forced the opening of Japan to foreign trade, the downfall of the military government, and the restoration of imperial rule:

> For people who have grown up with the "common sense" that love equals the 3D world, it may be impossible to convey the point I'd like to make: 3D love is like the Edo era's shogunate government. Throughout that period, everyone thought that the shogunate would continue forever. It was almost impossible to imagine another kind of government, and floating in this

vague understanding, all of a sudden, the black ships appeared. . . . Now, the love revolution (*ren'ai kakumei*) expanding in Japan is easiest to understand in terms of the Meiji Restoration. For a long time, everyone expected the common sense belief that "love = 3D world" would continue, but it has begun to be destroyed by the appearance of the *moe* phenomenon. (Honda 2005: 142)

Honda adds that people who do not fall for 2D characters are behind the times. He makes his case by construing history as a linear evolution defined by technology, an aspect of otaku discourses that LaMarre (2006b) notes, as well. According to Honda, digital technology such as cameras and plasma-screen TV sets were initially regarded as lacking "warmth" and "reality," for example, when professional photographers found fault with digital photos or nightclub DJs rejected CDs in favor of vinyl records. In the end, Honda reminds us, everyone came to embrace the digital; the same thing, he says, will happen with love. Just as VCRs (analog) gave way to DVD players (digital), so men will also give up on the analog world of real women in favor of the digital world of characters. While it might be easy to dismiss such proclamations, I would argue that examining some of these notions of manliness may be helpful for seeing the contours of normative masculinity. Certainly, *moe* masculinity runs afoul of society's standards of measuring men by their productivity. But Radiowave Man speaks to a broader concern among men generally.

Forgiving Unsuccessful Men

One can read Radiowave Man's manifesto not primarily as a rejection of relationships with real women but, more important, as a defense of failed men. This echoes what Michael Kimmel calls a "two-sided posture" necessary for masculinity studies: "One must engage masculinity critically as ideology, as institutionally embedded within a field of power, as a set of practices engaged in by groups of men. And yet given the contradictory locations experienced by most men, men not privileged by class, race, ethnicity, sexuality, age, physical abilities, one must also consider a certain forgiveness for actual embodied men as they attempt to construct lives of some coherence and integrity in a world of clashing and contradictory filaments of power and privilege" (Kimmel 2002: x). This helps explain why so much otaku-oriented anime contains troubled male protagonists who essentially reimagine the hero as vulnerable, conflicted, and anything but all-powerful. Napier sees this in Shinji, the fourteen-year-old male character from the mecha (giant robot) TV series *Neon Genesis Evangelion* in the mid-1990s: "His conflict with his father, issues with women, and generally antiheroic attitude toward saving the Earth lead up to the rich portrait of full-fledged neurosis" (2005: 123). Yet ultimately, Shinji is the hero of the series, and his weaknesses prove instrumental in reshaping the destiny of mankind, partly through passive acquiescence but also with a sense that developing a new future requires alternative styles of heroic action. Even passive, insecure, dubiously virile warriors have a place in saving the world in many anime series.

In other words, if the salaryman stood for one model of Japan's economic productivity, I would argue that otaku represent a new form of manhood through consumption that offers an alternative vision of value —one that can provide new insight into the contemporary era. For example, an otaku perspective on masculinity reminds us of the vulnerability experienced by many men who live outside the dominant ideal of male success. Not all men get the good education, the good job (and salary), the loving wife and children. What then? It makes sense to find alternative sources of value in one's life, to rationalize alternative modes of existence as engaged, rewarding, and meaningful. Think of the global obsession with sports and sports talk. Otaku are by no means unique in this regard. Sabine Frühstück notes that, for many male service members, joining the Japanese Self-Defense Forces (SDF) "is marked by a sense of defeat in some area of their lives," such as a failed college entrance exam, a low-income background that precludes costly training at technical schools, a feeling of disappointment in one's job situation, or an inability to find meaningful work. Joining the SDF offers a new chance. But because SDF soldiers are prohibited from engaging in combat missions, the men are also closed off from a sense of accomplishment that might come with valor on the battlefield, the traditional measure of value for the military man. Frühstück shows how, nevertheless, the service uses gender politics to create "true men" and a new kind of "postwarrior heroism" that does not depend on courageous action in battle. Instead, it places value in individual sacrifice and personal betterment through training (2007: 12).

Similarly, otaku may be unsuccessful in the salaryman's world, but the public discussion of the legitimacy of love for anime characters also points to realms in which actively debating which character you would marry is of real value. The online petition created a space for many to make similar claims of love and commitment to virtual characters. Other online message boards also facilitate a kind of community building around emotions evoked by 2D characters. In other words, what makes the debate about otaku masculinity interesting is not only the expansion of varieties of manhood, but also the challenge of rethinking how productivity and consumption offer alternative modes for evaluating contemporary men. This, too, can widen our thinking about a critical theory of production in terms of collaborative creativity.

Consuming the Postmodern Database

We can extend our consideration of *moe* consumption through a look at the philosopher Hiroki Azuma's claim that otaku-type cultures (*otakukei bunka*) reflect a new orientation toward viewing the world as a large database. He contrasts his perspective with that of the manga artist and critic Eiji Ōtsuka, who argues that what fans consume when they buy merchandise related to an anime or manga is a piece of a "grand narrative" (*ōki na monogatari*) (Azuma 2001: 42–55). According to Ōtsuka (2004), revisiting an argument he made years earlier, stories have replaced ideologies in guiding our understanding of social action. For Ōtsuka, the power of media arises from the productivity of creators, and when fans relate to characters, they become engrossed in a larger narrative world in which the characters live. Clearly, however, when otaku fans express a desire to marry an anime character, they are making a bid to recontextualize the worlds in which characters exist. Azuma theorizes this as a shift away from consuming a "story" toward dipping into a "database."

We might view this debate in terms of the different kinds of value that arise from productivity and from consumption. Ōtsuka recognizes the central place of characters in understanding contemporary anime fandom, but as a writer, he emphasizes the critical judgment of producers in developing characters with a breath of life and stories that evoke a contemporary urgency. Azuma, by contrast, notes that otaku tend to be fascinated by small details, diverse elements of overall projects, regardless of their connection to the internal logic of anime stories. Azuma describes this as a "database model" of consumption, whereby individual consumers actively choose elements of the anime that they feel are most important, regardless of whether they are central to the overall "story" designed by the producers.

Azuma views the subjectivity of the "I" (and eye) as determinant. "The 'I' extracts the story," he says (Azuma 2001: 52), and the arrow of causality runs from the eye to the deeper database. In this regard, the lesson that Azuma takes from the anime series *Neon Genesis Evangelion* is different from those taken by Napier or Mariana Ortega (2007), both of whom center their arguments on the complex storyline. In contrast, Azuma says that the series was important not because of its narrative but because of the database of elements it presented (2001: 62). His use of the term "database" is meant to highlight the diversity of elements of the different characters (e.g., the neurotic and inarticulate Shinji, the brash and self-assertive Asuka, the affectless but powerful Rei) and the world setting in which they interact. Audience members frustrated by the inconsistencies of the narrative may be missing the larger point, Azuma implies, by not focusing on the details and relating to them individually. As proof of this kind of consumption, which Azuma relates to *moe*, he describes the phenomenon that arose around another character that became popular before it even had a story.

According to Azuma, the appearance of a character called Di Gi Charat (*Dejikyaratto*) marked a symbolic moment in the development of the *moe* phenomenon in that it exposed the new modes of masculinity arising from this database style of otaku consumption. The character's name combines "digital," "character," and "cat," although it is more commonly referred to as Dejiko (see figure 31).

Dejiko was created in 1998 to be the mascot for a videogame magazine (Azuma 2001: 63–66). The character had absolutely no story and no background associated with it—I mean, her. Gradually, her popularity increased. She got her big break when she appeared on a TV commercial in 1999. By 2000, she had her own anime series and later appeared in novels and merchandise. Azuma says that Dejiko's character elements, not the story behind her, are what led to her popularity. The proof is that she grew popular before a story was created. We can see that Dejiko's elements include a maid's uniform; cat ears, mittens, and tail; and bells in her hair. Azuma relates the rise of Dejiko to a larger phenomenon: that of otaku who compile online databases of imaginary characters from anime, manga, videogames, and other sources, adding keyword tags to identify different elements of each character.

Azuma's perspective extends our understanding of how characters operate as particular kinds of platforms, suggesting that modes of interpretation can be far more varied than we might assume. For example, the *moe*

31. Dejiko, a character with no story, is now a multimedia phenomenon (from http://www.broccoli.co.jp/dejiko [accessed December 5, 2007]).

idea locates the value of characters not in the producer's intentions but in the consumers' uptake. The importance of understanding varieties of consumption and how these interpretive practices by fans may speak more broadly to gender can be seen in a consideration of Judith Butler's notion of performativity. She says her notion of performativity grew from thinking about Franz Kafka's short story "Before the Law": "There the one who waits for the law, sits before the door of the law, attributes a certain force to the law for which one waits." Her point is that in this situation, the law gains its force not from an external authority, but from an internal anticipation. By extension, she asks "whether we do not labor under a similar expectation concerning gender, that it operates as an interior essence that might be disclosed, an expectation that ends up producing the very phenomenon it anticipates" (Butler 1990: xv). Performativity locates the source of power in gender relations at least partly in our suppositions about what the future holds. This brings into focus the importance of subjective analytics, which through recursive actions reinforce (or subvert) gendered patterns.

Yet Butler also draws attention to the need to link this internal anticipation back out into the public world. We have to ask, how does this reframe the contexts in which we imagine social action? Azuma's database idea explains why Dejiko is a pivotal example for contemporary shifts in viewing masculinity and value in terms of consumption rather than production. Di Gi Charat was created by combining elements of *moe*—cat ears, mittens, bells, maid's uniform—in a way that drew attention not to some underlying original story, but to a sense of attraction within the consumer. But the consequences for a performativity that acts in some way on the larger social world seems only weakly defined in Azuma's model. The consequences of consumption seem to vanish into a dark well of otaku emotionality, with little impact on the real world of women and men. This is related more broadly to otaku theorizing of the aesthetics of the anime image.

LaMarre offers a very helpful discussion of Azuma's emphasis on image and information over narrative. In considering several otaku commentators, including the neo-pop artist Takashi Murakami, Toshio Okada, the self-proclaimed "ota king" who founded Gainax, Azuma, and others, LaMarre identifies common threads through what he calls the "Gainax discourse," such as a shared sense of the operation of the anime image and of anime aesthetics. When otaku go frame by frame to observe the jet trails of missiles or the space battles of giant robots, their obsessive attention to detail, with little regard for the overall story, is representative of a particular approach to aesthetics in which the anime image becomes "a nonhierarchized field of information. . . . In other words, the distributive visual field involves a breakdown in perceptual distance, which results in a purely affective relation to the image. Anime breaks out of its television frame, and the distance between viewer and image collapses into a moment of affect" (2006b: 368). The Gainax discourse argues for a breakdown in the guiding power of the narrative, as well as a parallel breakdown in the hierarchy of producers (there is no single creator), a breakdown in the hierarchies between fan and producer, and a radical break with definable subject positions (LaMarre 2006b). This relates to our original question about otaku and modes of masculinity by locating the power of the character not in the vision of the creators—that is, as arising from productivity— but, instead, in the ex post facto consumption by, and devotion of, fans. Yet this is where the emotion seems to end—namely, in the eye ("I") of the otaku interpreter. But if there is no connection back into the story, and the meaning of the character is embodied only in the feelings of individual otaku who have an affective response, we reach a theoretical dead end, a *moe* cul-de-sac.

Rediscovering Social Context

A path out of this emotional Never Never Land comes from attending to some of the ways the social context is present for, but insufficiently attended to by, those who analyze *moe* as a purely internalized response. By explaining consumption in terms of a disembodied eye, Azuma loses sight of the embeddedness of the "database" in larger social worlds. Azuma might have a better argument about the radical subjectivity arising from otaku love for characters if those people were to fall in love with characters they created themselves. But the objects of *moe* fascination are public and usually well-known characters, at least within particular communities of fans. Among those who signed the petition calling for the legal recognition of marriage to an anime character, those who identified a character they would marry drew from well-known examples. *Moe* is not just a feeling; it is also a way to talk about one's feelings and, without having to give much explanation, share the glow of affection with others who might have similar feelings. This is true of Dejiko. One could argue that she had a "soul" of sorts before her anime and manga serials were developed. When fans became interested in Dejiko, they inserted her into their own personal histories of caring for—or, at least, being interested in—characters. The growth of her popularity is the story, the background, the lived presence that gives the *moe* feeling a certain substance as a social phenomenon. This "internal" feeling, in the end, is a collaborative creation.

In addition, the theory of otaku consumption makes it easy to conclude that tuning in to the details of the anime results in the tuning out of society, whether in the form of real women or in the broader, shared narratives aimed for by producers. Takashita, the marriage petitioner, and Radiowave Man both give that impression by saying they have no interest in the 3D world or real women. This is the common image of the otaku as withdrawing from society into a world of affective consumption. But Takashita and Radiowave Man are also making their arguments publicly to a broader social world. Takashita didn't just want a change in the law; he wanted to announce the name of the character he would marry. (I imagine the latter expression was the greater impetus.) The "individual" *moe* feeling is something debated in many online realms in which fans can discuss the merits of different characters. The message board 2.chan, the social networking site Mixi, and video-sharing sites are just some examples of places to discuss various flavors of affective, 2D desire. To say this is somehow separate from the "3D world" makes no sense.

Consider, for example, the video-sharing site Nico Nico Douga, which in June 2008 was at the center of a minor *moe* scandal. Japan's Imperial Household Agency expressed dismay when a video clip showing fan-made images of Princess Mako, who was then seventeen, starting gaining attention online.[5] Amateur artists had transformed her into an anime character, complete with her image's appearance in music videos. Significantly, what makes Nico Nico Douga a huge phenomenon in Japan is that it combines the accessibility of YouTube with the public commentary of an online message board. Visitors can add their comments to low-resolution videos uploaded by users, and the comments scroll by as the video plays. The adoring messages posted by some users were then reported on in Japan as an example of "Princess Mako *moe*" (*Mako-sama moe*). Although this can be read as creating a 2D image that is detached from the real-world princess, one can find an alternative reading by attending to the commentary that scrolls by as the "*moe* images" appear. Some of the text commentary roughly translates as, "This is trouble for the Imperial Household Agency . . . A recommendation from Central Office of *Moe* . . . To the Emperor, banzai!" Arguably, it is the urge to make public displays within a community of peers who care that makes the *moe* phenomenon significant.

In sum, although the *moe* feeling may be internalized, it is connected to a broader range of politics and social settings. Collaborative creativity applies even to something as personal and intimate as "feeling strawberry." Radiowave Man's arguments about preferring 2D characters to 3D women and Azuma's emphasis on the radical immanence of the anime image both can be seen as gambits to encourage society to grant some respect to the depth of otaku emotionality. With the marriage petition, as well, what may be most striking is not the desire to move into a 2D world but the desire to have love for 2D characters *legally* recognized by the broader society. After all, it is difficult to imagine that much would change in a relationship between a person and a 2D character if they could somehow be married. What might change is that people who fall in love with characters could gain a measure of societal acceptance. This alters how we should interpret the debates about otaku and masculinity. Rather than seeing the assertions of the value of *moe* affect as a rejection of real women and the 3D world, we should view it instead as a plea for accepting a new kind of relationship between consumption as feeling (as love) and society.

Conclusion

This look at *moe* adds another dimension to our thinking about niche and mass in anime fandom. As anime becomes more mainstream both in Japan and around the world, we can observe in the *moe* boom the emergence of new kinds of niches.

It is easy to dismiss as ludicrous a petition calling on society to legally recognize marriage to an anime character. One can see it as a joke, as some signers did. Or one might express concern for men who are so pathetic that they can only hope to have relationships with virtual characters. What is lost in such reactions, however, is the idea that discussions about otaku and *moe* attractions provide a perspective on thinking more generally about the effects of virtual worlds and the value of an internalized, immaterial consumption. For one thing, we can observe how evaluating masculinity tends to emphasize men's productive capacities rather than their consumer experiences. Even when we evaluate consumerism, we tend to emphasize how it may contribute to economic growth; our spending is seen as productive in the sense that it enables businesses to keep investing, furthering the cycle of market expansion. The online commentator who wondered whether marriage to a 2D character would require royalties to be paid to creators is a perfect example of the urge to translate immaterial, internalized consumption into something outwardly productive. These measures of value depend on a logic of productivity. Discourses about otaku affect may offer an alternative style of manhood to that of salary-men, yet both "good otaku" and "bad otaku" tend to be held up to standards of creating things, whether commodifiable goods or havoc.

The idea of relating to anime primarily in terms of "love" can be viewed as a gesture toward a different basis for understanding value, consumerism, and media. The debate between Ōtsuka and Azuma also can be interpreted as a way to wrestle divergent understandings of how people should relate to media content, and in some ways their debate reproduces this conflict between valuing producers' grand narratives and consumers' piecemeal sampling. Both, however, might be faulted for construing their conclusions too narrowly—that is, seeing them primarily as saying something about anime, manga, and otaku. A more complete investigation would include an analysis of the heteronormative stereotyping at work here, too. As Laura Miller (2011) shows more generally, much of the discussion about "Cool Japan" centers on "male geek culture," which tends to gravitate toward a limited set of ideas of cute femininity.

Nevertheless, an alternative to viewing the desire to marry an anime character as perversity might be to acknowledge this as part of a struggle for the control and circulation of value. In the case of character *moe*, this power is pointed inward, to help overcome loneliness. This is media as meditative tool, not potential investment. Put that way, can't we see the parallels with Radiowave Man, Azuma, and some of our own attachments to great works of art, however we define greatness? Perhaps "feeling strawberry" is a chance to feel more whole. For us to recognize such varieties of masculinity, we may also need to recognize the varieties of masculine failure and how success and failure themselves are the products of ideological orientations toward value. In this respect, theories of otaku fans' emotional attachments to virtual objects are useful for proposing an alternative to thinking about manhood in terms of productivity. This circulatory energy around the love of characters implicitly depends on recognizing the legitimacy of those feelings by others.

Otaku men as a symbol offer a means of seeing the variety of ways in which consumption of the "virtual" has real-world substance. It is the desire for public recognition and acceptance that is shared across Takashita's marriage petition, Radiowave Man, Azuma, and others. Quite the opposite of a rejection of society, this is, rather, an affirmation of the importance of social acceptance. In this, our otaku brethren may not be so different from the rest of us. Or perhaps there is a little bit of otaku in all of us. In any case, the tendency to view otaku as separate, wacky, or just weird tends to obfuscate the ways in which otaku fans' attitudes reveal something about us all. In rushing to ridicule those pathetic fans who would rather marry an anime character than go through the trouble of relating to real others, we risk reinforcing a too simple naturalness to social mores. The workings of anime and masculinity can be best understood if we move beyond thinking of otaku as a bounded culture or identity and think more deeply instead about how *moe* consumption may be part of a broader range of social transformations. Ultimately, we see that the wider collaborative potential of new media can help produce extremely idiosyncratic and personal affects, so that even the seemingly asocial love for a 2D character in fact illuminates the emergence of alternative social worlds.

Future Anime

COLLABORATIVE CREATIVITY
AND CULTURAL ACTION

✱ In this book, I have focused on the collaborative creativity that links the labor of art and the labor of fans in the making of anime as a cultural phenomenon. Anime extends from wide-ranging television broadcasts and film showings to fan conventions with cosplay, anime music videos, and much more, as well as to a huge inventory of ancillary merchandise. This media success story has amplified the image of Japan as a leader in global popular culture. Of course, anime is just part of a broader transmedia nexus that includes manga, videogames, fashion, design, contemporary art, and more—cultural output that the journalist Douglas McGray (2002) identified as a kind of "gross national cool" and that, he proposes, constitutes a reinvention of superpower. One wonders, of course, how the image of Japan will change in the aftermath of the Tōhoku earthquake and tsunami of March 11, 2011. Whatever other images we already had, when foreigners think of Japan today those images are layered with the heart-rending photos and videos of a moving avalanche of black water carrying houses, burning buildings, cars, and boats in a deadly flow. It is imaginable that "Cool Japan" will be replaced by "Dangerous Japan" as a dominant idea, especially in light of the crisis at the Fukushima Daiichi Nuclear Power Station (Condry 2011a). But if collaborative creativity teaches us anything, it is that collective responses to big ideas can diverge in interesting and often unpredictable ways. Perhaps, as the novelist Junot Diaz (2011) argues in relation to the catastrophic earthquake in Haiti in 2010, disasters are kinds of apocalypses that reveal the social underpinnings of inequality. Ideally, the triple disaster in Japan will reinforce a more people-centered vision of the nation.

Whether or not "3/11," as the Tōhoku earthquake and tsunami have come to be known, augurs the end of Cool Japan, we can agree that the designation "Cool" was a poor label to begin with. Even as a fan of anime and manga, I have to admit that many of the examples used in this book would be seen by many friends and colleagues as more like "geek" Japan. Maybe "geek" is a better term—at least it captures the fact that "cool" functions only inside particular social worlds. One person's cool is another's geekdom. Cool Japan is a misnomer in another sense: The vitality of anime doesn't arise from "Japan" per se. Eiji Ōtsuka argues that anime's origins in American comics and animation make the media form transnational through and through (Ōtsuka and Ōsawa 2005). We can add, looking at current production processes, that the majority of frames for anime are drawn overseas, especially in South Korea, China, and the Philippines (Mōri 2011). Anime may come from Japan, sort of, but national culture doesn't explain the industry's development. Other contexts provide a more nuanced sense of the crucibles of creativity that matter. These are larger than individual creators and their studios and smaller in numbers than the nation as a whole but networked transnationally both in production and consumption.

It makes sense to look at anime as emerging from a certain kind of platform, starting with characters and worlds on which others build, while also considering how specific social contexts define participation and engagement. Ethnography is a very useful means of exploring these dimensions of our social reality, because fieldworkers can gain access to that which is most meaningful to people through proximity and persistence. I use "soul," despite possibly problematic connotations, partly because the term often came up during the fieldwork to describe that which was most meaningful in anime. When I heard the Japanese word *tamashii* (soul), it gestured toward what makes animation good, drawing us toward questions of style while also intimating a connection to feeling, maybe even an emergent life force. Most often this is spoken of as a characteristic that resides within the style of particular anime or the vision of a particular author—for example, "Miyazaki anime" in *Spirited Away* or "Oshii's style" in the film versions of *Ghost in the Shell*. But we can also think of aesthetics as arising out of conversations about value. To be sure, the quality of anime was evaluated in many other ways: in terms of the artwork, the characters, the worldview, and the pacing; in terms of whether the anime was "alive" (*ikite ru*) and more. "Soul" generally referred to something more elusive. For example, I sometimes heard Japanese anime creators say that hand-drawn characters tend to have more "soul" than those constructed through computer modeling, although, of course, most people's interest here was in what people accomplished with technology rather than in judging on the basis of the kind of technology used. The worlds of Japanese animation tend to emphasize hand-drawn, cel-type animation, but many styles of contemporary animation are being produced in Japan, including puppet animation, *ga nime* ("picture anime"), the fine arts style of Akino Kondoh (e.g., *Densha ka mo shirenai*), and much more.

Because the soul implies the ability to move across planes of existence, it hints at the transmedia flows that characterize contemporary forms of communication. What is it that flows between manga, anime, drama CDs, light novels, games, toys, merchandise? "Transmedia storytelling" brings into focus the design of the story and the narrative elaborations. To approach this as "marketing synergies" is to focus on the objects and brands that get linked through entertainment, licensing, and consumption. As I have tried to show, collaborative creativity aims to bring into focus the multiplicity of modes of production and what, exactly, collaboration means.[1] As I asked in the introduction, who is collaborating with whom? Who "owns" the results of collaboration? Whose creativity is valued; whose is recognized and within which spheres? How is collaboration something more than mere circulation, and in what ways does it overflow the categories of production and consumption? The answers depend on the ways that social and business worlds form a kind of scaffolding around which production achieves certain kinds of value. Obviously, I have not been exhaustive in evaluating all aspects of the anime phenomenon. Rather, I have tried to select entry points into the larger world for certain contrasts and connections. What we witness is a process of distributed innovation where what matters in each setting helps define the meanings of a broader, multifaceted whole.

How should we understand the global prominence of anime alongside the poor wages paid to animators? For one thing, the study of media too often neglects the laborers unless they are auteurs. At the same time, these on-the-ground workers can help us see the value of anime in a new light. Consider the short live-action film *Hope* (2009), directed by Michael Arias (the director of *Tekkon Kinkreet* discussed in chapter 5). The twenty-minute film dramatizes the work of an animator at an early stage of her career. The setting is after midnight, and the animator is working on in-between frames to smooth the movements of the key frames drawn by others. As she painstakingly draws a cat with big ears, she nods off. A second female animator sitting behind her, who presumably is more experienced, advises the first animator to take a short break and "reset" to get more work done. The first woman thanks her and takes her advice. She gets out a pillow, sets an alarm, and puts her head down on her desk but is awakened by a supervisor yelling, "What the hell are you doing sleeping on the job? We've got to get this up tomorrow. You're holding up the in-between check, the scanning, the whole team." The young woman says she's sorry, but the male supervisor keeps shouting at her: "You're so useless. This is your last warning. If you're not done by tomorrow, you're fired. Got it? Fired. Newbies these days, saying you're bored, wanting to go straight to drawing key frames, just whining and complaining. Your whole generation is nothing but a bunch of whiners!" The young female animator bows her head, apologizing. "I understand," she says and gets back to work.

After a while, the animator takes a break to get something to drink but ends up trapped in the building's jammed elevator—all night, as it turns out. Without a reason, the elevator opens in the morning, and the animator goes back to her desk. She finds her things stuffed in her purse and a note saying she's been fired. Understandably upset, she empties the contents of her purse, throwing her iPod, headphones, and magazines in the garbage. Then she scoops into her purse the stubs of the dozens of pencils she wore down to their nubs while doing her drawing work at the studio (see figure 32). Her labor means something, despite the bad ending. The film ends on this note of hope, her belief that the work she put into her craft is a step on the road to something bigger. The pencil stubs are a poignant symbol of the labor of animation, the personal efforts of many people. Don't we all hope that worn pencils like these will someday add up to something larger than ourselves?

32. Labor is what matters: an animator's used pencils from the film *Hope*.

What Japanese Films Can Go Global?

Anime illustrates the constructedness and variability of ideas of value in different crucibles of creativity. The "scale of analysis" question focuses us on which networked locations matter while setting aside the idea of an "origin" or "core" that can explain everything. As we saw with *Gundam*, the TV series that failed but was resurrected through fan activity and new merchandising, the world of entertainment is a complex, fickle business. It is no surprise that Japanese producers want to extend their reach even farther around the globe.

A special panel discussion on what films could compete in the world market, especially in North America and Europe, was held at the Tokyo International Film Festival (TIFF) in the fall of 2010. (Although China is viewed as a potentially huge market, earning profits there is seen as exceedingly difficult, given the bootlegging of DVDs and official limits on the importing of foreign films.) In fact, overseas markets were a recurring theme during my visits to policymakers and media companies in Tokyo in the fall of 2010. Japan's population is graying, manufacturing jobs continue to move offshore, and many questions are being raised about how to develop industries with export potential. The content industries of manga, anime, videogames, music, and film were being discussed in various forums in terms of their ability to attract overseas audiences. When I had dinner with a senior executive at the Japan External Trade Organization in 2010, he confessed that he was uncomfortable with the idea of trying to promote the "content industries" in other countries. "I think of Japan as a place that excels in 'making *things*' (*monodzukuri*)," he explained, but what kind of "thing" is media content? I suggested that he think of content as "making things that connect" (*tsunagari monodzukuri*). He liked that, he said, and went back to eating. Mika Takagi, the director of the Cool Japan (now Creative Industries) section of the Ministry of Economy, Trade, and Industry, was less interested in manga, anime, and games in the United States—"There are many businesses already successfully working in that space," she said—than in other parts of the world, such as Brazil and India.[2] A music intermediary company called E-Talent Bank was also busy working on plans to launch a social networking space for the French, Chinese, and North Americans to discuss Japanese popular culture online. For many, the future of Japan's media world increasingly seems to rely on markets outside the country.

The three participants in the panel discussion at TIFF also debated the possibilities for Japanese cinema, both live action and animated, to expand overseas. The panel was led by Utamaru, a radio personality and rapper who is known for doing penetrating, if offbeat, film reviews during his weekly radio show *Weekend Shuffle*. His cohost, Kou Furukawa, is a writer for music and anime magazines as well as the novelist who wrote spin-off novellas related to the anime series *Freedom*, which began as an advertising campaign for Cup Noodles. The third panelist was the screenwriter Yoshiki Takahashi.

The panel's title set the theme: "What Japanese films could be hits overseas? What Japanese films could the world be proud of?" (*Kaigai ni ukeru nihon eiga to wa nani ka? Sekai ga jiman saretai nihon eiga?*). The discussion highlighted the importance of differentiating two kinds of markets for cinema. At one level are mass-entertainment films, generally shown in three thousand or more theaters. To compete at the top level of the industry, a film has to be integrated into a massive system of distribution and promotion. As Takahashi pointed out, only one Japanese film has ever succeeded at that level: one of the early *Pokémon* features. At another level, there are smaller but still substantial markets in the more niche ends of the industry. An example here included *Machine Girl* about a wronged Japanese schoolgirl who metes out revenge with a machine gun grafted to her shoulder. Utamaru noted that for a while, *Machine Girl* was ranked the fourth most popular download on X-Box Live in the United States. In other words, this niche film had a chance in the context of film downloads, even though competing in mainstream theater multiplexes is out of the question. We can observe two things here. First, depending on the level of the media market—mainstream or cult—the measure of success is quite different. Second, to be successful at the top level requires a much broader system of related promotion and distribution, along the lines of Pokémon, than most anime distributors can afford. This points again to the importance of grasping the broader systemic forces that guide global popular culture and avoiding explanations that reduce success to the characteristics of content and the "resonance" with a certain kind of cultural backdrop. Looking at the emergence of success in terms of a kind of circulating social energy provides a theory for doing this because it reminds us that value is variable.

Value and Mr. Despair

The anime series *Sayonara Zetsubō Sensei* (Goodbye, Mr. Despair) includes a scene that similarly challenges us to rethink value in the contemporary world. The anime series, produced by the studio Shaft, is based on a gag manga by Kōji Kumeta that portrays a range of students facing ludicrous situations in a bizarre high school. In one episode, for example, the Japanese government decides to hire asocial *ani-ota* (serious fans) to protect the government's state secrets, the logic being that otaku who care only for characters in 2D worlds would not be seduced by temptresses of a rival government. And it works! The show walks a delicate line in its portrayal of the over-the-top attitudes of the characters, many of whom are joking adaptations of stock characters in anime and in the Japanese media more generally: an immigrant Filipino schoolgirl (who might be a boy); a blonde *gaijin* (foreigner) girl who thinks only about herself; a *hikikomori* (shut-in) girl, and so on. Ironic references to news "memes" (roughly, shareable kernels of thought)—or *neta*, as they are known in Japanese—are scattered throughout the series. Indeed, the series incorporates numerous visual and linguistic jokes, which are translated by participating fansub groups in remarkable detail. The fansubs explain, for example, how the central protagonist, the teacher of the class, has an almost-real-sounding name written in three *kanji* characters, Nozomu Itoshiki. But when the three kanji are combined into two characters, his name reads "despair" (*zetsubō*). Hence, the teacher is "Mr. Despair," and he comes with an attitude.

In one of the episodes, Mr. Despair uses the day of the students' physical exams to make a point about what is valuable, what is meaningful. The physical exams measure height, waist, chest, and weight, causing much emotional distress. Mr. Despair is shocked by the stupidity of this measure of value, so he makes an announcement:

> It seems today was the day of your physical examinations. But what is the point of focusing only on your outward appearance? Your physical body will eventually crumble. After you die, your ashes will be scattered on Ayers Rock. What's the point of worrying about such worldly matters? Like your company's market cap, how many calories on the menu, or the number of hits on your blog, or the sales of your book? The fact that mere numbers can make people rejoice or grieve is why Japan has become bizarre![3]

Too many people "don't know their own value," he says. Some people get biometric (finger scan) bank ATM cards even though they have only $50 in the bank, or buy enormous plasma TVs for tiny apartments. "Know yourself," intones Mr. Despair, "or you will succumb in every battle (by Sun Tzu)."

Mr. Despair is not satisfied with complaining; he has a solution. He announces that he has a developed a test "to evaluate people's true worth." He asks each student to come individually to an adjacent exam room. A boy named Usui Kage ("weak shadow") goes in first, and sits down opposite Mr. Despair. An awkward silence ensues. Then Mr. Despair says, "I know this is kind of sudden, but could you lend me ¥10,000 (about $100)?" The boy says no. "OK, how about $20?" Mr. Despair asks. "That's a lot of money," says the boy. Mr. Despair works downward—$5, $1, "How about 50 cents?" We hear a rattle of change, and the boy says, "Well, I suppose I could lend you that."

Then Mr. Despair's attitude changes. "Fifty cents!" he says, pointing an accusatory finger at the boy. "That's your caliber as a human being!" The boy screams, "What! What kind of person would that be?" Mr. Despair says, "You're the kind of person who will get pissed if someone borrows your mechanical pencil and uses the eraser! You're the kind of person who will ride past his desired train stop in order to take full advantage of your ticket price! You'd borrow someone else's cellphone to read at night (to save your own battery)! That's the kind of person you want to be!" The boy screams, "NO! I don't do those things, and I don't want to do those things!" But Mr. Despair is undeterred: "In any case, you have to live the life that is appropriate to your status." The next scene cuts back to the classroom. The boy is sitting in the front row, at a small desk with a tiny chair, hunched over in defeat. Sometimes when I show this clip during talks about anime, the audience gasps at the cruelty of the boy's humiliation. They needn't worry. The show is funny in part because it so accurately portrays the shared humiliations of the classroom, for student and teacher, and the absurdity of taking it all too seriously.

This scene reorients our understanding of value from an abstract, formalized system of measurement—here, outward physical appearance, but analogously in terms of economic value—in favor of something else. "What matters is what is on the inside," explains Mr. Despair. A common emphasis on value in economic exchange tends to overshadow a more important measure of a person's worth—namely, his or her generosity to others. We all recognize this concept of value, and arguably it is a far more important benchmark than material wealth for our assessment of others.

Similarly, so much of what makes media meaningful lies beyond the measures of retail sales, top-ten lists, and box-office figures. It is no surprise that megahit pop phenomena grab our attention. But it also makes sense to think about the broader pyramids of participation that undergird those works that rise to the pinnacle of "success," a loaded term that, like "creativity," depends on context (Negus and Pickering 2004).

Today, media forms are more than something we simply watch, listen to, or consume; media is something we do. Yet too often discussions of the social in media begin with a question of technology and what it enables— Twitter, Facebook, Mixi, YouTube, Nico Nico Douga, 2.chan—and secondarily, we turn to questions about how these technologies become part of our social worlds. But the technological platforms only work because people contribute their energy, and as time passes, this energy becomes part of the platform in its own right. This is how I interpret the deep catalog of successful manga, and we saw it in the Bandai meeting when the designers argued over their favorite characters from childhood. Platforms are not just objects or tools; they can also be immaterial and social.

Perhaps the idea of media necessarily contains this analytical double-sidedness. Media studies always oscillates between *looking in* at what media conveys (messages to audiences) and an alternative perspective that *looks outward* from media, asking how it shapes our cultural practices, connects us, and organizes our lives. If we think in terms of "connecting through media to extend the activities of our networks and to have meaningful relationships," then we can see how media viewed through the lens of the social need not be uniquely digital, mobile, and contemporary. Rather, media emerges from social contexts and media practices that came before. One can then view anime as part of the prehistory of social media and as a telling example of how "old" and "new" media forms are integrally related—or, as Lisa Gitelman (2006) says, "always already new." For me, what makes "social media" new is not the technology as much as the idea that media is not something to consume from a Network (like ABC) but something we participate in through our (small "n") networks—say, within Mixi or Google+.

Ethnography allows us to see the social as a guiding force that operates alongside legal or economic structures and motivations. As we are witnessing with copyright and the Internet, the practices around new tools tend to conform primarily to social norms (contested, conventional, contingent, all at once) and secondarily to government laws or to marketplace rules.

Wider Collaborative Networks, Deeper Personalized Media

Looking at media in terms of platforms and contexts should give us new opportunities to materialize ideas through cultural practice. Returning to an example from the beginning of the book, the director Mamoru Hosoda reworked characters and worlds in his films to explore driving issues of our day. How do we balance the forces of networked collaboration versus personalized futures? What will this mean for citizenship and democracy, consumerism and markets? Where will we find the heroes to tackle today's most pressing challenges? By thinking in terms of collaborative creativity, we may come to see how even our tiny niches are connected to broader networks of people and activities, which, in turn, are shaped by diverse values that come into being as we act on them. Anime demonstrates how, with some luck and some drive, we can have greater, more extensive influence than we might imagine.

We can be more specific, however, than saying there is just some disembodied social passion that guides anime production and consumption; this energy is also shaped by how anime-related projects unfold. Anime is not unique, but it has distinctive features as a media object and practice.

Anime characters and worlds, combined with the attachments that people feel toward them, become platforms on which others can innovate. Collaborative creativity thus hinges on a social understanding of value. A common thread, from the studios to the ancillary businesses and fan extensions, is the centrality of the social—that is, the connections lie less in the object than in the social relationships and energy that flow through them. The coherence comes from the material realities of our social networks (real and imagined). The mysteries of transmedia storytelling, such as what is it that moves across media, take a different form once we recognize that our relationships are clearly transmedia to begin with.

The seemingly paradoxical divergence in contemporary media between collaborative networks and personalized futures is the result of transformations that ultimately are both technological and cultural. In various ways, we have seen how collaborative creativity (a coming together) is paralleled by deeper niches (a moving apart), a complex feedback loop that can shed light on anime as a cultural movement. For example, at the same time that anime expanded from being a genre for children to something for older audiences, and thereby became more deeply integrated into mass culture, it also developed in more "maniac" directions toward particular niche audiences. This might be most clear in the examples of mecha (giant robot) anime, but parallel processes can be seen elsewhere. And so the cycle continues, from niche to mass, in ways that allow new niches to emerge.

This allows us to rethink media analysis in terms of cultural action and value, distinguishing between different levels and dimensions of "collaborative creativity." I use the term "creative" not in reference to the problematic category "creative industries"—as if banking and insurance were not "creative" (Negus 2006)—but, rather, in a broader sense of creating a world in which ideas and practices are guided by, and reproduce, certain kinds of values in patterned ways. What makes anime instructive is not that characters and worlds provide some internal core but that they become something on which others can build.

Globalization from Below

Ultimately, we learn that even an old-fashioned, often unprofitable industry such as Japanese animation can teach us a tremendous amount about the untapped potential of interest, passion, and commitment that can

sustain artistic movements through the years and that can become important nodes in a complexly networked global media environment. The
politics of anime arise not only from interpreting the messages and themes
of anime programs, but also from addressing the logics of both industry
and fan activities. From Blu-ray to BitTorrent, anime is at the leading edge
of new combinations of businesses and technologies, illustrating that what
counts as creative in media depends not only on the vision of auteurs, but
also on the dynamics that produce robust media circulation and enduring
fan attachments.

Anime can extend our understanding of "globalization from below."
The fields of Japan studies and cultural anthropology face particular challenges in adapting to globalization. The recognition that culture is no
longer bound by geography or specific ethnic groups raises questions about
how to reposition cultural studies in amid cross-cutting economic, political, and media currents that operate transnationally (Appadurai 1996;
Gupta and Ferguson 1997a; Marcus 1995). Although research in Japan
studies tends to look at imported forms in terms of how they are "domesti-
cated," I would like to move beyond questions of authenticity (i.e., "local,"
"Japanese," or "Westernized") to ask instead: How is popular culture
made? By whom? What does it do? Both *Hip-Hop Japan* (Condry 2006)
and this book zero in on cultural forms that were initially dismissed by
corporate elites as a passing fad or as a relatively unimportant sector of
popular media. Yet both rap music and anime went global, eventually
achieving wide-ranging influence. Hip-hop and anime also underscore the
polycentrism of globalization: Hip-hop went from the United States to
the world, while anime traveled from Japan to the world. Globalization is
not always driven by major corporations and the West, a point that others
are increasingly making (Fischer 2003; Iwabuchi 2002a; Larkin 2008;
Schein 2000).

Why do some forms of popular culture achieve international renown
while others languish beyond a horizon of indifference? Anime is a remarkable example of contemporary media partly because it is so labor-
intensive and difficult to capitalize on, yet it remains a sustainable and
vibrant media form. This draws our attention to grassroots and independent efforts that build economic and social networks that gradually expanded beyond their original locales. Both hip-hop and anime became
mainstays of global popular culture, yet they are not just mirror images of
the same process. In *Hip-Hop Japan*, I focused on spaces of cultural pro-

duction (live performance venues and recording studios) as locations where people interacted and produced the scene. Competitiveness among families of rap groups in Tokyo produced a diversity of styles and interests so that the authenticity of rap music varies depending on which "family" of groups one considers. Yet in talking with musicians, I was struck by the skepticism many of them had toward the "scene" (*shiin*), which was commonly viewed as too commercial or on a downswing or as suffering from a prevalence of untalented posers, despite, inevitably, the distant promise of a few younger acts. Magazine writers make their careers commenting on music scenes (as a whole), but artists, like anime studios, rise or fall depending on the success of their own particular works. For them, the scene is someone else's abstraction. In this respect, dynamics of niche and mass have a lot to do with one's location and perspective.

An ethnographic perspective on hip-hop performance and anime production sheds light on the interplay between creators and artists, the industry, and fans. Too often, these categories are presumed to be oppositional, similar to the ways "Japan" and the "West" are often set up as analytical binaries. On the contrary, both anime and Japanese rap music challenge the assumption that "the local" either resists or is co-opted by "the global," illustrating instead the mutual imbrication of East and West, artist and industry, producer and fan, capitalist accumulation and progressive activism, and so on.

From the 1950s to the 1990s, the anime industry was seldom viewed by corporate and government leaders in Japan as a potential engine of economic growth or as a source of international cachet. "Anime is like junk food," one producer told me. "No one respects it, but everyone likes to eat it."[4] He should know. He made a career publishing esoteric books about mecha anime. That public attitude changed, at least somewhat, after Mamoru Oshii's feature film of *Ghost in the Shell* reached number one in DVD sales in the United States in 1996. Also, when Pokémon became a global media-mix phenomenon—from a TV series to trading cards, videogames, endless merchandise—with only modest efforts at localization, a new sense of confidence arose on the part of popular culture producers that works created primarily for a Japanese audience could have a global appeal (Allison 2006; Tobin 2004). When *Spirited Away* won the U.S. Academy Award for Best Animated Feature, Japanese government and business elites found a title that they could be proud to promote as a measure of Japan's innovations in media content. Moreover, these international flows operate independently of broader political-economic stature. Unlike American culture in Japan in the 1960s and 1970s, which rode on the coattails of U.S. political and economic power, anime's prominence overseas came at a time of persistent recession in Japan.

This helps explain why understanding anime's success means searching for that which is most meaningful in different contexts rather than following the money. I don't deny that corporate and national power often guide collective activities, but too much focus on corporate underpinnings of media can give a distorted perspective of what makes media important. Questions surrounding the collaborative creativity of anime allow us to map other kinds of collectivities and organizing principles and thereby allow us to see our own, however modest, roles in shaping the world around us. In a sense, this is what anthropology has always aimed for: to unsettle common understandings of one's own culture by portraying the logic of other ways of doing things. By considering how our cultural practices support, undermine, or alter entrenched political and economic configurations, or simply make an open space for collaborative energy to build, I hope this book has helped illuminate some of the ways that alternative cultural phenomena can emerge, take shape, and spread.

ACKNOWLEDGMENTS

✳ All ethnographic projects incur more debts than can ever be repaid. Thank you to everyone who helped make this book possible, including everyone who shared time and energy to discuss anime, popular culture, and Japan with me. I cannot name all of you individually here, but please accept my gratitude. Writing this book was possible only with the collaborative creativity of many people.

I gratefully acknowledge all of the people whose interviews appear in the book. My regret is that I could not include more of our discussions, which were always fascinating, thoughtful, and provocative.

Several institutions were instrumental in providing financial support for various parts of this project, including the Japan Society for the Promotion of Science, the Japan Foundation, and the U.S. National Science Foundation. I also thank the MIT Japan Program and the Reischauer Institute of Japanese Studies at Harvard University for their ongoing support of the MIT/Harvard Cool Japan research project, which enabled the presentation of anime film screenings, seminars, and conferences that contributed greatly to the work here. The Program on U.S.-Japan Relations at Harvard also kindly provided a postdoctoral fellowship that allowed me to write an early version of this book. A heartfelt thanks to my MIT colleagues and friends, as well as others in Boston and beyond who took time to discuss the ideas here.

Several colleagues and friends made my stay in Japan both

possible and productive, including Yoshitaka Mōri, Tōko Tanaka, Toshiya Ueno, Atsuhisa Yamamoto, and Masataka Yoshikawa. I am grateful for the many opportunities provided, not only in terms of fieldwork but also for seminars, panel discussions, and talk over food and drink. Special thanks go to Yuichi Washida and Yumi Sano, who helped me gain access to several important fieldwork sites. I also appreciate the fascinating discussions with Matt Alt, Michael Arias, and Andy Newman. The dinners with Kou Furukawa, Mamoru Hosoda, and Utamaru (Shiro Sasaki) hold a special place in the development of the ideas here, as well.

Thank you to Koichi Iwabuchi and Glenda Roberts, my colleagues at Waseda University, who helped with arrangements for an extremely productive place to work during fieldwork in Tokyo.

Among the many people in the United States who deserve mention for their help during various stages of this manuscript are Anne Allison, Ted and Vickey Bestor, Thomas DeFrantz, Gary Halliwell, William W. Kelly, Tom LaMarre, David Leheny, Laura Miller, Susan Napier, Jing Wang, Merry White, Christine Yano, and Tomiko Yoda.

My many students at MIT provided invaluable support, from teaching me how to use BitTorrent and introducing me to AnimeSuki.com to participating in our dance theater project (directed by Thomas DeFrantz) *Live Action Anime: Madness at Mokuba*, which might never have happened but for the sudden appearance of a live, giant robot (Kristof Erkiletian) at a panel discussion on campus.

I also acknowledge the publishers of preliminary versions of several chapters that appear here. These much earlier versions are chapter 2, which appeared in the journal *Theory, Culture, and Society*; chapter 6, in *Mechademia 5: Fanthropologies*, edited by Frenchy Lunning; and chapter 7, in *Recreating Japanese Men*, edited by Anne Walthall and Sabine Frühstück. Special thanks go to my colleagues at Duke University Press, including Jade Brooks and Laura Sell, and especially my editor, Ken Wissoker, whose sage advice provided early inspiration and late triage.

My family provided the energy and companionship that made this all possible. Thank you, Margot, for your unending support, not least in terms of getting the five of us to Japan (twice) for adventures of a lifetime. You are my soulmate. Thanks to my mother and father, who instilled in my sisters and me a love of travel and learning. And finally, thanks to my three sons, Nick, Jackson, and Alec, whose energy, curiosity, and affection are a daily joy. This book is dedicated to them.

Introduction. Who Makes Anime?

1 The figure comes from an English-language report by the Japan External Trade Organization (JETRO), which quotes METI (2004). The 60 percent figure is widely quoted both online and in print. I cannot verify its accuracy, but I will note that when I asked the head of Cartoon Networks Studios, he said, "That sounds about right."

2 I acknowledge the advice of an anonymous reviewer in suggesting this analytical direction, and I have borrowed some of the reviewer's phrasing in this paragraph and the next.

3 The converse is also true. Where there is little of that energy, there is also the danger of little being accomplished. A Japanese friend who was trying to break into the anime screenwriting business once reported that meetings around a faltering project were low energy and pointless.

4 Yūichirō Saitō, interview by the author, August 2008.

5 The cost of living in Tokyo is comparable to that of major American cities, so it would be difficult, though not impossible, to support oneself on that level of pay.

6 See http://www.mofa.go.jp/announce/announce/2004/10/1026-2-1 .html (accessed April 9, 2008).

7 See the Ministry of Foreign Affairs press release, available online at http://www.mofa.go.jp/announce/announce/2008/3/0319-3.html (accessed April 9, 2008).

8 According to Craig, these were the questions most asked by journalists who were interested in the conference on Japanese popular culture that he organized in 1996, which resulted in his edited volume *Japan Pop!* (Craig 2000: 6).

9 See http://www.AnimeMusicVideos.org (accessed June 8, 2006).

10 Special thanks to an anonymous reviewer for suggesting some of these analytical directions.

One. Collaborative Networks

1 Mamoru Hosoda, interview by the author, March 2006.

2 Ibid.

3 Mamoru Hosoda, interview by the author, November 2010.

Two. Characters and Worlds

1 The Japanese word *sekaikan* is usually translated as "worldview," but in the case of anime production, the term more often evokes the idea of a particular context or background setting, such as "space colony in the near future" or "samurai-era Japan." Because "worldview" tends to imply "how one looks out at the world"—that is, a subjective orientation—I use the term "world" to specify the usage of sekaikan in anime studios.

2 Ryotarō Kuwamoto, interview by the author, July 2006.

3 This episode appears as "Shippo no Pū': Hoka Zen 48-wa," *Deko Boko Friends*, DVD, Shogakukan, 2004, PCBE-51041.

4 Kuwamoto interview.

5 This episode is available (in Japanese only) on the DVD *Zenmai Zamurai: Zenmai Zamurai Tanjō*, DVD (2006, ANSB 2321).

6 Kuwamoto interview.

7 Satoru Nishizono, interview by the author, July 2006.

8 Momoko Maruyama, interview by the author, July 2006.

9 Shinichirō Watanabe, interview by the author, March 2005.

10 Ibid.

Three. Postwar Anime

1 Personal communication, editor Kasai at *Oricon Style* (web magazine), August 15, 2006.

2 This version of the story is told in the documentary *Ōtsuka Yasuo no ugokasu yorokobi* (Yasuo Ōtsuka's joy of movement), produced by Studio Ghibli in 2004. The story is also related, though somewhat differently, in Ōtsuka 2001.

3 Peter Chung, interview by the author, November 2006.

4 Ibid.

5 Ibid.

Four. When Anime Robots Became Real

1 During fieldwork from 2005 on, I was struck by how many people, especially those in their fifties, responded to the question, "What do you think about anime?" by talking about manga. These categories—comics and animation—are not distinct in Japan.

2 Masao Ueda, interview by the author, August 2006.

3 Ibid.

4 The participants in Wonder Fest are granted one-day licenses to display works based on copyrighted characters. Today, many toy companies circulate at Wonder Fest to find new designs to license from fan groups and home-based artists. Wonder Fest continues to take place twice a year, although General Products no longer organizes the events. That is now handled by the toy company Kaiyōdō.

Five. Making a Cutting-Edge Anime Studio

1 Shin Ishikawa, interview by the author (in English), June 2006.

2 The video is available at http://www.gonzo.co.jp/works/mov/rd_500k.wmv (accessed July 13, 2010).

3 Ishikawa interview.

4 Ibid.

5 Toshio Suzuki, interview by the author, March 2005.

6 Eiko Tanaka, interview by the author, August 2006.

7 Michael Arias, interview by the author (in English), August 2006.

Six. Dark Energy

1 Christopher McDonald, "Unethical Fansubbers," ANN, June 8, 2003, available online at http://www.animenewsnetwork.com/editorial/2003-06-08/2 (accessed October 22, 2007).

2 BrundelFly, webmaster, Anime Junkies, response to editorial in ANN Forum, June 9, 2003, available online at http://www.animenewsnetwork.com/bbs/phpBB2/viewtopic.php?t=2193&postdays=0&postorder=asc&start=390 (accessed October 22, 2007).

3 As discussed elsewhere, debates about downloading music through peer-to-peer networks differ in Japan and the United States but in both cases prompt discussion of the legitimacy of record company practices toward artists and fans (Condry 2004). As digital technologies put the power of distribution in the hands of consumers, major media companies have fought back to protect their intellectual property, initially through legal challenges to file-sharing companies like the original Napster or video sites like YouTube and more recently with litigation against consumers themselves (e.g., lawsuits by the Recording Industry Association of America and the Motion Picture Association of America).

4 Director of overseas sales, Toei Animation, interview by the author, March 2005.

5 Matt Alt, who lives in Tokyo and works in videogame localization as well as being a blogger and commentator, says he deserves some credit for this idea, which he conveyed to Kelts in a conversation, and Kelts happily acknowledges Alt as a source of inspiration. That said, Kelts is the one who develops the idea most fully in print.

6 Available online at http://www.bittorrent.org/introduction.html (accessed November 2, 2007).

7 Available online at http://www.samuraichamploo.com (accessed October 20, 2005).

8 An on-screen note says, "Written by Midori-sour."

9 See http://www.baka-updates.com/seriesinfo.php?id=171&PHPSESSID=d9 848c36a49971040693899dee870224 (accessed February 8, 2005).

10 See http://www.envirosphere.com/yabbse/index.php?board=5;action=print page;threadid=144 (accessed July 30, 2007).

11 See http://www.anime-empire.net/anime-empire/articles.php?ID=11 (accessed July 31, 2007).

12 The Anime Junkies response was posted on the ANN site by the original editorial writer: see http://www.animenewsnetwork.com/editorial/2003-06-19 (accessed February 13, 2008).

13 Founder, anime distribution company, interview by the author, September 2004.

14 Masakazu Kubo, Chihiro Kameyama, and Toshio Suzuki, interviews by the author, March 2005.

15 For a review of empirical studies of music file sharing from an economics perspective, see http://www.rufuspollock.org/tags/filesharing (accessed March 15, 2011).

Seven. Love Revolution

1 See "Nijigen kyara to no kekkon o hōteki ni mitomete kudasai—Shomei katsudō nara 'Shomei TV' (Please legally recognize marriage to a two-dimensional character—If it's a petition campaign, use Shomei TV)," available online at http://www.shomei.tv/project-213.html (accessed December 3, 2008). The Shomei TV website is designed to encourage people to set up online petitions for any kind of movement, and people can do so anonymously or with fictitious names.

2 TP (in English), October 30, 2008, posted online at http://www.news.com .au/comments/0,23600,24576437-5014239,00.html (accessed December 8, 2008).

3 The question of reciprocity in *moe* desire is complicated. At one level, people who feel a *moe* response to inanimate objects can hardly expect those objects to reciprocate. This is certainly the case with *moe* for industrial factories, as shown in the publication of several "factory *moe*" (*kōjō moe*) photography books and websites (see, e.g., "Daily Factory Moe," available online at http://d.hatena.ne .jp/wami [accessed December 17, 2008]). But at a deeper level, I argue that *moe* implies a desire for reciprocity in the sense that those who feel *moe* hope for public recognition that such desires for inanimate or virtual objects are viewed as worthwhile. In other words, there is a desire for reciprocity in terms of a community response, though this is generally undertheorized by otaku commentators.

4 The term is used in many more innocuous ways, sometimes simply as a reference to anything related to manga or anime. The magazine *Pia*, a weekly

entertainment guide, devotes a section of its website to *MoePia*, which lists performances by voice actors and theme-song bands and other live events related to anime: see http://t.pia.co.jp/moe/moe.html (accessed December 3, 2007).

5 Netallica, "Netto de daininki 'Mako sama moe'! Kannaichō konwaku gimi" ("Princess Mako *moe*" becomes Internet sensation: Disturbing the Imperial Household Agency), June 15, 2008, available online at http://netallica.yahoo .co.jp (accessed July 7, 2008).

Conclusion. Future Anime

1 Special thanks to an anonymous reviewer for suggesting some of these analytical directions.

2 Mika Takagi, interview by the author, November 2010.

3 Adapted from a.f.k. fansub.

4 Anime producer, interview by the author, March 2005.

REFERENCES

Aberdeen, J. A. 2000. *Hollywood Renegades: The Society of Independent Motion Picture Producers*. Palos Verdes Estates, Calif.: Cobblestone Entertainment.

Allison, Anne. 2006. *Millennial Monsters: Japanese Toys and the Global Imagination*. Berkeley: University of California Press.

Andersen, Birgitte, and Marion Frenz. 2007. "The Impact of Music Downloads and P2P File-Sharing on the Purchase of Music: A Study for Industry Canada." Available online at http://strategis.ic.gc.ca/epic/site/ippd-dppi.nsf/en/h_ip01456e.html (accessed November 16, 2007).

Anderson, Chris. 2009. *Free: The Future of a Radical Price*. New York: Hyperion.

Anime Style Editors, ed. 2006. *Toki o kakeru shojo ekonte Hosoda Mamoru* [Hosoda Mamoru's storyboards for *The Girl Who Leapt through Time*]. Tokyo: Style.

Appadurai, Arjun. 1996. "Disjuncture and Difference in the Global Economy." *Modernity at Large: The Cultural Dimensions of Globalization*, ed. Arjun Appadurai, 27–47. Minneapolis: University of Minnesota Press.

Arvidsson, Adam. 2006. *Brands: Meaning and Value in Media Culture*. London: Routledge.

Asō, Tarō. 2007. "Asō Tarō moto gaimu daijin ga kataru manga rikkoku ron: Hyogenryoku de, sonkei of atsume yo" [Former Foreign Minister Asō Tarō explains his theory of a manga-based nation: Let's get respect from the power of our expressive culture]. *Nikkei Business*, December 3, 2007, 44–45.

Azuma, Hiroki. 2001. *Dōbutsuka suru posutomodan* [Animal-ized postmodern]. Tokyo: Kōdansha gendai shinsho.

Benkler, Yochai. 2006. *The Wealth of Networks: How Social Production Transforms Markets and Freedom*. New Haven: Yale University Press.

——. 2011. *The Penguin and the Leviathan: How Cooperation Triumphs over Self-Interest*. New York: Crown Business.

Bestor, Theodore. 2004. *Tsukiji: The Fish Market at the Center of the World*. Berkeley: University of California Press.

Biddle, Peter, et al. 2000. "The Darknet and the Future of Content Distribution." Vol. 2004: Proceedings of the ACM Workshop on Digital Rights Management, Washington, D.C., November 2002. Online at http://msl1.mit.edu/ESD10/docs/darknet5.pdf (accessed June 2, 2011).

Blair, Preston. 2003 [1949]. *Animation 1 with Preston Blair: Learn to Animate Cartoons Step by Step*, repr. ed. Laguna Beach, Calif.: Walter Foster.

Bolitho, Harold. 1984. "The Myth of the Samurai." *Japan's Impact on the World*, ed. Alan Rix and Ross Mouer, 2–9. Canberra: Japan Studies Association of Australia.

Bolter, J. David, and Richard A. Grusin. 1999. *Remediation: Understanding New Media*. Cambridge: MIT Press.

Bolton, Christopher, Istvan Csicsery-Ronay Jr., and Takayuki Tatsumi, eds. 2007. *Robot Ghosts and Wired Dreams: Japanese Science Fiction from Origins to Anime*. Minneapolis: University of Minnesota Press.

Bourdieu, Pierre. 1998. *On Television*, trans. Priscilla Parkhurst Ferguson. New York: New Press.

Brown, Steven T., ed. 2006. *Cinema Anime: Critical Engagements with Japanese Animation*. New York: Palgrave Macmillan.

——. 2010. *Tokyo Cyberpunk: Posthumanism in Japanese Visual Culture*. New York: Palgrave Macmillan.

Butler, Judith. 1990. *Gender Trouble: Feminism and the Subversion of Identity*. New York: Routledge.

Christakis, Nicholas A., and James H. Fowler. 2009. *Connected: The Surprising Power of Our Social Networks and How They Shape Our Lives*. New York: Little, Brown.

Chun, Jayson. 2007. *A Nation of a Million Idiots? A Social History of Japanese Television, 1953–73*. London: Routledge.

Clarke, Bruce, and Mark B. N. Hansen. 2009. *Emergence and Embodiment: New Essays on Second-Order Systems Theory*. Durham: Duke University Press.

Clifford, James, and George E. Marcus. 1986. *Writing Culture: The Poetics and Politics of Ethnography*. Berkeley: University of California Press.

Condry, Ian. 2004. "Cultures of Music Piracy: An Ethnographic Comparison of the U.S. and Japan." *International Journal of Cultural Studies* 7(3), 343–63.

——. 2006. *Hip-Hop Japan: Rap and the Paths of Cultural Globalization*. Durham: Duke University Press.

——. 2007. "Youth, Intimacy, and Blood: Media and Nationalism in Contemporary Japan." *Japan Focus* (2403). Available online at http://japanfocus.org/-Ian-Condry/2403.

——. 2011a. "Post-3/11 Japan and the Radical Recontextualization of Value:

Music, Social Media, and End-Around Strategies for Cultural Action." *International Journal of Japanese Sociology* 20, 4–17.

——. 2011b. "Touching Japanese Popular Culture: From Flows to Contact in Ethnographic Analysis." *Japanese Studies* 31(1), 11–22.

Craig, Timothy, ed. 2000. *Japan Pop! Inside the World of Japanese Popular Culture*. Armonk, N.Y.: M. E. Sharpe.

Dentsu Sōken, ed. 2009. *Jōhō Media Hakusho* [Information media white paper]. Tokyo: Diamond.

Diaz, Junot. 2011. "Apocalypse: What Disasters Reveal." *Boston Review* 36(3). Available online at http://www.bostonreview.net/BR36.3/junot_diaz_apocalypse_haiti_earthquake.php.

Digital Content Association of Japan (DCAJ) and Ministry of Economy, Trade, and Industry (METI). 2005. *Dejitaru kontentsu hakushō 2005* [Digital contents white paper 2005]. Tokyo: METI.

Dunlap, Kathryn, and Carissa Wolf. 2010. "Fans Behaving Badly: Anime Metafandom, Brutal Criticism, and the Intellectual Fan." In *Mechademia 5: Fanthropologies*, ed. Frenchy Lunning, 267–84. Minneapolis: University of Minnesota Press.

Epstein, Daniel Robert. 2007a. "*Afro Samurai*: Eric Calderon Interview." Formerly available online at http://www.ugo.com/ugo/html/article/?id=16498&sectionId=2 (accessed February 7, 2007).

——. 2007b. "*Afro Samurai*: Takashi Okazaki Interview." Formerly available online at http://www.ugo.com/ugo/html/article/?id=16499 (accessed February 7, 2007).

Fischer, Michael M. J. 2003. *Emergent Forms of Life and the Anthropological Voice*. Durham: Duke University Press.

——. 2007. "Culture and Cultural Analysis as Experimental Systems." *Cultural Anthropology* 22(1), 1–65.

Frühstück, Sabine. 2007. *Uneasy Warriors: Gender, Memory, and Popular Culture in the Japanese Army*. Berkeley: University of California Press.

Furukawa, Kou, and Editors New Type. 2006. *Toki o Kakeru Shoujo Notebook*. Tokyo: Kadokawa Shoten.

Gabler, Neal. 2007. *Walt Disney: The Triumph of the American Imagination*. New York: Alfred E. Knopf.

Galbraith, Patrick. 2009. "*Moe*: Exploring Virtual Potential in Post-Millennial Japan." Available online at http://www.japanesestudies.org.uk/articles/2009/Galbraith.html (accessed November 11, 2010).

Ganti, Tejaswini. 2002. "'And Yet My Heart Is Still Indian': The Bombay Film Industry and the (H)Indianization of Hollywood." *Media Worlds: Anthropology on New Terrain*, ed. Faye D. Ginsburg, Lila Abu-Lughod, and Brian Larkin, 281–300. Berkeley: University of California Press.

George, Timothy S. 2001. *Minamata: Pollution and the Struggle for Democracy in Postwar Japan*. Cambridge: Harvard University Press.

Gill, Tom. 2001. *Men of Uncertainty: The Social Organization of Day Laborers in Contemporary Japan*. Albany: State University of New York Press.

Ginsburg, Faye D. 2002. "Screen Memories: Resignifying the Traditional in Indigenous Media." *Media Worlds: Anthropology on New Terrain*, ed. Faye D. Ginsburg, Lila Abu-Lughod, and Brian Larkin, 39–57. Berkeley: University of California Press.

Ginsburg, Faye D., Lila Abu-Lughod, and Brian Larkin. 2002. "Introduction." *Media Worlds: Anthropology on New Terrain*, ed. Faye D. Ginsburg, Lila Abu-Lughod, and Brian Larkin, 1–36. Berkeley: University of California Press.

Gitelman, Lisa. 2006. *Always Already New: Media, History, and the Data of Culture*. Cambridge: MIT Press.

Gladwell, Malcolm. 2008. *Outliers: The Story of Success*. New York: Little, Brown.

Graeber, David. 2001. *Toward an Anthropological Theory of Value: The False Coin of Our Own Dreams*. New York: Palgrave Macmillan.

Gupta, Akhil, and James Ferguson, eds. 1997a. *Anthropological Locations: Boundaries and Grounds of a Field Science*. Berkeley: University of California Press.

———. 1997b. "Discipline and Practice: 'The Field' as Site, Method, and Location in Anthropology." *Anthropological Locations: Boundaries and Grounds of a Field Science*, ed. Akhil Gupta and James Ferguson, 1–46. Berkeley: University of California Press.

Hajdu, David. 2008. *The Ten-Cent Plague: The Great Comic-Book Scare and How It Changed America*. New York: Farrar, Straus, and Giroux.

Hamabata, Matthews Masayuki. 1990. *Crested Kimono: Power and Love in the Japanese Business Family*. Ithaca, N.Y.: Cornell University Press.

Hamano, Yasuki. 2003. *Hyōgen no bijinesu: kontentsu seisaku ron* [The expression business: Theory of producing content]. Tokyo: University of Tokyo Press.

Harvey, David. 2005. *A Brief History of Neoliberalism*. New York: Oxford University Press.

Hatakeyama, Kenji, and Kubo Masakazu. 2005. *Odoru kontentsu bijinesu no mirai* [The future of the dancing contents business]. Tokyo: Shogakukan.

Hayashi, Yuka. 2009. "Discontent Seeps into Japan's Anime Studios." *Wall Street Journal*, November 21, 2009. Available online at http://online.wsj.com (accessed June 28, 2010).

Hills, Matt. 2002. *Fan Cultures*. London: Routledge.

Hobby Shosekibu. 2009. *Samaa uōzu kanzen settei shiryō shū* [*Summer Wars* complete premises material collection]. Tokyo: Enterbrain.

Honda, Tōru. 2005. *Denpa Otoko* [Radiowave Man]. Tokyo: Sansai Books.

Hosoda, Mamoru, and Summer Wars Film Partners. 2009. *Summer Wars ekonte Hosoda Mamoru* [*Summer Wars* storyboards by Hosoda Mamoru]. Tokyo: Asuka Shinsha.

Itō, Gō. 2005. *Tezuka Izu Deddo: Hirakareta manga hyōgenron e* [Tezuka is dead: Postmodernist and modernist approaches to Japanese manga]. Tokyo: NTT Shuppan.

Ito, Mizuko, Daisuke Okabe, and Izumi Tsuji, eds. 2012. *Fandom Unbound: Otaku Culture in a Connected Age*. New Haven: Yale University Press.

Iwabuchi, Koichi. 2002a. *Recentering Globalization: Popular Culture and Japanese Transnationalism*. Durham: Duke University Press.

——. 2002b. "'Soft' Nationalism and Narcissism: Japanese Popular Culture Goes Global." *Asian Studies Review* 26(4), 447–69.

Japan External Trade Organization (JETRO). 2005. "Japan Animation Industry Trends." *JETRO Japan Economic Monthly* (June 2005), http://www.jetro.go.jp/en/reports/market/pdf/2005_35_r.pdf (accessed July 3, 2012).

Jenkins, Henry. 2004. "The Cultural Logic of Media Convergence." *International Journal of Cultural Studies* 7(1), 33–43.

——. 2006. *Convergence Culture: Where Old and New Media Collide.* New York: New York University Press.

——. 2009a. "If It Doesn't Spread, It's Dead (Part One): Media Viruses and Memes." Available online at http://henryjenkins.org/2009/02/if_it_doesnt_spread_its_dead_p.html/ (accessed February 11, 2009).

——. 2009b. "The Revenge of the Origami Unicorn." Sessions of an Aca-Fan blog, December 12, 2009. Available online at http://henryjenkins.org/2009/12/the_revenge_of_the_origami_uni.html (accessed January 15, 2010).

Johnson, Steven. 2001. *Emergence: The Connected Lives of Ants, Brains, Cities, and Software.* New York: Scribner.

Kanai, Maki, and Ayako Hirashima. 2010. "Ima, nakama ga kiteru riyū." *Nikkei Entertainment*, December, 21–22.

Kato, Chitaka, and Kou Furukawa. 2005. *Samurai Champloo: Roman Album.* Tokyo: Tokuma Shoten.

Kelly, William W., ed. 2004. *Fanning the Flames: Fans and Consumer Culture in Japan.* Albany: State University of New York Press.

Kelts, Roland. 2006. *Japanamerica: How Japanese Pop Culture Has Invaded the U.S.* New York: Palgrave Macmillan.

Kelty, Christopher M. 2005. "Geeks, Social Imaginaries, and Recursive Publics." *Cultural Anthropology* 20(2), 184–214.

——. 2008. *Two Bits: The Cultural Significance of Free Software.* Durham: Duke University Press.

Kimmel, Michael. 2002. "Foreword." *Masculinity Studies and Feminist Theory: New Directions*, ed. Judith K. Gardiner, ix–xi. New York: Columbia University Press.

Kinsella, Sharon. 1998. "Japanese Subculture in the 1990s: Otaku and the Amateur Manga Movement." *Journal of Japanese Studies* 24(2), 289–316.

——. 2000. *Adult Manga: Culture and Power in Contemporary Japan.* Honolulu: University of Hawai'i Press.

Krauss, Ellis S. 2000. *Broadcasting Politics in Japan: NHK and Television News.* Ithaca, N.Y.: Cornell University Press.

Kubo, Masakazu. 2005. "Animeshon, kyarakutaa no sōgō purodyūsu" [The mutual production of animation and characters]. In DCAJ and METI, *Dejitaru kontentsu hakushō 2005* [Digital contents white paper 2005], 13–29. Tokyo: METI.

LaMarre, Thomas. 2006a. "The First Time as Farce: Digital Animation and the Repetition of Cinema." *Cinema Anime: Critical Engagements with Japanese Animation*, ed. Stephen T. Brown, 161–88. New York: Palgrave Macmillan.

———. 2006b. "Otaku Movement." *Japan after Japan: Social and Cultural Life from the Recessionary 1990s to the Present*, ed. Tomiko Yoda and Harry D. Harootunian, 358–94. Durham: Duke University Press.

———. 2008. "Speciesism, Part I: Translating Races into Animals in Wartime Animation." *Mechademia 3: Limits of the Human*, ed. Frenchy Lunning, 75–95. Minneapolis: University of Minnesota Press.

———. 2009. *The Anime Machine: A Media Theory of Animation*. Minneapolis: University of Minnesota Press.

Larkin, Brian. 2008. *Signal and Noise: Media, Infrastructure, and Urban Culture in Nigeria*. Durham: Duke University Press.

Lash, Scott, and Celia Lury. 2007. *Global Culture Industry: The Mediation of Things*. Cambridge: Polity.

Lee, William. 2000. "From Sazae-san to Crayon Shin-chan: Family Anime, Social Change, and Nostalgia in Japan." *Japan Pop! Inside the World of Japanese Popular Culture*, ed. Timothy Craig, 186–203. Armonk, N.Y.: M. E. Sharpe.

Leibowitz, Stan J. 2006. "File Sharing: Creative Destruction or Just Plain Destruction." *Journal of Law and Economics* 49(1), 1–28.

Leonard, Sean. 2005. "Progress against the Law: Anime Fandom, with the Key to the Globalization of Culture." *International Journal of Cultural Studies* 8(3), 281–305.

Lessig, Lawrence. 2004. *Free Culture: How Big Media Uses Technology and the Law to Lock Down Culture and Control Creativity*. New York: Penguin.

———. 2008. *Remix: Making Art and Commerce Thrive in the Hybrid Economy*. New York: Penguin.

Looser, Thomas. 2006. "Superflat and the Layers of Image and History in 1990s Japan." *Mechademia 1: Worlds of Anime and Manga*, ed. Frenchy Lunning, 92–110. Minneapolis: University of Minnesota Press.

Lukacs, Gabriella. 2010. *Scripted Affects, Branded Selves: Television, Subjectivity, and Capitalism in 1990s Japan*. Durham: Duke University Press.

Lunning, Frenchy, ed. 2006. *Mechademia 1: Emerging Worlds of Anime and Manga*. Minneapolis: University of Minnesota Press.

———. 2007. *Mechademia 2: Networks of Desire*. Minneapolis: University of Minnesota Press.

———. 2008. *Mechademia 3: Limits of the Human*. Minneapolis: University of Minnesota Press.

———. 2009. *Mechademia 4: War/Time*. Minneapolis: University of Minnesota Press.

———. 2010. *Mechademia 5: Fanthropologies*. Minneapolis: University of Minnesota Press.

Lury, Celia. 2004. *Brands: The Logos of the Global Economy*. London: Routledge.

Lysloff, Rene T. A. 2003. "Musical Community on the Internet: An On-line Ethnography." *Cultural Anthropology* 18(2), 233–63.

Macwilliams, Mark Wheeler. 2008. *Japanese Visual Culture: Explorations in the World of Manga and Anime*. Armonk, N.Y.: M. E. Sharpe.

Malinowski, Bronislaw. 1984 (1922). *Argonauts of the Western Pacific*. Prospect Heights, Ill.: Waveland.

Mandel, Ruth. 2002. "A Marshall Plan of the Mind: The Political Economy of a Kazakh Soap Opera." *Media Worlds: Anthropology on New Terrain*, ed. Faye D. Ginsburg, Lila Abu-Lughod, and Brian Larkin, 211–28. Berkeley: University of California Press.

Marcus, George. 1995. "Ethnography in/of the World System: The Emergence of Multisited Ethnography." *Annual Review of Anthropology* 24, 95–117.

Matsumoto, Taiyō. 2006. *Tekkon Kinkreet: Black and White (All-in-One)*. San Francisco: VIZ Media. Originally serialized in Japanese beginning in 1994.

Mauss, Marcel. 1990. *The Gift: The Form and Reason for Exchange in Archaic Societies*. New York: W. W. Norton.

McCarthy, Helen. 1999. *Hayao Miyazaki: Master of Japanese Animation: Films, Themes, Artistry*. Berkeley, Calif.: Stone Bridge.

McCloud, Scott. 1993. *Understanding Comics: The Invisible Art*. New York: HarperCollins.

McGray, Douglas. 2002. "Japan's Gross National Cool." *Foreign Policy* (May–June), 44–54.

McVeigh, Brian. 2000. "How Hello Kitty Commodifies the Cute, Cool, and Camp: 'Consumutopia' versus 'Control' in Japan." *Journal of Material Culture* 5(2), 225–45.

"Megahitto no hōsoku: Manga shinseiki sengen" [The rules of megahits: Declaration of a new manga century]. 2006. *Kino* 1(1), 3.

Mihara, Ryotaro. 2010. *Haruhi in USA*. Tokyo: NTT Publications.

Miller, Laura. 2011. "Cute Masquerade and the Pimping of Japan." *International Journal of Japanese Sociology* 20, 18–29.

Ministry of Economy, Trade, and Industry (METI). 2004. "Kontentsu sangyō no genjō to kadai: Kontentsu sangyō kokusai kyōsōryoku kyōka o mukete" [Topics and current conditions of the content industry: Toward strengthening the international competitiveness of the content industry], February. Available online at http://www.meti.go.jp/policy/media_contents/downloadfiles/kobetsugenjyokadai/genjyoukadai1215.pdf (accessed June 1, 2007).

Mitchell, W. J. T., and Mark B. N. Hansen. 2010. *Critical Terms for Media Studies*. Chicago: University of Chicago Press.

Moeran, Brian. 1996. *A Japanese Advertising Agency: An Anthropology of Media and Markets*. Honolulu: University of Hawai'i Press.

Montfort, Nick, and Ian Bogost. 2009. *Racing the Beam: The Atari Video Computer System*. Platform Studies Series. Cambridge: MIT Press.

Mōri, Yoshitaka. 2011. "The Pitfall Facing the Cool Japan Project: The Transnational Development of the Anime Industry under the Condition of Post-Fordism." *International Journal of Japanese Sociology* 20(1), 30–42.

Murakami, Takashi. 2000. *Superflat*. Tokyo: MADRA.

Nakahara, Masaya, Yoshiki Takahashi, Melon Uminekozawa, and Shūichirō Sarashina. 2006. *Ken Otaku Ryu* [Hating the otaku wave]. Tokyo: Ohta Shuppan.

Nakano, Hitori. 2004. *Densha Otoko* [Train man]. Tokyo: Shinchōsha.

Napier, Susan. 2005. *Anime: From Akira to Howl's Moving Castle*. New York: Palgrave Macmillan.

——. 2007 *From Impressionism to Anime: Japan as Fantasy and Fan Cult in the Mind of the West*. New York: Palgrave Macmillan.

——. 2011. "Where Have All the Salarymen Gone? Masculinity, Masochism, and Technomobility in Densha Otoko." *Recreating Japanese Men*, ed. Sabine Frühstück and Anne Walthall, 154–76. Berkeley: University of California Press.

Nash, Eric Peter. 2009. *Manga Kamishibai: The Art of Japanese Paper Theater*. New York: Abrams.

Negus, Keith. 2006. "Rethinking Creative Production away from the Cultural Industries." *Media and Cultural Theory*, ed. James Curran and David Morley, 197–208. New York: Routledge.

Negus, Keith, and Michael Pickering. 2004. *Creativity, Communication, and Cultural Value*. London: Sage.

Nielsen. 2008. "The Nielsen Company Measures the American Idol Phenom." Available online at http://en-us.nielsen.com/content/dam/nielsen/en_us/documents/pdf/Press%20Releases/2008/May/The% 20Nielsen%20Company%20Measures%20the%20American%20Idol%20Phenom.pdf (accessed June 28, 2010).

Nye, Joseph. 2004. *Soft Power: The Means to Success in World Politics*. Cambridge: PublicAffairs/Perseus.

Oberholzer-Gee, Felix, and Koleman Strumpf. 2007. "The Effect of File Sharing on Record Sales: An Empirical Analysis." *Journal of Political Economy* 115(1), 1–42.

Odell, Colin, and Michelle Le Blanc. 2009. *Studio Ghibli: The Films of Hayao Miyazaki and Isao Takahata*. Herts, U.K.: Kamera.

Okuno, Takuji. 2007. *Japan kūru to Edo bunka* [Cool Japan and Edo culture]. Tokyo: Iwanami Shoten.

Ortega, Mariana. 2007. "My Father, He Killed Me; My Mother, She Ate Me: Self, Desire, Engendering, and the Mother in Neon Genesis Evangelion." *Mechademia 2: Networks of Desire*, ed. Frenchy Lunning, 216–232. Minneapolis: University of Minnesota Press.

Ōtsuka, Eiji. 2004. *Monogatari Shōmetsu ron: Kyarakutaaka suru "watashi", ideogogii ka suru "monogatari"* [Theory of the end of narratives: "I" becomes a character, "stories" become ideologies]. Tokyo: Kadokawa Shoten.

——. 2008. *Kyarakutaa Meekaa: 6-tsu no riron to waakushoppu de manabu "tsukurikata"* [Character maker: Learning "ways of making" through six strategies and workshops]. Tokyo: Ascii Media Works.

Ōtsuka, Eiji, and Ōsawa Nobuaki. 2005. *"Japanimashon" wa naze yabureru ka* [Why "Japanimation" can be destroyed]. Tokyo: Kadokawa Shoten.

Ōtsuka, Eiji, and Gō Sasakibara. 2001. *Kyōyō to shite manga anime* [Manga and anime as education]. Tokyo: Kodansha.

Ōtsuka, Yasuo. 2001. *Sakuga Asemamire* [Drawing pictures through the sweat], rev. ed. Tokyo: Studio Ghibli.

——. 2004. *Ritoru Nimo no yabō* [The aspirations of Little Nemo]. Tokyo: Tokuma Shoten.

Ōzawa, Masachi. 2008. *Akihabara hatsu: oo nendai e no toi*. Tokyo: Iwanami Shoten.

Pariser, Eli. 2011. *The Filter Bubble: What the Internet Is Hiding from You*. New York: Penguin.

Poitras, Gilles. 1999. *The Anime Companion: What's Japanese in Japanese Animation?* Berkeley, Calif.: Stone Bridge.

Pollack, Rufus. 2009. "File Sharing Costs, Dubious Figures Making the Rounds Again." Available online at http://rufuspollock.org/2009/05/29/filesharing-costs-dubious-figures-making-the-rounds-again/ (accessed March 15, 2011).

Raffaelli, Luca. 1997. "Disney, Warner Bros., and Japanese Animation: Three World Views." *A Reader in Animation Studies*, ed. Jayne Pilling, 112–36. Sydney: John Libbey.

Raugust, Karen. 2004. *The Animation Business Handbook*. New York: St. Martin's.

Roberson, James E., and Nobue Suzuki. 2003. *Men and Masculinities in Contemporary Japan: Dislocating the Salaryman Doxa*. London: Routledge Curzon.

Robertson, Jennifer. 1998. *Takarazuka: Sexual Politics and Popular Culture in Modern Japan*. Berkeley: University of California Press.

Ruh, Brian. 2004. *Stray Dog of Anime: The Films of Mamoru Oshii*. New York: Palgrave Macmillan.

Sayle, Murray. 1995. "Letter from Hiroshima: Did the Bomb End the War?" *New Yorker*, July 31, 40–64.

Schein, Louisa. 2000. *Minority Rules: The Miao and the Feminine in China's Cultural Politics*. Durham: Duke University Press.

——. 2002. "Mapping Hmong Media in Diasporic Space." *Media Worlds: Anthropology on New Terrain*, ed. Faye D. Ginsburg, Lila Abu-Lughod, and Brian Larkin, 229–44. Berkeley: University of California Press.

Schodt, Frederik L. 1983. *Manga! Manga! The World of Japanese Comics*. Tokyo: Kodansha International.

——. 1996. *Dreamland Japan: Writings on Modern Manga*. Berkeley, Calif.: Stone Bridge.

——. 2007. *The Astro Boy Essays: Osamu Tezuka, Mighty Atom, and the Manga/Anime Revolution*. Berkeley, Calif.: Stone Bridge.

Sisario, Ben. 2011. "Net Providers Plan Penalties to Slow Piracy." *New York Times*, July 8, A1, A3.

Sito, Tom. 2006. *Drawing the Line: The Untold Story of Animation Unions from Bosko to Bart Simpson*. Lexington: University Press of Kentucky.

Steinberg, Marc. 2008. "Anytime, Anywhere: Tetsuwan Atomu Stickers and the Emergence of Character Merchandising." *Theory, Culture, and Society* 26(2–3), 113–38.

Tada, Makoto. 2002. *Kore ga anime bijinesu da* [This is the anime business]. Tokyo: Kosaido.

Takahata, Isao. 1999. *12 seiki no animeshon: Kōhō emakimono ni miru eiga teki, anime teki naru mono* [Twelfth-century animation: The things that are cinema-like, anime-like in the national treasure picture scrolls]. Tokyo: Tokuma Shoten.

Takeda, Yasuhiro. 2005. *The Notenki Memoirs: Studio Gainax and the Men Who Created Evangelion*. Houston: ADV Manga.

Tobin, Joseph J. 1992. "Introduction: Domesticating the West." *Re-Made in Japan: Everyday Life and Consumer Taste in a Changing Society*, ed. Joseph J. Tobin, 1–41. New Haven: Yale University Press.

——, ed. 2004. *Pikachu's Global Adventure: The Rise and Fall of Pokémon*. Durham: Duke University Press.

Toei Animation. 2006. *Toei Animation 50-nen shi, 1956–2006, Hashiridasu yume no saki ni* [Toei Animation fifty-year history, 1956–2006, running beyond dreams]. Tokyo: Deko.

Treat, John Whittier. 1996. "Introduction: Japanese Studies into Cultural Studies." *Contemporary Japan and Popular Culture*, ed. John Whittier Treat, 1–14. Honolulu: University of Hawai'i Press.

Tsing, Anna Lowenhaupt. 2005. *Friction: An Ethnography of Global Connection*. Princeton: Princeton University Press.

Tsutsui, Yasutaka. 2003 (1967). *Toki o kakeru shōjo* [The girl who leapt through time]. Tokyo: Kadokawa Bunko.

Ueno, Toshiya. 1998. *Kurenai no metaru sūtsu: Anime to iu senba* [Red metal suits: The battlefield called anime]. Tokyo: Kinokuniya Shoten.

Valenti, Jack. 1982. "Home Recording of Copyrighted Works; Hearings before the Subcommittee on Courts, Civil Liberties, and the Administration of Justice; Committee on the Judiciary, House of Representatives, 97th Congress, Second Session, Serial No. 97, Part 1." Washington: U.S. Government Printing Office. Available online at http://cryptome.org/hrcw-hear.htm (accessed November 2, 2005).

Vogel, Harold L. 2001. *Entertainment Industry Economics: A Guide for Financial Analysis*, 5th ed. New York: Cambridge University Press.

Wells, Paul. 1998. *Understanding Animation*. London: Routledge.

——. 2002. *Animation and America*. New Brunswick: Rutgers University Press.

Williams, Raymond. 2006. "Base and Superstructure in Marxist Cultural Theory." *Media and Cultural Studies: Keyworks*, ed. Meenakshi Gigi Durham and Douglas M. Kellner, 130–43. Malden, Mass.: Blackwell.

Yamaguchi, Yasuo. 2004. *Nihon no anime zenshi* [A complete history of Japanese anime]. Tokyo: Ten Books.

Yoda, Tomiko, and Harry D. Harootunian. 2006. *Japan after Japan: Social and Cultural Life from the Recessionary 1990s to the Present*. Durham: Duke University Press.

Zittrain, Jonathan. 2008. *The Future of the Internet and How to Stop It*. New Haven: Yale University Press.

INDEX

Italicized page numbers indicate illustrations.

action movie scale, 127
Aeon Flux, 97
Afro Samurai, 80–82, *82*
Akiho, 64
Aladdin, 98
Allison, Anne, 20, 41, 120–21, 189
Alt, Matt, 223
Anderson, Chris, 164
Animatrix, 97
anime: definition of, 1; pronunciation, 1; why study it? 16–17
Anime-Empire (fansub group), 172
Anime Junkies (fansub group), 162, 176
Anime News Network, 162
Animec (magazine), 130
AnimeForever, *171*
AnimeSuki.com, 168
animetism vs. cinematism, 106
Aniplex (Sony), 53
Anno, Hideaki, 129
anthropology of media, 76
Arias, Michael, 153–55, 207
Arvidsson, Adam, 61
Asahina, Mikuru, 186
Astro Boy, 101, 104
Azuma, Hiroki, 196–200
audiences, 51–52

Bandai, 112–117: Hobby Center, 114
Benkler, Yochai, 168
Bestor, 179
big eyes, 102–3
BigChampagne, 167
Bip and Bap, 89
BitTorrent, 166–67
Blair, Preston, 99
Bogust, Ian, 57–58, 63
Book of the Dead, 89
brands, 61–62
Buckingham, David, 165
Butler, Judith, 198–99

Captain Tsubasa, 18
Cartoon Network (studio), 142
Chaplin, Charlie, 151
characters: design of, 61–62, 64–65; goods business, 70–71; *kyara* vs. *kyarakutaa*, 64; as platform, 55–56, 83–84; ubiquity of, 61
Christakis, Nicholas, 77
Chun, Jayson, 101
Chung, Peter, 96–99
cinematism vs. animetism, 106
Cohen, Bram, 167
collaboration, 4

collaborative creativity, 2, 34, 76–78, 110–11, 201–2, 213–14
Comic Market, 108
Comics Code (US), 108–9
Comike, 108
content industry, 150
convergence, 73
Cool Japan, 204–5
copyright, 23, 24–25, 161–64, 178, 180
copyright wars, 33
cosplay, 184
Craig, Timothy, 20
Crypton Future Media, 63
cultural production, 3

Daicon (convention), 129–31
dark energy, 164, 183
darknet, 184
Dejiko, 197–98, *198*
Deko Boko Friends, 59–61, *60,* 64–65
democratic capitalism, 106–7
Denpa Otoko, 193
Densha Otoko, 189, 193
Di Gi Charat, 197–98, *198*
Disney, 89, 94–96
dōjinshi (fanzines), 108–9
domestication, 96
Dunlap, Kathryn, 171

Edison, Thomas, 181
emakimono, 92
emergence, 19–21
ethnography, 86–87, 143
Evangelion, 132, 195
eyes in anime, 102–3

Fan Wank, 171
fansubs, 161–174: ethics of, 174–76; market effects of, 178–80
fieldwork, 5, 51–53
figurines, 133
Fischer, Michael M. J., 22, 41
Fleischer brothers, the, 99
Fontana, Lucio, 44
Fowler, James, 77

Freedom (anime), 209
Frühstuck, Sabine, 195
Fuji, Jun (Fujijun), 137
fujoshi (rotten girls), 188
Furukawa, Kou, 209

Gabler, Neal, 94
Gainax, 127–34, 191; discourse, 199
Galbraith, Patrick, 190
Gankutsuoh, 146
Ganti, Tejaswini, 28
garage kits, 130
Garland, Eric, 167
gender, 6, 185–203
General Products, 130–31
George, Tim, 47
Ghibli, Studio, 87–88, 147–52
Gill, Tom, 86
Ginsberg, Faye, 28, 76
Girl Who Leapt through Time, 46–50, *50*
Gitelman, Lisa, 213
Gladwell, Malcolm, 17
globalization, 214–217
Gonzo (studio), 80–82, 135–47
Graeber, David, 28–29, 75
graffiti, 170–71
Grave of the Fireflies, 91–92
Gundam, 123–27
GunPla (Gundam plastic models), *115,* 125
gutter, 156–60, *157*

Hajdu, David, 108–9
Hakuhodo, 61
Hakujaden, 94
Hamabata, Matthew, 86
Hamano, Yasuki, 63
Hansen, Mark B. N., 28
Haruhi. See *Melancholy of Haruhi Suzumiya, The*
Harvey, David, 163
Hasegawa, Noriko, 86
Hatsune, Miku (see Miku)
Heidi, Girl of the Alps, 148

Hello Kitty, 58
Hills, Matt, 171
hip-hop, 78–82, 215–16
Honda, Tōru, 193–94
Hope (film), 207–8
Hosoda, Mamoru, 9–12, 35–40, *41*, 44–46
Howl's Moving Castle, 149

Inoue, Hiroaki, 131
Ishikawa, Shin, 146–47
Itō, Gō, 64
Itō, Mizuko, 83

Jackson, Samuel L., 81
Jenkins, Henry, 29, 43–44, 57, 73
JETRO (Japan External Trade Organization), 209

Kameyama, Chihiro, 176–77
Kanada, Yoshinori, 93
Kawamoto, Kihachirō, 89
Kelts, Roland, 165–66
Kelty, Chris, 179, 183
kengaku, 143
Kimmel, Michael, 194
Kino (magazine), 107
Kinsella, Sharon, 109
Kotani, Mari, 188
Kubo, Masakazu, 72, 176
Kumeta, Kōji, 210–11
Kurosawa, Akira, 151
Kuwamoto, Ryotarō. *See* m&k
Kyōjin no Hoshi, 148
Kyoto Animation, 190
Kyoto Seika University, 107

LaMarre, Thomas, 30, 41–43, 95, 105–6, 118–19, 151, 199
Larkin, Brian, 30
Lash, Scott, 71, 118
Laughing Man Fansubs, 171
learning by watching, 143
leechers vs. seeders, 167
Leonard, Sean, 166

Lessig, Lawrence, 180–83
Little Nemo (film), 8–9
Lukacs, Gabriella, 62
Lupin III, 149
Lury, Celia, 61, 71, 118
Lysloff, Rene, 174

Macross, 131
Mandel, Ruth, 28
m&k, 61, 64–65, 71
manga, 21–22, 108–9; megahit, 106–8
Maruyama, Momoko. *See* m&k
Marx, Karl, 110–11
masculinity studies, 194–96
mass vs. niche, 83, 185
Matrix, The, 97
Matsumoto, Taiyō, 154–60
Matsuo, Kou, 137–46, *141*
Mazinger Z, 120, *121*
McCay, Winsor, 8–9, *8*
McCloud, Scott, 103, 156–60, *157*
McGray, Douglas, 204
McVeigh, Brian, 58
mecha anime, 120
media anthropology, 76
media studies, 26–28, 212–13
Melancholy of Haruhi Suzumiya, The, 76, 166, 190
Metropolis (Tezuka), *102*
Mickey Mouse, 98
Mihara, Ryotarō, 166
Miku, 63
Miller, Laura, 203
Mind Game, 154
MIT Anime Club, 166
Mitchell, W. J. T., 27
Miyazaki, Hayao, 148–52, 192
Miyazaki, Tsutomu, 189
moe, 186–87, 191
Montfort, Nick, 57–58, 63
Mōri, Yoshitaka, 205
Motion Picture Association of America, 182
Murakami, Takashi, 93
Mushi Pro, 101–6

Nagai, Gō, 120
Napier, Susan, 189, 195
Negus, Keith, 78, 212
neoliberalism, 163
niche vs. mass, 83, 185
Nico Nico Douga, 63, 163, 201, 212
Ninja Scroll, 175
Nintendo, 121, 165
Nishizono, Satoru, 69
Norakuro, 95

Oh Edo Rocket, 80
Okada, Toshio, 128–29, 199
Okazaki, Takashi, 80–82
Okuno, Takuji, 93, 191
One Piece, 44–46, *45*
organization of the book, 3
Ortega, Mariana, 197
Oshii, Mamoru, 119, 155
Osias, Mitch, 155
otaku, 186–88
Ōtsuka, Eiji, 62, 95, 151–52, 196, 205
Ōtsuka, Yasuo, 90–91, 99, 105

Pickering, Michael, 212
picture scrolls, 92
piracy, 33, 161–67, 178, 180–82
platform, 16, 55–57, 113, 125, 213; genera-
    tive, 58; studies, 57–58
Pokémon, 72, 121, 165
Pollack, Rufus, 179
Polta, from a Distant Country, 89
Power Rangers, 120
premise, 67
Pretty Cure, 88–89

Qoo, 61

Radiowave Man, 193
real, concept of, 71, 112–13, 117–19, 127
real robot anime, 126
Recording Industry Association of
    America, 167
Red Garden, 98, 136–47, *141*, *142*
resonance, cultural, 19–20, 166

Roberson, James, 187
Robertson, Jennifer 102

Sadamoto, Yoshiyuki, 37–40
Samurai Champloo, 78–80, *81*, 169–71,
    171
Samurai 7, 80
Sasakibara, Gō, 122–23
Sayonara Zetsubō Sensei, 210–12
Sazae-san, 86
Schein, Louisa, 28
Schodt, Frederik, 102–3
seeders vs. leechers, 167
Sefton-Green, Julian, 165
sekaikan. See world
Self-Defense Forces, 195
settei. See premise
Shinsen-Subs, 169
Shrek, 99
social energy, 30–31, 101, 104, 144
social media, 212–13
social networks, 77, 82–83
soft power, 18
soul of anime, 1–2, 30, 75, 205–6
Space Battleship Yamato, 122
Spirited Away, 87
Steinberg, Marc, 104
storyboards, 9, 11–14, *12*, *50*, 149–50, *150*
structures of creative action, 28–29, 75–
    76
Studio 4°C, 152–55, *153*
Studio Ghibli. *See* Ghibli, Studio
Studio Nue, 131
success in anime, 87–88, 151–52, 185;
    causes of, 2, 17, 19–21, 85–86; defini-
    tion of, 2; lack of monetary, 14–15
Summer Wars, 10–12, *12*, *13*, 35–40, *38*
Sunrise (studio), 123–27
super robot anime, 126
Suzuki, Nobue, 187
Suzuki, Toshio, 87–88, 147–52, 177

Tajiri, Satoshi, 121, 189
Takagi, Mika, 209
Takahashi, Yoshiki, 209–10

Takahata, Isao, 91–92
Takashita, Taichi, 186
Takeda, Yasuhiro, 127
Tanaka, Eiko, 133, 152–53
Tanigawa, Nagaru, 190
Tekkon Kinkreet, *153*, 154–60, *155*, *158*, *159*
Tetsuwan Atomu. See *Astro Boy*
Tezuka, Osamu, 101–6, *102*, 122
thingification of media, 71, 118
Tobin, Joseph, 96, 165, 184
Toei Animation, *16*, 88–91, 99–100, 164
Tokyo International Film Festival, 208–10
Tomino, Yoshiyuki, 122
toys, 112–34
Train Man, 189, 193
transmedia storytelling, 73–75
Tsing, Anna, 87
Tsutsui, Yasutaka, 47
20th Century Boys, 74
2.chan, 193, 201, 212

Ueda, Masuo, 54, 123–25
Ueno, Toshiya, 119
umbrellas in Japan, 145
Uminekozawa, Melon, 192
Urasawa, Naoki, 74
Utamaru, 209

Valenti, Jack, 182
value, 110, 162–63; if, then right, 180–82
vaudeville, 99
VCRs, 182
Vocaloid, 63
Vogel, Harold, 182
voice acting, 143–44

Washida, Yuichi, 112–115
Watanabe, Shinichirō, 78–80, 123
Weintraub, Anthony, 155
Wells, Paul, 93
Williams, Raymond, 28
Wolf, Carissa, 171
workspaces, 140–42
world, view of, 67–68

Yabushita, Taiji, 95
Yamaga, Hiroyuki, 129
Yamaguchi, Yasuo, 89
Yamashita, Tomohiro, 137
Yasumi, Tetsuo, 54
Yellow Kid, 95
Yoshioka, Hiroshi, 105
Yuasa, Masaaki, 154

Zenmai Zamurai, 54, 65–71, *66*, *68*
Zittrain, Jonathan, 20, 58

IAN CONDRY is Associate Professor of Comparative Media Studies at the Massachusetts Institute of Technology and the author of *Hip-Hop Japan: Rap and the Paths of Cultural Globalization* (Duke, 2006).

Library of Congress Cataloging-in-Publication Data
Condry, Ian.
The soul of anime : collaborative creativity
and Japan's media success story / Ian Condry.
p. cm. — (Experimental futures)
Includes bibliographical references and index.
ISBN 978-0-8223-5380-5 (cloth : alk. paper)
ISBN 978-0-8223-5394-2 (pbk. : alk. paper)
1. Animation (Cinematography)—Social aspects—
Japan. 2. Popular culture—Social aspects—Japan.
3. Creation (Literary, artistic, etc.)—Social aspects—
Japan. I. Title. II. Series: Experimental futures.
NC1766.J3C57 2013   791.43'340952—dc23
2012033721